MAKING COMPARISONS IN EQUALITY LAW

Within Gender, Age and Conflicts

This book seeks to rebalance the relationship between comparison and justification to achieve more effective equality and non-discrimination law.

As one of the most distinguished equality lawyers of his generation, having appeared in over 40 cases in the House of Lords and the Supreme Court and many leading cases in the Court of Justice, Robin Allen QC is well placed to explore this critical issue.

He shows how the principle of equality is nothing if not founded on apt comparisons. By examining the changing way in which the work of men and women has been compared over the last 100 years, he shows the importance of understanding the framework for comparison. With these insights, he addresses contemporary problems of age discrimination and conflict of equality rights.

ROBIN ALLEN, Queen's Counsel, is an equality barrister and long-term campaigner for equality rights; instructed in many leading cases at the highest level for every protected characteristic; Bencher of Middle Temple; previously Chair of the Bar Council's Equality and Diversity Committee. He gave the prestigious Hamlyn Lectures in 2018 focussing on comparisons in equality law.

THE HAMLYN LECTURES 2018

MAKING COMPARISONS IN EQUALITY LAW

Within Gender, Age and Conflicts

ROBIN ALLEN QC
Cloisters Chambers

CAMBRIDGE
UNIVERSITY PRESS

University Printing House, Cambridge CB2 8BS, United Kingdom

One Liberty Plaza, 20th Floor, New York, NY 10006, USA

477 Williamstown Road, Port Melbourne, VIC 3207, Australia

314–321, 3rd Floor, Plot 3, Splendor Forum, Jasola District Centre,
New Delhi – 110025, India

79 Anson Road, #06–04/06, Singapore 079906

Cambridge University Press is part of the University of Cambridge.

It furthers the University's mission by disseminating knowledge in the pursuit of
education, learning, and research at the highest international levels of excellence.

www.cambridge.org
Information on this title: www.cambridge.org/9781108842273
DOI: 10.1017/9781108900034

First published 2020

Printed in the United Kingdom by TJ International Ltd, Padstow Cornwall

A catalogue record for this publication is available from the British Library.

Library of Congress Cataloging-in-Publication Data
NAMES: Allen, Robin (Barrister) author.
TITLE: Making comparisons in equality law : within gender, age, and conflicts /
Robin Allen, Cloisters Chambers.
DESCRIPTION: Cambridge, United Kingdom ; New York, NY : Cambridge
University Press, 2020. | Series: The Hamlyn lectures | Includes index.
IDENTIFIERS: LCCN 2020022550 (print) | LCCN 2020022551 (ebook) | ISBN
9781108842273 (hardback) | ISBN 9781108827546 (paperback) | ISBN 9781108900034
(ebook)
SUBJECTS: LCSH: Equality before the law. | Sex discrimination – Law and legisla-
tion. | Age discrimination – Law and legislation.
CLASSIFICATION: LCC K3250 .A94 2020 (print) | LCC K3250 (ebook) |
DDC 342.08/5–dc23
LC record available at https://lccn.loc.gov/2020022550
LC ebook record available at https://lccn.loc.gov/2020022551

ISBN 978-1-108-84227-3 Hardback
ISBN 978-1-108-82754-6 Paperback

CONTENTS

The Hamlyn Trust owes its existence today to the will of the late Miss Emma Warburton Hamlyn of Torquay, who died in 1941 at the age of eighty. She came from an old and well-known Devon family. Her father, William Bussell Hamlyn, practised in Torquay as a solicitor and JP for many years, and it seems likely that Miss Hamlyn founded the trust in his memory. Emma Hamlyn was a woman of strong character, intelligent and cultured; well-versed in literature, music and art; and a lover of her country. She travelled extensively in Europe and Egypt, and apparently took considerable interest in the law, ethnology and culture of the countries that she visited. An account of Miss Hamlyn may be found, under the title 'The Hamlyn Legacy', in Volume 42 of the published lectures.

Miss Hamlyn bequeathed the residue of her estate on trust in terms which, it seems, were her own. The wording was thought to be vague, and the will was taken to the Chancery Division of the High Court which, in November 1948, approved a Scheme for the administration of the trust. Paragraph 3 of the Scheme, which follows Miss Hamlyn's own wording, is as follows:

> The object of the charity is the furtherance by lecturers or otherwise among the Common People of the United Kingdom of Great Britain and Northern Ireland of the

knowledge of the Comparative Jurisprudence and
Ethnology of the Chief European countries including the
United Kingdom, and the circumstances of the growth of
such jurisprudence to the Intent that the Common People
of the United Kingdom may realise the privileges which in
law and custom they enjoy in comparison with other
European Peoples and realising and appreciating such
privileges may recognise the responsibilities and
obligations attaching to them.

The Trustees are to include the Vice-Chancellor of the
University of Exeter; representatives of the Universities of
London, Leeds, Glasgow, Belfast and Wales; and persons co-
opted. At present, there are eight Trustees:

Dame Laura Cox
Ms Clare Dyer
Professor Roger Halson, University of Leeds
Professor Jane Mair, University of Glasgow
Professor John Morison, Queen's University Belfast
Professor Avrom Sherr, University of London
Professor Chantal Stebbings (Chair, representing the Vice-
    Chancellor of the University of Exeter)
Professor Thomas Glyn Watkin, Bangor University

From the outset, it was decided that the objects of the Trust
could be best achieved by means of an annual course of public
lectures of outstanding interest and quality by eminent
lecturers, and by their subsequent publication and
distribution to a wider audience. The first of the Lectures
was delivered by the Rt Hon. Lord Justice Denning (as he
then was) in 1949. Since then, there has been an unbroken

series of annual Lectures published until 2005 by Sweet & Maxwell and from 2006 by Cambridge University Press. A complete list of the Lectures may be found on pages ix to xiii. In 2005, the Trustees decided to supplement the Lectures with an annual Hamlyn Seminar, normally held at the Institute of Advanced Legal Studies at the University of London, to mark the publication of the Lectures in printed book form. The Trustees have also, from time to time, provided financial support for a variety of projects, which, in various ways, have disseminated knowledge or have promoted to a wider public understanding of the law.

This, the seventieth series of Lectures, was delivered by Robin Allen QC at the Queen's University Belfast, Parliament House, Edinburgh, and Middle Temple Hall, London. The Board of Trustees would like to record its appreciation to Robin Allen and also the three venues which generously hosted these Lectures.

CHANTAL STEBBINGS
Chair of the Trustees

The Trustees of the Hamlyn Trust dedicate this seventieth volume of the Lectures to Sir Stephen Sedley, with affection, respect and gratitude, to mark his retirement from the Board of Trustees after almost twenty years of dedicated and wise counsel.

This book is about making comparisons appropriately, and then following through on their consequences. I believe this to be important for two main reasons.

First, making an appropriate comparison is the key to resolving most disputes about equality. Secondly, looking to find that key is an essential task, even if it is often an elusive one. This is because all modern democratic societies must take equality very seriously if they are to survive.

Throughout 45 years of professional working life as a barrister I have been engaged in this search, in case after case, and in respect of all the protected characteristics. The search for this key in any particular context has often proved to be difficult and contentious. The search is nonetheless always an intriguing process that has often involved the views of many different people beyond just lawyers and jurists, such as politicians, commissions, non-governmental organisations (NGOs) and activists of all kinds.

The Hamlyn Trustees' invitation to give the 2018 Hamlyn Lectures was completely unexpected. It was, however, very welcome. I saw it as an opportunity to collect and order what I have learnt about this search. I hoped I might be able to provide some signposts for the next stages of this search. I am therefore greatly indebted to the Trustees for the honour they have done me. It has been a challenge to undertake the task I set myself, but it has always felt worthwhile; not least because it has forced me to clarify and seek to systematise what I have learnt. I hope that these lectures and this book will repay that honour and go some way to illuminate how these discussions could develop in the future, as equality law evolves yet further.

This book is based on, but does not exactly reprise, the 2018 lectures. I have added an introductory chapter on the nature of comparison, and then re-ordered how I discuss the specific topics I discussed in the lectures.

The first lecture was given in the magnificent modern Moot Court Room of the law school of Queen's University in Belfast. This discussed the development of age equality and was entitled, 'The newest problem: Making a fair comparison across all ages'. The topic of this lecture now forms the basis for the third chapter of this book.

The second lecture, given by kind permission of the Faculty of Advocates in the ancient Laigh Hall in the Parliament House in Edinburgh, discussed equal pay. It was entitled 'The oldest problem: Establishing equal work'. It now forms the second chapter and the first specific study of comparisons in the context of the campaign for equal pay.

The last lecture was given in Middle Temple Hall in London, where I was first called to the Bar in 1974. It was entitled 'The most contentious problem: Comparing rights in conflict'. This last lecture has been expanded somewhat. Its focus differs from the previous two chapters in that it is concerned with the way in which equality law has compared the competing equality claims of individuals.

Returning to the first chapter, my aim has been to provide a generic context for the three more specific chapters that follow. This first chapter owes much to what I said in opening remarks in the three lectures, while also discussing in a more general way the relationship of the idea of comparability to the possibility of justification for different treatment.

To those who attended the lectures, I should explain shortly the decision to reorder and start with a discussion of gender pay equality comparisons. Though there is by no means unanimity on how such comparisons are to be made, it is commonly agreed, as we celebrate the centenary of women's first emancipation, that a page of history has at last been turned. There is now a broad general acceptance that, at least in theory, men's and women's work can and should be compared. So, in looking back, from today's viewpoint, over the long journey to 2019, we are able to see more sharply the pitfalls and wrong turnings.

The reader may be, as I have been, appalled and amazed by this history, at the promises made and broken, and the range of opposing arguments that were advanced to prevent a speedier conclusion to this part of the equality debate. However, the discussion of this particular history is not presented merely as an entertainment, but so that we may learn its lessons. I strongly believe that these can help us see how we might expect the idea of what is comparable to evolve in other contexts and this is particularly relevant to the third chapter. This looks specifically at what I had called 'the newest problem' in equality law, that is to say the development of a system of age equality.[1] What is an apt comparison in an age

---

[1] In passing I should say that I recognise there are other claims to the newest equality concept, but certainly the right to age equality is of direct

equality case is far from being fully established. So, in this third chapter I have tried to sketch some of the factors that are at work in developing this right. In approaching these I have drawn heavily on the understanding of the kinds of pressures that have emerged from the discussion of comparisons in relation to equal pay. Whether my comments prove relevant will have to be reviewed in later years and probably by others! My hope is that they may help focus the debate as this new right develops.

The lectures and book are the product of many different discussions and engagements. I have been privileged to be instructed in many equality cases since the mid-1970s. In each one I have had to think anew about the best way to present each case.

In many cases I have been instructed by the officers of the Equality and Human Rights Commission and its predecessors, the Commission for Racial Equality, the Equal Opportunities Commission and the Disability Rights Commission. The insights they have brought to these cases have been part of my life-long learning for which I am very grateful.

I have also been privileged to work with the European Commission in the late 1990s and early part of this century on the development of new equality law rights pursuant to the then Article 13 EC (now re-enacted in the Treaty on the Functioning of the European Union), and also with the Equality and Human Rights Commission and the

relevance to each and every one of us; it is very new; and it is still largely unexplored in the jurisprudence.

government in the development of the Equality Bill that became the Equality Act 2010. Discussions with officials of these Commissions and Parliamentarians (here and in Europe) have been very important in thinking about these issues, as have those with the members of the many NGOs that were engaged in the formation of policy and the process of making these new rights real. I have also had the privilege of working with other Equality Commissions and jurists across Europe and they, too, have contributed to my thinking.

When I was first asked by Sir Stephen Sedley, then trustee of the Hamlyn Trust, acting on behalf of the other Trustees, to consider giving the 2018 Hamlyn Trust Lectures, I was immensely flattered, as would anyone be. While I knew immediately that I wished to talk about comparisons in equality law, I also knew that I needed much discussion to help me to write coherently and usefully about my ideas. There are many people who have contributed to the thoughts expressed first in the lectures and now in this book. While acknowledging that all errors are my own, I wish to thank everyone who has talked equality law with me over the past 3 years. There are simply too many people to name them all, but there are some whose contributions I have found have been particularly important.

Two people are the forefront of that list. First, Sir Stephen, who had led me on many occasions while I was a junior and he was not yet on the bench; his deep analysis of the issues in those cases in which we were jointly instructed has greatly influenced my own approach. Secondly, my wife Gay Moon, whose own career in this field has been as lengthy as my own, spanning work in Camden Community Law

Centre, working for JUSTICE, and lately as a Joseph Rowntree Charitable Trust Fellow assisting the Equality and Diversity Forum. She has discussed equality law almost daily with me, so that I no longer know which of my ideas came first from her. To them both I give my very great thanks.

To those concerned with the cases I undertook described in these pages I give my sincere thanks for entrusting me with their test case litigation.

All the members of the Employment and Discrimination team of my chambers, Cloisters, have contributed to my thinking over a very long period. I cannot name them all, but I thank Anna Beale, Rachel Crasnow QC, Declan O'Dempsey, Paul Epstein QC, Dee Masters, Claire McCann, Jonathan Mitchell QC and Daphne Romney QC in particular.

Catherine Casserley deserves even greater mention; she was my junior in two of the Supreme Court cases I discuss in the last chapter, and through these has made a special contribution to my thinking. Her knowledge of disability law has provided a bedrock for understanding the overall purpose of equality law. Sinead Eastwood was my junior on the 'Gay Cake Case', which I also discuss in that chapter. I also thank her for her insights, together with all the team at the Equality Commission of Northern Ireland, who instructed me on that case. I wish we had been ultimately successful and perhaps in due course we shall be. I am certain that over time the relevance of this judgment to equality law will be revisited.

Stefan Cross QC, who instructed me in several of the cases I discuss, has been very kind in reminding me of some of the more recent history of equal pay litigation and the headwinds he has faced in making rights real for women. His great contribution to equality law in the United Kingdom has been one of the wonders of this century.

Sam Mercer, Head of Policy, Equality & Diversity at the General Council of the Bar, and I, have worked together for over 6 years. Her practical approach to equality issues has been an inspiration and caused me on many occasions to reflect on how the more theoretical ideas in this book can be given practical effect.

Everyone who works on equality law issues owes a huge debt to Michael Rubenstein and I am no exception. His thoughts and insight have provoked us all in the best sense of the word.

Many people have helped me develop ideas about age equality. I cannot mention them all, but I must mention Bridget Sleap, Ken Bluestone, Bill Mitchell, Nena Georgantzi, Andrew Byrnes, and Israel Doron (and again Dee Masters) with whom I have collaborated on work for the UN's Open-Ended Working Group on Ageing.

My hosts in Belfast, Edinburgh and London have all been kindness itself; they are respectively Professor John Morrison; Gordon Jackson QC, Dean of the Faculty of Advocates; and Master Wilmot-Smith QC, the Treasurer of Middle Temple. Their hospitality greatly added to my enjoyment of the honour of being the 2018 Hamlyn Lecturer. I have also been greatly privileged in that respectively Dr Evelyn Collins CBE, Chief Executive of the Equality Commission of Northern Ireland, Lady Dorrian, the Lord Justice Clerk, and Dame Laura Cox DBE, had agreed in turn to chair these lectures. I hope that they have enjoyed them, and I am very grateful to them all for their introductions, and their skilful work in fielding questions and debate after I had spoken.

I am very grateful to the staff of Cambridge University Press for their support and encouragement.

Finally and most importantly, I thank Professor Chantal Stebbings of the University of Exeter, who until this year was Chair of the Hamlyn Trust, for her guidance throughout, and all the Hamlyn Trustees for their support and encouragement.

Robin Allen

Cloisters

2019

Postscript: This book went into production before the Covid-19 pandemic. How the world will look once this virus is overcome will have to wait another discussion. Equality will surely be no less important then than it has been when these lectures were given.

Chapter 1

Why Do Comparisons Matter?

Introduction

This book concerns the role of comparison in equality law. The next three chapters discuss how they come to be made, the difficulties that comparisons pose for individuals, societies, politicians and jurists, and how they may be made in the future. In this chapter, I shall explore some ideas about how, and why, we make such comparisons, and how in general terms they work in equality law. But first: why make comparisons at all? After all, the aphorism 'comparisons are odious' has very ancient origins,[1] and it is still widely used across the English-speaking world, often as a prelude to a qualified or doubtful comparison.[2] It has probably lasted the course because there

---

[1] It has been suggested that the earliest recorded use of this phrase appears to be in 'A Disputation between a horse, a sheepe and a goose, for superiotitie', written by John Lydgate in about 1440. The aphorism has been used by several later authors, including Cervantes, Christopher Marlowe and John Donne, while Shakespeare, writing in 1598–9, jokingly gave Dogberry the line 'comparisons are odorous' in *Much Ado About Nothing*: Act 3, scene 5.

[2] See e.g. *Timokhina* v. *Timokhin* [2019] EWCA Civ 1284, [2019] 7 WLUK 289, per King LJ at [76], and *Re Z (Adoption: Scottish Child Placed in England: Convention Compliance)* [2012] EWHC 2404 (Fam), [2012] 8 WLUK 348, [2013] 1 FLR 618, [2012] Fam Law 1442, per Mostyn J at [64].

are so many reasons to despise a bad comparison. We all know that a failure to make an apt comparison can cause disappointment and resentment, which, for both individuals and societies, are dangerous psychological states. So, if this is wisdom of ages, why do we persist in making comparisons?

One answer is that we cannot help it. We are born with no innate sense of value of things, processes or people. Without exception, we must all be taught, from our earliest years, that to navigate the world we, and others, will make comparisons, sometimes to point up a difference, sometimes to establish a basis for equal treatment. Anyone could offer a mundane example as to how they first learnt to make comparisons. A typical example might be to recollect a parent explaining to a younger child that she must go to bed earlier than her elder sibling. The younger child might say that her parent's treatment of her is unfair because she has less time to play before sleep, in short that she is treated less favourably. The parent will reply, knowing that the younger child needs more sleep, that this is not so and that her elder sibling also had to go to bed at the earlier time when she was that age. Put another way, the parent is saying that the two children are not in the same situation.

When, later, the younger child reaches the same age as that at which the elder was permitted to stay up past 8 o'clock,

A search on 26 July 2019 on Google News found many examples of this aphorism being deployed in as disparate contexts as the debate about reparations for slavery, see www.sfltimes.com/news/reparations-justified, and a report on a new tech company in the Investors Chronicle, see www.investorschronicle.co.uk/shares/2018/10/17/comparisons-are-odious-for-softcat/.

the younger child will then expect the same treatment. The comparison helps explain, and so make acceptable, the differential treatment of the two children by their parents. It also serves another function, creating a mutual future expectation between parent and child that when the younger child reaches the age at which the elder was permitted to stay up later, she too will be similarly treated. They may have added that as time passes the younger will be treated in the same way.

Thus, as we grow up, we learn to use this intellectual tool to make comparisons in much wider contexts than fairness between individuals, for instance in ranking fashions, ideas, the weather, schools, universities and jobs, and so on. Very soon, making comparisons becomes an essential tool for navigating our world; if we were not to continue to do so, we should be lost.

Such expectations of similar outcomes in comparable situations and of different outcomes in different contexts, are not borne out of any deep philosophical debate. They simply reflect an idea of fairness handed down between generations and learnt at a very early age. They are at the foundation of what it is to be a rational human being. We know that apt comparisons can diffuse tension rather than create it. Such lessons about fairness generally stand us in good stead. They help us secure equal treatment in the present moment, while also, as my example demonstrates, showing how immediate differential treatment can be justified with an expectation of similar treatment at a later time, but we need to work at them to make sure our points of reference are shared by others.

In due course, our experience of this kind of dialogue at home will also lead to a more generalised understanding of what it is to compare that we can use in contexts beyond our family, at school and, in due course, in our workplace and the wider community. Then we will in turn pass it on to the next generation. In short, it is through making good comparisons that the idea of equality is seen to be based on fairness. Nonetheless, the process of comparing carries risks; making inapt comparisons can cause complaints of unfair treatment.

Such comparisons can be made on a simple or more complex basis. We may compare on what might appear to be a single issue such as gender, or on a more complex basis where two or many more aspects are thrown into the mix. For instance, we might look at the disadvantage suffered by black disabled immigrant children. Understanding the way in which some people suffer multiple disadvantages – sometimes called inter-sectional discrimination – is very important but very complex.[3]

We may have to make them in a fresh context where there may be no agreement as to the values to be attached to the different aspects of the comparison. There may be a dispute as to what those aspects are. The more complex the process, the more likely this is. In some places, and in some times, compar-isons are simply not made because they cannot be counte-nanced. The UN's Human Rights Committee noted[4] some time ago that '[i]nequality in the enjoyment of rights by

---

[3] It has formed the basis of much academic literature since Kimberlé Williams Crenshaw first wrote about this subject in 1989; see:
K. Crenshaw, 'Demarginalizing the Intersection of Race and Sex: A Black Feminist Critique of Antidiscrimination Doctrine, Feminist Theory and Antiracist Politics' (1998) *Feminism and Politics*, 314–343.

[4] See Human Rights Committee, General Comment 28, Equality of rights between men and women (article 3), UN Doc CCPR/C/21/Rev.1/Add.10 (2000) at [5].

4

women throughout the world is deeply embedded in tradition, history and culture, including religious attitudes' and in many places there has been little change.

Such prejudices, learnt early, will often be maintained throughout later life. Yet as we grow older, we do have a choice. We can either accept the underlying concept of fairness we have been taught or question it. We can, and often will, re-calibrate as we see the world differently. We do not have to be consistent about this; we may consider it differently in any particular context, and our views may change over time. When an underlying concept of fairness is shared by all, it can be of great social benefit, helping us moderate disputes and social tensions without resort to force. When the concept is not shared by all, it is inevitable there will be a struggle to work to a new consensus, though the time and place of that struggle will not always be obvious. We must remember that the idea of fairness is not itself immutable however much we might wish it to be.

This point was neatly summarised in the earliest justification for the aphorism, of which I am aware, that comparisons were odious because they are a cause of 'haterede' – that is to say hatred.[5] Of course this will be a real risk if there is a dispute as to what conclusions are to be drawn from a comparison, and even more so if those disputed conclusions lead to disputed actions. On the other hand, failing to make and act on a comparison can also be just as much a source of disagreement, and the bigger or more complex the comparison exercise, the greater these risks will be.

---

[5] John Lydgate said, 'Odyous of olde been comparisonis, And of comparisonis engendyrd is haterede.' Lydgate, 'A Disputation'.

The role of law in a democracy is to provide ascertainable rules to regulate behaviour to the general good and with the minimum of force. So, we must ask: can law help with this problem inherent in the making of comparisons? The short answer to that question is that the law tries.

PART 1 THE STATUTORY OBLIGATION TO COMPARE APPROPRIATELY

Parliament had legislated as to how comparisons are to be made in a series of enactments before 2010. That year it passed the Equality Act 2010, consolidating and modernising the disparate equality legislation for Great Britain.[6] In section 23 of the 2010 Act it legislated for 'Comparison by reference to circumstances'. Section 23(1) requires that in both direct and indirect discrimination cases, when comparisons are made they must proceed on the basis that:

> there must be no material difference between the circumstances relating to each case.

This obviously requires some thought as to how a comparison is to be made. In every situation it begs two questions:

> *What are the relevant circumstances relating to the case?*
> *What differences are 'material' in the context of any particular circumstances?*

---

[6] Its reach to Northern Ireland is more limited, where equality law is contained in a code of different enactments.

To a casual reader of section 23, the answer to these questions might seem obvious. That would be a mistake based on a failure to get to grips with the nuances of the framework for the comparison. A court or tribunal might, on the other hand, think it had much freedom to the answer these questions. This again would be a mistake: there are rules as to how they should proceed.

In approaching these questions in a contentious context, the court or tribunal will need a thorough understanding of the function of section 23. My predecessor as Hamlyn Lecturer, Professor Andrew Burrows, made the point very well in his first 2017 Hamlyn Lecture,[7] pointing out it is essential to get under the skin of the black letter text of a provision. He cited a passage from a judgment of Toulson LJ, as he then was, in *An Informer* v. *A Chief Constable*:[8]

> Construction of a phrase in a statute does not simply
> involve transposing a dictionary definition of each word.
> The phrase has to be construed according to its context and
> the underlying purpose of the provision.

In the early days of my advocacy in equality cases I used regularly to cite the White Papers that introduced the ideas in the Sex Discrimination Act 1975[9] and the Race Relations Act 1976.[10] These were helpful in explaining to judges why they had

---

[7] See A. Burrows, *Thinking about Statutes – Interpretation, Interaction, Improvement* (Cambridge University Press, 2018), at pp. 6–7.

[8] [2012] EWCA Civ 197, [2012] 3 All ER 601, [2013] 2 WLR 694, [2013] QB 579, at [67].

[9] See Equality for Women, Command 5724, September 1974.

[10] See Racial Discrimination, Command 6234, September 1975.

to revisit their preconceptions about the applicable framework, but they did not always convince. Moreover, these Acts were concerned with a single ground of discrimination and not with intersectional issues. As the enactment of equality protections has increased to reach new situations, government has again commented on the process of comparison that is required in Explanatory Notes published with the Equality Act 2010.[11] The Equality Act 2010 did not go so far as to address the most complex kinds of intersectional discrimination, but in section 14 it did legislate for what it called 'combined discrimination' involving 'dual characteristics'. As well as ordinary cases of direct discrimination contrary to section 13, and indirect discrimination contrary to section 19, section 23 was designed to apply to such combined discrimination. The Explanatory Notes set out to address how this was to be done:[12]

Section 23: Comparison by reference to circumstances

Effect

91.This section provides that like must be compared with like in cases of direct, dual or indirect discrimination. The treatment of the claimant must be compared with that of an actual or a hypothetical person – the comparator – who does not share the same protected characteristic as the claimant (or, in the case of dual discrimination, either of the protected characteristics in the combination) but who

---

[11] These are now commonly cited in litigation. Parliament must be taken to have been aware of them, since they largely replicated notes published when this Act was first published as a Bill. Moreover, as the 2010 Act was a consolidating measure in many places, the explanation for the legislation is particularly important.

[12] See www.legislation.gov.uk/ukpga/2010/15/notes/division/3/2/2/11.

is (or is assumed to be) in not materially different circumstances from the claimant. In cases of direct or dual discrimination, those circumstances can include their respective abilities where the claimant is a disabled person.

. . .

Examples
A blind woman claims she was not shortlisted for a job involving computers because the employer wrongly assumed that blind people cannot use them. An appropriate comparator is a person who is not blind – it could be a non-disabled person or someone with a different disability – but who has the same ability to do the job as the claimant.

A Muslim employee is put at a disadvantage by his employer's practice of not allowing requests for time off work on Fridays. The comparison that must be made is in terms of the impact of that practice on non-Muslim employees in similar circumstances to whom it is (or might be) applied.

In following subsections, section 23 enacted how comparisons are to be made in relation to disability and to sexual orientation in specific circumstances:

(2) The circumstances relating to a case include a person's abilities if—

    (a) on a comparison for the purposes of section 13, the protected characteristic is disability;

    (b) on a comparison for the purposes of section 14, one of the protected characteristics in the combination is disability.

(3) If the protected characteristic is sexual orientation, the fact that one person (whether or not the person referred to as B) is a civil partner while another is married to a person of the opposite sex is not a material difference between the circumstances relating to each case.

(4) If the protected characteristic is sexual orientation, the fact that one person (whether or not the person referred to as B) is married to a person of the same sex while another is married to a person of the opposite sex is not a material difference between the circumstances relating to each case.

These are very important normative provisions. I suspect that members of many courts and tribunals would struggle to reach these conclusions had they not been enacted. Their basis for making comparisons would not have supported such conclusions, just as it would not for many members of the public. The writer of the Explanatory Notes probably understood this, since they expressly add:[13]

> 92. The section also enables a civil partner who is treated less favourably than a married person in similar circumstances to bring a claim for sexual orientation discrimination.
>
> . . .
>
> 93. The section replicates similar provisions in previous legislation but also accommodates the new concept of dual discrimination.

[13] Ibid.

In fact, government itself has had second thoughts since 2010 about combined or dual discrimination, and has not brought section 14 into force, sparing the judiciary the task of making sense of the comparison required by section 23 in such contexts, though also making the Equality Act 2010 a less comprehensive tool for addressing equality.

These specific legislative statements – particularly in relation to civil partnerships and disability – close off argument and force comparisons to be made when many might not otherwise be willing to do so. Yet they still leave a series of questions unanswered:

> *Outside the specific examples given in these Notes and sub-sections 23(2)–(4) does section 23 really help?*
>
> *Do these Notes and provisions really tell us how to answer the two questions posed by section 23(1)?*
>
> *What is 'like' and what does is it mean to say 'that like must be compared with like'?*

PART 2 THE PROBLEMATIC PRINCIPLE OF EQUAL TREATMENT

Section 23 enacts how, within the United Kingdom and the European Union, the law tries to regulate the approach to these questions by means of a principle, known as the 'principle of equal treatment'. It is a generally recognised basic principle, in both domestic and European law, and it is always based on a process of comparison. It looks to see if there is less favourable treatment by reference to particular human characteristics, such as the characteristics of age,

disability, gender reassignment, marriage and civil partnership, pregnancy and maternity, race, religion or belief, sex,
and sexual orientation, that are protected by the Equality Act
2010.[14]

There are several versions of the statement, all to the
like effect, resolving to a common form, such as the statement
that:[15]

> the principle of equal treatment or non-discrimination
> requires that comparable situations must not be treated
> differently and that different situations must not be treated
> in the same way unless such treatment is objectively
> justified.

This statement of principle owes much to that acute observer
of human nature, Aristotle, as Advocate General Sharpston
pointed out in her Opinion in Case C-427/06 *Bartsch* v. *Bosch
und Siemens Hausgerate (BSH) Altersfursorge GmbH.*[16] It
seems also to reflect common sense. Lord Hoffmann described

---

[14] See e.g. s. 4 of the Equality Act 2010 which applies within Great
Britain, and Article 21 of the Charter of Fundamental Rights of the
European Union. Mostly equivalent protection applies within
Northern Ireland.

[15] See, for instance, Case C-344/04 *IATA and ELFAA* ECLI:EU:C:2006:10,
[2006] ECR I-403 at [95]; Case C-300/04 *Eman and Sevinger* ECLI:EU:
C:2006:545, [2006] ECR I-8055 at [57]; Case C-227/04 P *Lindorfer* EU:
C:2007:490; [2007] ECR I-6767 at [63]; and domestically, *R (on the
application of Chester)* v. *Secretary of State for Justice* [2013] UKSC 63,
[2014] AC 271, [2013] 3 WLR 1076, [2014] 1 All ER 683 at [60].

[16] EU:C:2008:517, [2008] ECR I-7245, [2009] 1 CMLR 5, [2009] All ER
(EC) 113.

it in *Matadeen and Others* v. *M.G.C. Pointu*,[17] as 'a general axiom of rational behaviour'. Does this principle answer the question what is 'like'?

Certainly, those seeking to apply the principle will be engaged in a process that can have a semblance of rationality. Yet a little deeper reflection will reveal that it has little of the prescriptive utility that we might hope to get from a normative legal statement. By itself, it can help us along the path to a fair outcome, but it will not prescribe it. We have to find the context within which it is to be applied and we have to know what is the right and wrong way to make the comparisons it requires.

Let us start with its prescriptive ability. If we parse the content of the principle, one problem is swiftly obvious. If two persons are indeed in truly comparable situations, how can anything 'objectively' justify different treatment? To put the point the other way around, if different treatment is justified 'objectively', then how can the two persons be properly described as being in a comparable situation? In such cases, the treatment that two people will receive will not be comparable, so how can it be said that the situations are comparable?

One answer is that the root meaning of the word 'compare', and its gerund 'comparing' and gerundive 'comparable', is to an extent ambiguous. First, it can be used in a process to establish the equal or similar nature or quality of some matter. We are most familiar with this when we talk in relatively abstract terms, such as in a square of side two is equal in area to another square of side two, or opposing sides

---

[17] [1998] UKPC 9, [1998] 3 WLR 18, [1999] AC 98, [1999] 1 AC 98, at [8].

in a football match start with equal numbers of players. However, this is not the sole use of 'compare'; it is just as frequently used with a more complex aim of describing, estimating or measuring the similarities and dissimilarities of the two matters.

Thinking about this, we should be prompted to consider the equal treatment principle more deeply and to ask which of these two kinds of comparison does it require. Is it the first 'equal' concept? If so, does the principle add anything to the resolution of problems of fair treatment? Surely it is obvious that equal or highly similar situations should be treated in the same way, and that there can hardly be any principled basis for an objective justification for not doing so. If, on the other hand, it is the second complex meaning that is to be applied, then the principle has almost no normative value beyond stating that some objective assessment is to be made. How the comparison is to be undertaken becomes the critical question.

Thinking like this, we will soon conclude that the principle of equality seems either trite or useless. It may therefore seem surprising that a search of any database of domestic or European case law will demonstrate that the principle is enunciated very frequently.[18] It seems that it has become a mantra for many advocates and judges. The problem is that these judgments rarely address the key question: what normative obligation really lies at the heart of this statement?

---

[18] A search of the Westlaw database in late August 2019 returned nearly 200 cases citing the principle.

A few jurists have seen the importance of exploring this question further. For instance, Advocate General Sharpston in her Opinion in *Bartsch*[19] commented:

> A classic formulation of the principle of equality, such as Aristotle's 'treat like cases alike'[20] leaves open the crucial question of which aspects should be considered relevant to equal treatment and which should not.[21] Any set of human beings will resemble each other in some respects and differ from each other in others. A maxim like Aristotle's therefore remains an empty rule until it is established what differences are relevant for the purposes at hand. For example, if we criticise a law banning redheads from restaurants as being unjust, that is based on the premise that, as regards the enjoyment of a meal in a restaurant, hair colour is irrelevant. It is therefore clear that the criteria of relevant resemblances and differences vary with the fundamental moral outlook of a given person or society.[22]

In *Matadeen*, Lord Hoffman made a different but equally apt criticism, querying the extent to which the application of the principle would be always justiciable:[23]

---

[19] See note 16 above, at [44].

[20] Nicomachean Ethics, V.3. 1131a10–b15; Politics, III.9.1280 a8–15, III.12. 1282b18–23.

[21] See further S. Gosepath, '*Equality*', in E.N. Zalta (ed.), *The Stanford Encyclopedia of Philosophy* (Fall 2007 Edition), available online at: http:// plato.stanford.edu/archives/fall2007/entries/equality/.

[22] See H.L.A. Hart, *The Concept of Law* (2nd edn, Clarendon Press, 1994), pp. 159–163.

[23] See note 17 above, at [9].

But the very banality of the principle must suggest a doubt as to whether merely to state it can provide an answer to the kind of problem which arises in this case. Of course persons should be uniformly treated, unless there is some valid reason to treat them differently. But what counts as a valid reason for treating them differently? And, perhaps more important, who is to decide whether the reason is valid or not? Must it always be the courts? The reasons for not treating people uniformly often involve, as they do in this case, questions of social policy on which views may differ. These are questions which the elected representatives of the people have some claim to decide for themselves. The fact that equality of treatment is a general principle of rational behaviour does not entail that it should necessarily be a justiciable principle – that it should always be the judges who have the last word on whether the principle has been observed. In this, as in other areas of constitutional law, sonorous judicial statements of uncontroversial principle often conceal the real problem, which is to mark out the boundary between the powers of the judiciary, the legislature and the executive in deciding how that principle is to be applied.

Lord Hoffman's point about the role of elected representatives highlights how the value to be attributed in the process of comparison is as much, if not more, an issue for parliaments than judges. Yet section 23 would seem to give much freedom to the courts and tribunals to make their own decisions on comparability.

PART 3 THE FRAMEWORK FOR COMPARISON

Others have attempted to circumvent these difficulties by taking a somewhat different approach to what equality requires. For instance, in 2008 an international group of scholars and jurists, drawing on international human rights instruments, agreed a Declaration of Principles of Equality which defined the right to equality and the idea of equal treatment thus:[24]

1 The Right to Equality

The right to equality is the right of all human beings to be equal in dignity, to be treated with respect and consideration and to participate on an equal basis with others in any area of economic, social, political, cultural or civil life. All human beings are equal before the law and have the right to equal protection and benefit of the law.

2 Equal Treatment

Equal treatment, as an aspect of equality, is not equivalent to identical treatment. To realise full and effective equality it is necessary to treat people differently according to their different circumstances, to assert their equal worth and to enhance their capabilities to participate in society as equals.

The second paragraph explicitly acknowledges that there will almost always be differences between persons, events and situations. So these statements emphasise the human context within which equality is to operate. They place an emphasis on looking at the extent of those differences, in the complex

---

[24] See www.equalrightstrust.org/content/declaration-principles-equality.

sense of 'compare'. We should note how the first clause of this scholar's definition refers to human dignity as the touchstone to resolve comparisons. Some countries have tried to build an equality jurisprudence around human dignity, but this is not entirely straightforward because the idea of human dignity and what rights and obligations it entails is not always clear.[25]

Judge Tanaka discussed some of these ideas in his famous dissenting Opinion in the *South-West Africa Cases (Second Phase)*:[26]

> The most fundamental point in the equality principle is that all human beings as persons have an equal value in themselves, that they are the aim itself and not means for others, and that, therefore, slavery is denied. The idea of equality of men as persons and equal treatment as such is of a metaphysical nature. It underlies all modern, democratic and humanitarian law systems as a principle of natural law. This idea, however, does not exclude the different treatment of persons from the consideration of the differences of factual circumstances such as sex, age, language, religion, economic condition, education, etc. To

---

[25] There is a large body of academic commentary on the problem of using human dignity. See, as examples only, G. Moon and R. Allen, 'Dignity Discourse in Discrimination Law: A Better Route to Equality?' (2006) 6 *European Human Rights Law Review*, 610, and C. O'Mahony, 'There is No Such Thing as a Right to Dignity (2012 10(2) *International Journal of Constitutional Law* 551. For a more general discussion of the role of human dignity see, for instance, C. McCrudden (ed.), *Understanding Human Dignity* (Proceedings of the British Academy) (Oxford University Press, 2014).

[26] *South-West Africa Cases (Second Phase)*; see www.icj-cij.org/files/case-related/47/047-19660718-JUD-01-06-EN.pdf.

treat different matters equally in a mechanical way would be as unjust as to treat equal matters differently.

We know that law serves the concrete requirements of individual human beings and societies. If individuals differ one from another and societies also, their needs will be different, and accordingly, the content of law may not be identical. Hence is derived the relativity of law to individual circumstances ...

... the principle of equality before the law does not mean the absolute equality, namely equal treatment of men without regard to individual, concrete circumstances, but it means the relative equality, namely the principle to treat equally what are equal and unequally what are unequal. The question is, in what case equal treatment or different treatment should exist. If we attach importance to the fact that no man is strictly equal to another and he may have some particularities, the principle of equal treatment could be easily evaded by referring to any factual and legal differences and the existence of this principle would be virtually denied. A different treatment comes into question only when and to the extent that it corresponds to the nature of the difference. To treat unequal matters differently according to their inequality is not only permitted but required. The issue is whether the difference exists. Accordingly, not every different treatment can be justified by the existence of differences, but only such as corresponds to the differences themselves, namely that which is called for by the idea of justice ...

I think, like Advocate General Sharpston and Lord Hoffmann, that it is time that the law looked more sharply at the equal treatment principle, and that judges and advocates stopped deploying it without a good deal deeper thought as to what, juridically, they are doing. What does this mean for decision-makers who wish to avoid discrimination and promote equality? I think that a partial answer can be found firstly in the way that they approach their task. How should they proceed?

3.1 Forensic Focus

The assessment of the degree of similarity and difference is critical in assessing the value of the treatment that is to be afforded to the individual. How much forensic scrutiny is to be brought to this exercise? As Judge Tanaka said, 'no man (I would add or woman) is strictly equal to another and he (or she) may have some particularities'. So, if we focus too closely on the differences then we shall never find comparability in the first sense and be hamstrung in finding comparability in the second. In the forensic process there is a point at which we must always stop. Where that point should be is the difficult question for any decision-maker, whether judge, politician or administrator. They need to be clear about the calibration they use in their reasoning and to make this explicit in their decisions, showing where they place the point at which the process of analysis of similarity and difference stops.

Judge Tanaka's focus on 'individual circumstances' and his statement that '[a] different treatment comes into question only when and to the extent that it corresponds to the nature of the difference' is surely right. This emphasises the intense forensic process always necessary in disputed claims to equality. Sometimes that will seem easy to most people; by the time that the issue of the justification of apart-heid was raised before the International Court of Justice in the *South-West Africa Cases* the question had become relatively easy to answer. Yet, even there it depended on those in the judgment seat rejecting the idea that the separation of races was consistent with equality. We need to remember that though this is now universally accepted, it had by no means always been so. It had taken more than half a century before the US Supreme Court had ruled in 1954 in *Brown* v. *Board of Education*[27] against its 1896 judgment in *Plessy* v. *Ferguson*[28] that segregation by colour was consistent with the Equal Protection Clause of the Fourteenth Amendment of the US Constitution.

Yet to state the undisputed importance of a deep focus does not answer the fundamental question how such correspondence is to be judged. This requires recognising not only the role of law makers, but also how comparison and justification are closely connected.

3.2 Comparison and Justification Compared

It can be argued that a decision to say that there is an 'objective' reason for different treatment is really a decision to deny a comparison in the first equal sense. Advocate General Sharpston pointed this out in her Opinion in Case C-227/04 P *Lindorfer* v. *The Council of the European Union*,[29] saying that it was wrong to always

---

[27] 347 US 483 (1954). [28] 163 US 537 (1896).
[29] ECLI:EU:C:2007:490, ECLI:EU:C:2005:656, ECLI:EU:C:2006:748.

expect to find a sharp distinction between them. As she put it:[30]

> In practice, however, there may be some blurring between the assessment of characteristics which differentiate situations and the assessment of objective justification for differentiated treatment of otherwise comparable situations (or for uniform treatment of otherwise different situations).

Black-letter lawyers who do not understand the ideas behind legislation will perhaps struggle with this, since our legislation divides comparison from justification, yet I think it is valuable to look further at the extent that this divide is essential or informative.

Given the content of the equal treatment principle, it has always surprised me that the base concept of direct discrimination in section 13(1) of the 2010 Act does not mention justification at all. It simply defines direct discrimination in terms of comparative treatment:

> A person (A) discriminates against another (B) if, because of a protected characteristic, A treats B less favourably than A treats or would treat others.

Yet immediately section 13 recognises that is insufficient; in the following subsections it provides expressly for justification in relation to age and gives normative statements about the comparison to be made in cases of disability, race, maternity and pregnancy:

---

[30] Ibid. See her second Opinion at [23].

(2) If the protected characteristic is age, A does not discriminate against B if A can show A's treatment of B to be a proportionate means of achieving a legitimate aim.

(3) If the protected characteristic is disability, and B is not a disabled person, A does not discriminate against B only because A treats or would treat disabled persons more favourably than A treats B.

(4) If the protected characteristic is marriage and civil partnership, this section applies to a contravention of Part 5 (work) only if the treatment is because it is B who is married or a civil partner.

(5) If the protected characteristic is race, less favourable treatment includes segregating B from others.

(6) If the protected characteristic is sex—

   (a) less favourable treatment of a woman includes less favourable treatment of her because she is breast-feeding;

   (b) in a case where B is a man, no account is to be taken of special treatment afforded to a woman in connection with pregnancy or childbirth.

Looking at each in turn, we can paraphrase these normative provisions as follows:

- In some cases it may not be appropriate to treat persons of different ages as being in a relevantly comparable position and the apparently less favourable treatment is not to be treated as significant.

- The able bodied are not in a comparable situation to disabled persons and so cannot complain about the apparently better treatment of disabled persons.
- Women who are pregnant or who have recently given birth are not comparable to men who cannot therefore complain of special treatment.
- It is never comparably equal treatment to segregate by race.
- A breast-feeding woman is comparable to a man and is entitled to no less favourable treatment.

Although justification is only mentioned in respect of age, in each of the other cases we could make the same normative statements using the language of justification:

- Better treatment of disabled persons is justified by the fact of disability.
- Special treatment of pregnant women and women in the early stages of maternity is justified by the importance of their situation.
- Segregation by race is never justified.
- Less favourable treatment of breast-feeding women is never justified.

In these four cases Parliament has made definitive statements, telling courts and tribunals and all who apply this law how closely related comparison and justification are. However, I recognise that in respect of age it has done something less, delegating the decision to the court or tribunal to decide on the specificities of the case.[31]

---

[31] Though even here judges and tribunals are much constrained: see *Seldon* v. *Clarkson Wright & Jakes* [2012] UKSC 16, [2012] 3 All ER 1301, [2012] 2

The same point can be made about justification as a core component of the current definition of indirect discrimination in section 19(1) of the 2010 Act, which in turn is based on European law. This states:

(1) A person (A) discriminates against another (B) if A applies to B a provision, criterion or practice which is discriminatory in relation to a relevant protected characteristic of B's.

(2) For the purposes of subsection (1), a provision, criterion or practice is discriminatory in relation to a relevant protected characteristic of B's if—

  (a) A applies, or would apply, it to persons with whom B does not share the characteristic,

  (b) it puts, or would put, persons with whom B shares the characteristic at a particular disadvantage when compared with persons with whom B does not share it,

  (c) it puts, or would put, B at that disadvantage, and

  (d) A cannot show it to be a proportionate means of achieving a legitimate aim.

Section 19(1)(d), in providing a possible defence to a claim of indirect discrimination, is therefore showing that there can be exceptions. Are these cases where there is no comparison or something else? I think that it can easily be said that this definition is, in reality, saying that although A and B may be considered comparable for some purposes, in particular contexts they have no right to be treated comparably.

CMLR 50, [2012] ICR 716, [2012] IRLR 590, [2012] Eq LR 579, [2012] Pens LR 239.

In fact, our domestic equality legislation is full of statutory exceptions where the law does not interfere. Sometimes these are expressed as being justified. An example is the possibility of an employer asserting that he has a genuine occupational requirement[32] for employing a person having a particular characteristic in a particular context. The statutory language of these exceptions is also based on 'proportionality', the key test for justification. Yet is this really a question of justification or a recognition that in some work contexts not all people are comparable irrespective of their protected characteristics? Often, I think, it is easier to explain the issue as a matter of comparability. The Explanatory Notes[33] to this provision seem to merge these two approaches:

> The need for authenticity or realism might require
> someone of a particular race, sex or age for acting roles (for
> example, a black man to play the part of Othello) or
> modelling jobs.

This implies both that a white man cannot play Othello comparably to a black man and a casting director would be justified by Shakespeare's script in preferring to cast a black man as Othello. Both propositions are equally true.

Another example that is given in the Notes[34] is:

> A counsellor working with victims of rape might have to be
> a woman and not a transsexual person, even if she has

---

[32] See, for instance, Part of Sch 9 to the Equality Act 2010.

[33] See www.legislation.gov.uk/ukpga/2010/15/notes/division/3/16/26/1/1/3.

[34] Ibid.

a Gender Recognition Certificate, in order to avoid causing
them further distress.

Here the Notes recognise that such a victim may not consider
a male to female transsexual person as being comparable to
that of a person whose current and birth gender is female and
imply that she is to be treated as justified in making such
a distinction.

Of course, the Notes do not state that only a black
man can play Othello. In any event it would not be true: Golda
Rosheuvel has played Othello,[35] and so has Laurence Olivier.[36]
Nor does it say that no male to female transsexual woman
could give effective counselling to any woman who was a rape
victim. There is no reason to believe that would always be true
in every situation, even if it is sometimes true. This is where
the second sense in which the idea of comparison is so
important.

The jurisprudence of the European Court of Human
Rights (ECtHR) is relevant here. This Court is concerned with
the definition of discrimination in Article 14 of the European
Convention on Human Rights (ECHR), and also Protocol 13
to that Convention, which is in similar terms. Article 14 says:

> The enjoyment of the rights and freedoms set forth in this
> Convention shall be secured without discrimination on
> any ground such as sex, race, colour, language, religion,
> political or other opinion, national or social origin,
> association with a national minority, property, birth or
> other status.

[35] See www.bbc.co.uk/news/entertainment-arts-41930973.
[36] See www.bl.uk/collection-items/postcard-of-olivier-as-othello-1964.

It will readily be seen that Article 14 is neutral as to the way discrimination is to be established; it does not specifically refer to the equal treatment principle. From an early stage the ECtHR has been relatively relaxed about the need to make a comparison. Many years ago, in the *Belgian Linguistic Case (No 2)*,[37] it said:

> In spite of the very general wording of the French version ('sans distinction aucune'), article 14 does not forbid every difference in treatment in the exercise of the rights and freedoms recognised ... The competent national authorities are frequently confronted with situations and problems which, on account of the differences inherent therein, call for different legal solutions; moreover certain legal inequalities tend only to correct factual inequalities.

Earlier this century, in *Stec* v. *United Kingdom*,[38] the Court added:

> A difference of treatment is, however, discriminatory if it has no objective and reasonable justification; in other words, if it does not pursue a legitimate aim or if there is not a reasonable relationship of proportionality between the means employed and the aim sought to be realised. The contracting state enjoys a margin of appreciation in assessing whether and to what extent differences in otherwise similar situations justify a different treatment.

Lady Hale commented on this jurisprudence in *AL (Serbia)* v. *Secretary of State for the Home Department*,[39] noting:

---

[37] (1968) 1 EHRR 252, at 284, [10].   [38] (2006) 43 EHRR 1017, at [51].
[39] [2008] UKHL 42, [2008] 1 WLR 1434, at [24] and following.

24. ... the classic [ECtHR] statements of the law do not place any emphasis on the identification of an exact comparator. They ask whether 'differences in otherwise similar situations justify a different treatment'. Lord Nicholls put it this way in *R (Carson)* v. *Secretary of State for Work and Pensions:*[40]

'the essential question for the court is whether the alleged discrimination, that is, the difference in treatment of which complaint is made, can withstand scrutiny. Sometimes the answer to that question will be plain. There may be such an obvious, relevant difference between the claimant and those with whom he seeks to compare himself that their situations cannot be regarded as analogous. Sometimes, where the position is not so clear, a different approach is called for. Then the court's scrutiny may best be directed at considering whether the differentiation has a legitimate aim and whether the means chosen to achieve the aim is appropriate and not disproportionate in its adverse impact.'

In effect, the ECtHR's approach accepts in practice that comparison and justification are really two sides of the same coin, and that what matters is the scrutiny of the facts and reasons for the treatment in question. There is an attractive intellectual honesty about this approach when set against the problems that I have noted above in relying too heavily on the

---

[40] [2006] 1 AC 173, at [3]; see also *R (o.t.a Harvey)* v. *London Borough of Haringey* [2018] EWHC 2871 (Admin) 2018 WL 05516609, per Julian Knowles J at [106].

principle of equal treatment. It has one great advantage over the domestic approach to the idea of equality in that the issue of comparison is not to be treated as a knock-out point which if not adequately established will mean that no inquiry into the reasons for the treatment is required. On the other hand, this approach is not much more predictive than a rigid application of the equal treatment principle. It still requires courts and tribunals, politicians and administrators, to focus on what might be thought to be a reasonable and proportionate treatment, and to make decisions on those issues.

Also, we cannot ignore two things before rushing to advocate this approach more generally. First, the test of comparison in our domestic law and the law of the European Union is entrenched in the legislation and jurisprudence. We cannot just ignore it. Secondly, I don't think this idea reflects the general public understanding of discrimination. For all their faults, the core ideas in the equal treatment principle reflect a way of thinking that is part of general discourse. Whether they are aware of Aristotle or not, the public are happy to make comparisons and do so. The kind of detailed assessment of proportionality of treatment – with the identification of an aim, consideration of its legitimacy and the assessment of the means for achieving it – might seem to be apt for political decisions, but it will be much less welcome on the shop floor or management office, or when deciding who a commercial enterprise approaches as its customers.

I do not ignore the fact that our concept of indirect discrimination places a burden on a person or organisation to provide a justification for outcomes that seem inconsistent with equal treatment. My comments merely reflect the extent to which the general public do not understand this concept. My concern is thus that the ECtHR's approach barely recognises a distinction between direct and indirect discrimination as they have been defined in domestic and European Union law for nearly half a century. Nonetheless, none of these are reasons for judges and tribunals to ignore this very close connection. Understanding this close connection should cause a more circumspect approach when considering comparisons that is focussed more closely on the whole context.

3.3 Time and Place

My third point is connected. For none of the protected characteristics has a single framework for comparison been accepted by all and for all time. We need therefore to be acutely aware that there is always a contemporary framework for any such comparison, and therefore any decision as to whether there is a failure to provide equal treatment and an unacceptable act of discrimination has to be made in that very limited context. A decision-maker, applying the equal treatment principle and deciding what is and is not comparable, may have every confidence in his or her decision, yet he or she should be aware history may well prove that their view is the subjective product of their background and time in history.

The historical analysis I have tried to undertake in Chapter 2, of the path to an effective equal pay right, provides many examples of this. Moreover, I shall show how, if the necessary framework for making the comparison does not exist or is not accepted by a decision-maker, then a claim for equal treatment will inevitably flounder and the principle of equal treatment will not by itself rescue it. These are key points about comparisons, because I believe that through greater self-awareness, decision-makers will make better and more acceptable decisions.

The framework within which any comparison is made will be the consequence of many different pressures for change. It can often take years in the formation. It is as well to remember just how long this can be. Slavery – that state which denies to the uttermost the comparability of free and slave – continued in the colonies up to the Slavery Abolition Act 1833, despite being held by judges to be inconsistent with the Common Law of England[41] and Scotland[42] some 60 years earlier. We can see, therefore, that within the United Kingdom the framework for *truly* comparing white and black workers was not yet fully in place, despite the work of the Abolitionists. In fact, successive Navy Acts had to state in terms that black and white sailors were to be paid equally long before 1833.

Within my working life I have direct professional experience of a more contemporary example as to how a changed framework enabled rights to be established that had once been considered absurd. From this I know that such a change can be very slow or quite sudden.

[41] *Sommersett's Case* (1772) 20 StTr 1.
[42] See *Knight* v. *Wedderburn*, cited by Lord Mansfield in *Sommersett's Case*.

PART 4 EXAMPLES OF A CHANGING
FRAMEWORK

Two examples drawn from personal experience will serve to demonstrate this.

4.1 Lesbian and Gay Couples

During much of my working life, the situation of two men or two women committed to live their lives together to the exclusion of all others has been seen as incomparable to that of a married man and woman by those that mattered. This was so even though the adverse consequences for gay and lesbian partners could only be described as pitiable, and deserving of the deepest sympathy.

In 1984 I was briefed to appeal possession proceedings brought by Harrogate Borough Council against my client, a Ms Simpson.[43] She was the surviving partner of a lesbian relationship. Regrettably, her partner alone had held the tenancy of their accommodation from the local authority. Under the provisions of the Housing Act 1980 as they then were, had her partner been of the opposite sex so that they were living together as 'husband and wife', she would have been permitted to succeed to the tenancy. As it was, the council claimed possession from her at one of the most vulnerable moments in her life, immediately following her partner's death.

---

[43] *Harrogate Borough Council* v. *Simpson* (1985) 17 HLR 205.

I was briefed to argue that this was wrong. I had to argue that two women could live in a relationship that was akin to marriage and so be permitted the same treatment as would be afforded to an unmarried man or woman on the decease of their partner of the opposite sex. It was therefore essential to try to set up a framework for comparison in which this argument could be accepted. In preparing my advocacy for the appeal, I tried to collect well-known examples of women who had lived together in a way that was akin to a marriage.[44] I went into court with a list of well-known examples of women whose commitment to each other was mutual, life-long and devoted, in the same way that might be expected in the most successful of marriages.

The court was not remotely impressed by my arguments. The senior judge was a rugby football-loving war hero, Sir Tasker Watkins VC. He cut me short and would not allow me to deploy my examples. They signified nothing whatsoever to him. His framework for comparison was demonstrated in this passage from his judgment accepting the Council's argument and rejecting my submissions:

> the [Council], contends that, if Parliament had wished homosexual relationships to be brought into the realm of the lawfully recognised state of a living together of man and wife for the purpose of the relevant legislation, it would

---

[44] It was of course a difficult task to try to identify in advance which pairs of women the judges might have heard of. Hoping for a degree of artistic erudition in my court, among others I referred to Gertrude Stein and Alice B. Toklas, who for forty years had lived together in Paris, as lovers and partners, and hosts to some of the most famous artists and writers of the time, such as Hemingway, Picasso and Matisse.

plainly have so stated in that legislation, and it has not done so. I am bound to say that I entirely agree with that. I am also firmly of the view that it would be surprising in the extreme to learn that public opinion is such today that it would recognise a homosexual union as being akin to a state of living as husband and wife. The ordinary man and woman, neither in 1975 [when other relevant legislation was passed] nor in 1984, would in my opinion not think even remotely of there being a true resemblance between those two very different states of affairs. That is enough, I think, to dispose of this appeal, which, for the reasons I have provided, I would unhesitatingly dismiss.

Ewbank J gave a short concurring judgment adding:

> I agree that the expression 'living together as husband and wife' in section 50 of the Housing Act 1980 is not apt to include a homosexual relationship. The essential characteristic of living together as husband and wife, in my judgment, is that there should be a man and a woman and that they should be living together in the same household. Accordingly, the appellant was not able to establish that she is a member of the deceased's family and she is accordingly not entitled to succeed on this appeal.

The framework for these two old men did not extend to conceiving that anyone could think that two women could be in a relationship comparable to marriage. Their point of view was far from unique. The judgment in *Simpson* was affirmed in 1997 by a different division of the Court of Appeal concerned with similar facts in *Fitzpatrick* v. *Sterling*

Housing Association Ltd.[45] However, 7 years after *Fitzpatrick*, and 20 years after Sir Tasker Watkins' judgment, the framework had materially changed; such a proposition was no longer 'surprising in the extreme'. First, the judicial committee of the House of Lords, applying the Human Rights Act 1998, took a different line in 2004 in *Ghaidan* v. *Godin-Mendoza*;[46] then later the same year Parliament thought public opinion had changed sufficiently to enact the Civil Partnership Act 2004. Within a further 9 years, the Marriage (Same Sex Couples) Act 2013 had taken another giant step forward to change the state's framework for comparison.

The marvel, as others have noted, was the speed with which the framework applied in the UK to same-sex relationships had changed. Yet just as Lord Mansfield's judgments in the late eighteenth century did not immediately complete the Abolitionist's campaign for equal treatment, these changes in the framework for comparing the treatment of opposite- and same-sex relationships, do not amount to a definitive and final reversal. This point can be evidenced in many ways.

For instance, the fact that the first enactment had to create a new concept of 'civil partnership' rather than just establishing civil same-sex marriage, even though there was very little to distinguish the rights and consequences that

---

[45] [1998] Ch 304, [1998] 2 WLR 225, [1997] 4 All ER 991, [1997] 7 WLUK 484, [1998] 1 FLR 6, [1998] 1 FCR 417, (1998) 30 HLR 576, [1997] Fam Law 784.
[46] [2004] UKHL 30, [2004] 2 AC 557, [2004] 3 WLR 113, [2004] 3 All ER 411, [2004] 6 WLUK 427, [2004] 2 FLR 600, [2004] 2 FCR 481, [2004] HRLR 31, [2004] UKHRR 827, 16 BHRC 671, [2004] HLR 46.

flowed from this new status,[47] demonstrated just how dominant the previous orthodoxy had been. Despite change in the Republic of Ireland,[48] it still remains dominant in Northern Ireland, where the Democratic Unionist Party, and both Protestant and Catholic religious organisations,[49] fear their religious concept of marriage would be undermined by equivalent change. The Gay Cake[50] Case I discuss in Chapter 4 is further evidence of this.

4.2 Pregnant Women

Another example of how a change in the framework for comparison can change everything can be seen in the road taken to the current protection of pregnancy discrimination. In the very early part of my career, I was briefed to argue that the dismissal of a pregnant woman was sex discrimination. Being very inexperienced and not being female, I thought it appropriate to argue that, had my client been a man with an illness that would not last more than a relatively short period, he would not be dismissed,

---

[47] See e.g. the discussion in *Bull & Anor* v. *Hall & Anor* [2013] UKSC 73, [2013] WLR 3741, [2014] 1 All ER 919, 36 BHRC 190, [2013] 1 WLR 3741, [2014] Eq LR 76, [2014] HRLR 4, [2013] WLR(D) 454.

[48] See the 34th Amendment to the Constitution of the Republic of Ireland, www.irishstatutebook.ie/eli/2015/ca/34/enacted/en/print.

[49] See, for instance, the statement of the Free Presbyterian Church of Ulster on 'Reaffirmation of this Presbytery's position on marriage in the light of the increasing abandonment of biblical teaching on the matter', see www .freepresbyterian.org/statements/.

[50] *Lee* v. *Ashers Baking Company Ltd & Ors (Northern Ireland)* [2018] UKSC 49; [2018] WLR(D) 648, [2018] 3 WLR 1294.

proved that there was discrimination. As I recall it, this argument failed, and I was not briefed on an appeal.

It would now be thought that this argument was absurd and wrongheaded. Pregnant women are not ill and would not now be considered as having a status somehow equivalent to an ill man. Yet this argument was later adopted to try to advance women's rights by Pat Smith, a female (though lay) judge[51] of the Employment Appeal Tribunal in *Turley* v. *Allders Department Stores Ltd,*[52] so my submissions, seen in their historical context, were not so odd.

These arguments came to a head in a later case, *Webb* v. *Emo Air Cargo (UK) Ltd,* concerning the dismissal of a woman who was the temporary replacement of another woman who was on maternity leave. The replacement woman herself became pregnant and complained about her treatment. My arguments and Ms Smith's approach were redeployed; but now it was argued that her dismissal was not discrimination since a man ill for a similar period would have been dismissed.

In 1992, Glidewell LJ said this giving judgment on the case the Court of Appeal:[53]

> I see no difficulty in comparing a pregnant woman with
> a man who has a medical condition which will require him to
> be absent for the same period of time and at the same time as
> does the woman's pregnancy. Ms Smith, in her dissenting
> opinion in *Turley's* case ... gave some examples of such
> conditions. Obviously one can think of others which might
> be more appropriate in the circumstances of this particular
> case. Suppose that a man suffering from an arthritic hip

[51] Ms Pat Smith. [52] [1980] ICR 66. [53] [1992] ICR 445.

condition and who had been engaged by the company to
replace Mrs. Stewart when she took her maternity leave and,
in the meantime, to train for that job, had learned at the
beginning of July 1987 that a hip replacement operation
would be available to him early in February 1988 and that he
would then be required to leave the job and be absent for
several months. The industrial tribunal's findings of fact
make it clear that in such circumstances the man would also
have been dismissed by the company.

   . . . In my judgment, if a woman was dismissed from
employment for a reason arising out of pregnancy and she
claims that she was discriminated against in breach of the Sex
Discrimination Act 1975, it is necessary for the industrial
tribunal which hears her complaint to decide whether a man
with a condition as nearly comparable as possible which had
the same practical effect upon his ability to do the job would,
or would not, have been dismissed.

In short, the judge also thought that this was an appropriate
comparison. From the point of view of an employer who
merely wishes to have an effective member of staff, one can
see why. From the point of view of women, though, the matter
looked quite different, as indeed the then (now Sir) Stephen
Sedley made clear in his submissions to the Court of Appeal.
Moreover, this approach was not necessarily always fatal for
a woman. If she could show that the ill man would have had
better treatment than she had been afforded, it meant she
could succeed, though of course not otherwise.

    Yet this approach was offensive: it was an affront
to many women to say that pregnancy was in some sense
comparable to illness. It is and always has been a normal

event for a woman to be pregnant. The continuation of the human race depends on this happening! The capacity to become pregnant is simply a normal capacity that a pre-menopausal adult woman has. Though pregnancy can provide the occasion for illness, it is not itself an illness and it is completely wrong to say so.

It took the famous decision of the Court of Justice of the European Court in *Webb* to make this clear:[54]

> 24. . . . there can be no question of comparing the situation of a woman who finds herself incapable, by reason of pregnancy discovered very shortly after the conclusion of the employment contract, of performing the task for which she was recruited with that of a man similarly incapable for medical or other reasons.
>
> 25. As the applicant rightly argues, pregnancy is not in any way comparable with a pathological condition, and even less so with unavailability for work on non-medical grounds, both of which are situations that may justify the dismissal of a woman without discriminating on grounds of sex . . .

The illness comparison was ended. Now it is not thought even necessary to make a detailed comparison when a woman suffers adverse treatment because of her pregnancy. The treatment is gender based for the sole reason that men cannot become pregnant and only women can. *Webb* v. *Emo Air Cargo (UK) Ltd* thus

---

[54] See Case C-32/93 *Webb* v. *Emo Air Cargo (UK) Ltd* [1994] ICR 770, and the judgment of the House of Lords affirming this judgment, *Webb* v. *Emo Air Cargo (UK) Ltd (No 2)* [1995] ICR 1021.

changed the framework for comparison for pregnant women forever.

PART 5 DEVELOPING THE FRAMEWORK APPROACH

In Chapter 2, I shall look in detail at how the framework for comparing women's and men's work has changed over a century of agitation to the point where the contemporary concept of equal pay for work of equal value now has general – though by no means complete – social acceptance. Unlike the debate in *Webb* the changes needed to secure this have taken a very long time. I have gone into this history at some length with a purpose. It is a good story in itself, but much more importantly, it provides many lessons about how the future of equality law generally and the newer ideas about equality in particular may be written. The chapter shows how the path to a modern concept of equal pay for work of equal value is above all else a story about a challenge to a dominant social framework within which the work of men and women was considered incomparable in terms of value. It was only once the dominance of that framework was removed that the legislative change that gave real enforceable rights to women to have their work valued comparably to that of men could be made.

The story told in that chapter shows how the challenge came from many different directions, how surprisingly sometimes men made the running and women resisted, how the different social pressures that emerged in times of national crisis could be very significant, how visceral prejudices learnt in childhood could be, and how different ideas of fairness competed. It will show how the dominant social framework was so resistant to change, and how the shocks to society from two world wars were crucial in changing the framework within which the debate was to be continued. The history shows that it sometimes takes huge effort, over many years, to move to a new framework, which in turn will allow comparisons to be made in the national discourse that were once considered absurd.

I believe that understanding this history better will give perspective when we survey the future of newly emerging campaigns for equality, sharpening our understanding of the points Lord Hoffmann and Advocate General Sharpton have made. It should help illuminate the way in which the new idea of age equality, which is barely into its adolescence, might develop. This is the subject of Chapter 3.

The final chapter is somewhat different. In that chapter, I shall discuss how newly emerging conflicts between different protected characteristics can disrupt established ideas about equal treatment and disturb established equality frameworks. The emergence of such conflicts of rights arguments is another dimension in the dynamic of equality law, which, because of its novelty and unpredictability, provide new challenges to ideas about comparability.

The lesson from my two short examples in this chapter, and the discussion in the following chapters is, I suggest, that whenever the principle might be deployed, jurists should consider the degree of social agreement about what is, and what is not, generally relevant to any particular comparison, and what kind of reasons society considers valid in this sphere of action. They should also imagine how that might change.

Today Sir Tasker Watkins' judgment in *Simpson* does not look so wise, while the more thoughtful Pat Smith and Glidewell LJ can be better judged by history, even though they were wrong.

In short, I suggest that judges should lean much more to the kind of approach taken by the ECtHR in looking in depth at the context within which they are making their decision. They could learn much from the way that Court, aware that the ECHR is a living instrument, looks to see how the framework for its application is developing across the different states parties to the Convention.

This is not to suggest that the Court's approach in *Stec* can or should always be taken at the domestic level. Our specific discrimination legislation does not permit that, as Lady Hale pointed out in *AL (Serbia)*. Rather, what is suggested is that courts and tribunals should take much greater care to note how the framework for their decision is formed currently and to be aware how easily that can change.

If these chapters can prompt that on any occasion, they will have been worthwhile.

Chapter 2

Establishing an Effective Right
to Equal Pay for Equal Work

Introduction

It is an old saying attributed to Mao Zedong that 'Women hold up half the sky',[1] but it is common knowledge that they are not getting paid equally for doing so – here or in China![2] I take it as fully accepted now that this is wrong and that if work is equal then it should be equally paid unless there are very special justifications for not doing so. The question is thus when is one person's work 'equal' to another's and this is answered in our current laws on three bases:[3]

- when it is like work;
- when it has been evaluated as such by a non-discriminatory job evaluation system; and
- when it has equal value.

Of these different ways of establishing equal work, the most difficult, by far, is to argue that it has equal value. This is

---

[1] This was probably news to the many men in the People's Liberation Army; of course the women would have known they did more than that!
[2] According to the World Economic Forum, China is 100th on the list of the world's gender pay gaps, while the UK is 15th. See www.weforum.org /reports/the-global-gender-gap-report-2017.
[3] See s. 65 of the Equality Act 2010.

critical because although job evaluation systems have been used by many large employers, it is probably still true that the majority of women's work has never been the subject of systematic evaluation. The idea that one job can have equal value to another and so receive equal pay is much more tendentious, yet it is critically important as the world of work changes and society addresses old patriarchal norms.

Nobody can have missed the news stories this year reporting on the gender pay gap in companies of 250 or more employees.[4] The BBC has reported on 4 April 2018 that 78 per cent of companies pay men more than women and the national median pay gap is 18.4 per cent.[5] In Edinburgh on 5 April 2018 the Evening News 'revealed' the 'list in full' of the pay gap in Edinburgh firms.[6] The list, which likewise focussed on the median pay gap between men and women, ranged from a very surprising 0 per cent gap for Heart of Midlothian PLC,[7] to 53.2 per cent for Premier Oil Plc,[8] while in April 2018 the BBC reported that 'Scottish finance firms among worst for gender pay gap'.[9] These figures represent the spread of men and women across the pay bands of these businesses.

[4] See https://genderpaygap.campaign.gov.uk/.
[5] See www.bbc.co.uk/news/business-43586574.
[6] See www.edinburghnews.scotsman.com/our-region/edinburgh/revealed-edinburgh-s-gender-pay-gap-the-list-in-full-1-4718901.
[7] See www.heartsfc.co.uk/news/6613 for full details. In fact many football clubs listed a zero gender pay gap, usually by omitting players who are employed through companies etc.
[8] See www.premier-oil.com/sites/default/files/files/gender-pay-report-2018-03-20.pdf for full details.
[9] See www.bbc.co.uk/news/uk-scotland-43640330.

The progress of women at work as measured by the gender pay gap provides a context for this discussion, but the returns tell us nothing, *directly*, about equal pay for work of equal value. The Office for National Statistics is very careful not to say definitively that it is a result of discrimination, but rather that there is a high percentage of the gap that is simply unexplained. That undoubtedly means that it could be caused by discrimination, including the payment to women of a lesser sum than that paid to men for work of equal value,[10] and this is where the overall focus must be, because, as the Scottish Accounts Commission[11] recently explained, securing equal pay is a necessary condition for closing the pay gap:[12]

> The causes of the gender pay gap are complex. As well as discrimination in pay grading systems, other factors, including occupational segregation and inflexible working practices can contribute to female workers earning less than their male counterparts. Ensuring women and men receive equal pay for equal work should contribute to closing the gender pay gap . . .

There are two basic conditions for women to get equal pay for work of equal value:

---

[10] See www.ons.gov.uk/employmentandlabourmarket/peopleinwork/earnings andworkinghours/articles/understandingthegenderpaygapintheuk/2018-01-17.

[11] See www.audit-scotland.gov.uk/about-us/accounts-commission/a-his tory-of-the-commission/accounts-commission-our-changing-role.

[12] See Equal Pay in Scottish Councils, Accounts Commission, 7 September 2017, at p. 23, www.audit-scotland.gov.uk/uploads/docs/report/2017/nr_170907_equal_pay.pdf.

- they must have knowledge of the detail of the two jobs to be compared; and
- somehow there must be an objective assessment of the components of those two jobs.

The first condition – knowledge – can be very difficult to obtain, particularly where there is job segregation and because our society has such a reluctance to discuss pay in an open way. The second involves a combination of judicial and expert skills. Women have to have access to these. In this lecture I shall discuss how these two conditions have been approached and what we can do to make sure that they are met in the future.

I think this is important as, while our country does not value women's work equally to that of men, the fact that women hold up half the sky is empty rhetoric and of no consequence for their rights. Moreover, getting equal pay for work of equal value is not only 'the oldest problem', having been around in some form or another for over a century,[13] it is now among the most urgent: worldwide, because the United Nations has made 'achieving equal pay for work of equal value' by 2030[14] one of its current Sustainable Development Goals

---

[13] My title had a double meaning. First, it is the oldest equality problem with which I personally have engaged. The first ever writing I undertook on equality law was to draft the Equal Opportunities Commission's guide to the Equal Pay Act 1971, see R. Allen, *Sex Discrimination and Equal Pay: How to Prepare your own Case for an Industrial Tribunal* (Equal Opportunities Commission, 1985).

[14] See www.undp.org/content/undp/en/home/sustainable-development-goals/goal-8-decent-work-and-economic-growth/targets/.

(SDGs),[15] and in Scotland, because at least 8,000 women have been striking in Glasgow.[16]

We can all do the maths – 2030 arrives in 12 years from now. To me this SDG seems very ambitious, given the rate of progress since this principle was first enunciated in a legal text. I do not think that any of the big equal pay cases I have been involved in have taken less than 5 or more years to complete. Some have taken much longer.

Ambitious or not, this UN Goal is a timely reminder how important achieving equal value is. But if we really are to achieve this Goal in the next 12 years, every part of civic society in the UK – government, jurists, businesses, trade unions, academia, activists and NGOs – will need to play their part. That means all of us and our efforts could be worth it, if the World Economic Forum is correct[17] in predicting in 2017 that:[18]

> economic gender parity could add an additional US$ 250 billion [approximately £190 billion] to the GDP of the United Kingdom.

---

[15] The SDGs were adopted by the UN in 2016, to build on the progress already achieved in the Millennium Development Goals.

[16] The 48-hour strike by 8,000 women in late October 2018 is said to have caused hundreds of schools in Glasgow to shut and home care services to be affected. It is thought to have been one of the UK's biggest strikes over equal pay. See www.bbc.co.uk/news/uk-scotland-glasgow-west-45941552.

[17] See http://www3.weforum.org/docs/WEF_GGGR_2017.pdf. The basis for this calculation is somewhat obscure, but it assumes that true equal pay would bring more women into the labour market.

[18] Ibid. at p. viii.

Such a potential gain far exceeds annual planned spending on the NHS,[19] and we could all do with that in a post-Brexit world. Is this illusory? All I can say is that the international business consultancy McKinsey has come up with an equally startlingly large figure.[20] However both these figures depend on women and men participating in the economy on a full and equal basis to the best of their skills and abilities, unhampered by stereotyping and job segregation.

Now, after a very slow start, Scotland *has* made a step change in getting to grips with this kind of inequality at work. What has been happening here is not much different from anywhere else in the UK, but it will serve well to highlight many of the problems that are still to be overcome.

One indicator of the progress to date can be found in looking at the pace at which significant equal pay appellate litigation has been brought before the Scottish tribunals and courts.

In the 24 years between the Equal Pay Act of 1971 coming into force at the beginning of 1976 and the Millennium, there were only four reported Court of Session cases concerned with equal pay,[21] only two of which (*Glasgow*

---

[19] See https://fullfact.org/health/what-is-the-nhs-budget/.

[20] See also the similar figures postulated in McKinsey Global Institute, *The Power of Parity: Advancing Women's Equality In The United Kingdom* (McKinsey, 2016), see www.mckinsey.com/~/media/McKinsey/Featured %20Insights/Women%20matter/The%20power%20of%20parity%20 Advancing%20womens%20equality%20in%20the%20United%20 Kingdom/Power-of-parity-Advancing-womens-equality-in-the-United -Kingdom-Full-report.ashx.

[21] These are *Rainey* v. *Greater Glasgow Health Board* 1985 SLT 518; *Stevenson* v. *Lord Advocate* 1998 SC 825; *Glasgow City Council* v. *Marshall*

City Council v. *Marshall* and *Strathclyde RC* v. *Wallace*) were particularly significant.[22] Only *Marshall* concerned the assessment of equal value, and by the time the case went on appeal it was an accepted fact that the women and men did like work, and so this was no longer an issue.

I hope you will also be very pleased to know that since then there have been fourteen equal pay cases reported in the Session Cases over the following 18 years, and six of these have been specifically concerned with issues connected with equal value claims.

This step change in the judicial engagement has gone hand in hand with the progress that female judges have made in breaking through the glass ceiling. I don't know if it is wholly coincidental that the acceleration has occurred since the appointment of Lady Cosgrove as the first female Senator of the College of Justice.[23] What I do know is that there has since been very significant progress in securing a more equal role for women in the Scottish judiciary; now there are some ten female Senators, three of whom sit in the Inner House.[24]

There are some who think that Rose Boland, Eileen Pullen, Vera Sime, Gwen Davis and Sheila Douglass, the

1998 SC 274, and *Strathclyde RC* v. *Wallace* 1996 SC 535. All bar *Stevenson* went to the House of Lords and were reported respectively at 1987 SC (HL) 1, 2000 SC (HL) 67 and 1998 SC (HL) 72.

[22] The first to be reported merely mentioned in passing that the jurisdiction to determine equal pay issues had been conferred on Industrial Tribunals: *Gordon DC* v. *Hay* 1978 SC 327.

[23] Although she had held other important judicial offices previously, I understand that she was appointed in 1996.

[24] Ladies Dorrian, Paton, Smith, Clark of Calton, Stacey, Scott, Wise, Rae, Wollfe, and Carmichael.

sewing machinists who went on strike at Ford Motor Company Limited's Dagenham plant in 1968, were the first to campaign for the right to equal pay for work of equal value, and that the first steps to legal protection were taken only after Barbara Castle's negotiation of their return to work and her promise to turn their argument into legislation.

This current common misconception was probably made worse by the deserved success of that great film[25] 'Made in Dagenham', starring Sally Hawkins, Bob Hoskins, Miranda Richardson, Geraldine James, Rosamund Pike and others, because the film so firmly located the issue as only having arisen in the late 1960s.

It is certainly correct that in February 1970, the late Barbara Castle, when First Secretary of State and Secretary of State for Employment and Productivity, proposed the Bill that became the Equal Pay Act 1971;[26] so the striking machinists' campaign and her role are hugely important. But it is by no means correct to say that this was the first time that the principle of equal pay for work of equal value was set out in a legal document of relevance to the UK.

In fact, by the time the 1971 Act was passed, that legal principle was already over 50 years old. What happened in between has now been largely forgotten, but I think this is a mistake. If we do not take some time to understand the lack of progress over those 50 years, we shall make it harder for ourselves to understand what progress we have actually made

[25] www.imdb.com/title/tt1371155/.
[26] See https://api.parliament.uk/historic-hansard/commons/1970/feb/09/equal-pay-no-2-bill.

to date, and the full extent of the challenge posed by the United Nations.

Very few now know that it was a hundred years ago on 28 June 1919 that the right for women to have 'equal remuneration for work of equal value' was first clearly written down in a legal document applying to the UK. It was on this date, in the very splendid Hall of Mirrors in the Palace of Versailles, that a treaty was signed by the High Contracting Parties. That date has prime claim to being the true beginning of the *legal* right with which this lecture is concerned.[27]

The Versailles Treaty is now remembered as the treaty that defined the international settlement between Germany and the Allied powers following the end of the First World War, but it was much more than that. Most people realised this back then. My father, who fought in that First World War, kept his personal copy of the Versailles Treaty all his life, and I have it still. It was very important to him because it sought to set out how world peace could be maintained through the League of Nations.

It has been very important for me, too, because Part XIII of the Treaty sets out the founding provisions of the International Labour Organisation or ILO, and the role of that

[27] The Treaty was signed by representatives of the United States of America, the British Empire (specifically including the United Kingdom of Great Britain and Ireland, South Africa, Canada, New Zealand and India), France, Italy, Japan, Belgium, Bolivia, Brazil, China, Cuba, Ecuador, Greece, Guatemala, Haiti, The Hedjaz, Honduras, Liberia, Nicaragua, Panama, Peru, Poland, Portugal, Roumania, the Serb-Croat-Slovene State, Siam, Czechoslovakia, Uruguay, and Germany. These spellings follow precisely the wording of the Treaty.

organisation in establishing the current basis for the legal right is critical. First, among the Articles in that Part, is Article 427, by which the UK and the other High Contracting Parties, committed to:

> recognising that the well-being, physical, moral and intellectual, of industrial wage-earners is of supreme international importance, [and] in order to further this great end, [have framed] the permanent machinery . . . [concerning the ILO] and associated with that of the League of Nations.
>
> They recognise that differences of climate, habits, and customs, of economic opportunity and industrial tradition, make strict uniformity in the conditions of labour difficult of immediate attainment. But, holding as they do, that labour should not be regarded merely as an article of commerce, they think that there are methods and principles for regulating labour conditions which all industrial communities should endeavour to apply, so far as their special circumstances will permit.
>
> Among these methods and principles, the following seem to the High Contracting Parties to be of special and urgent importance: . . .
>
> *Seventh. The principle that men and women should receive equal remuneration for work of equal value.*
>
> Eighth. The standard set by law in each country with respect to the conditions of labour should have due regard to the equitable economic treatment of all workers lawfully resident therein.
>
> . . .
>
> Without claiming that these methods and principles are either complete or final, the High Contracting Parties are of

opinion that they are well fitted to guide the policy of the League of Nations; and that, if adopted by the industrial communities who are members of the League, and safeguarded in practice by an adequate system of such inspection, they will confer lasting benefits upon the wage-earners of the world.

(Italics added for emphasis)

Later we shall see how this Article was developed after the Second World War, but reading this Article, now, prompts five questions:

- Where did this idea – that as a matter of principle 'men and women should receive equal remuneration for work of equal value' – come from?
- Why was it set out in a treaty ending a world war?
- What did the High Contracting Parties mean by it?
- How was it taken forward thereafter?
- Why did it take so long to be made the subject of domestic legislation enforceable by women themselves?

In the first Part of this lecture I shall try to give some answers to these questions. This part is lengthy because it tells us so much about the intransigence, arguments and tactics of those who oppose equal pay for work of equal value. We shall find in those answers many of the problems that are still encountered, and we can perhaps draw on the experience of those who have gone before in finding the future that we seek.

In Part 2, I shall more briefly review the extent to which the domestic right to equal pay for work of equal value has been converted from being a theoretical and somewhat illusory right to a more accessible legal right for women.

In the final Part 3, I shall briefly review what steps could now be taken to help the UK to meet the UN Sustainable Development Goal.

PART 1 EQUAL VALUE IN WAR AND PEACE

1.1 Women's Pay in the First World War

One of the forgotten facts[28] about the campaign for this principle to be part of the ILO's founding provisions is the extent to which

---

[28] Professor Mary Davis, Visiting Professor in Labour History at Aston University, has well described how in the late 1800s women were largely excluded from trade unions and how the wage that men earned was seen as the 'family wage' which had to support both the man and the women at home. She has written: 'By the mid-19th century, trade unions were established on a firm footing among skilled and better paid workers, but at the same time women workers suffered a great defeat. This meant that for the most part women were excluded from trade unions. The only trade in which they still remained organised in any numbers was that of weaving. The aim of trade unionism, according to Henry Broadhurst, secretary of the TUC, speaking in 1875, summed up the ideology, which was: ". . . to bring about a condition . . . where wives and daughters would be in their proper sphere at home, instead of being dragged into competition for livelihood against the great and strong men of the world." From this kind of thinking sprang the widespread acceptance of the notion of the "family wage" to be won by the male breadwinner. Hence, not only was unequal pay accepted as a norm, but women's work was only tolerated if not threatening to the man. In any case, it was seen as a mark of shame if a man permitted his wife to work, hence the widespread practice, hardly contested by the unions until the twentieth century, of barring married women from employment altogether. Such

there was an international women's movement campaigning for it. Dorothy Sue Cobble, in her article 'The Other ILO Founders: 1919 and Its Legacies',[29] describes this comprehensively, including the role that international women's movements played in persuading the drafters of this part of the Versailles Treaty to bring equal pay into its text. Regrettably their role is too large a story to include in this lecture and I must concentrate more closely on matters in the UK.[30] It is our own national story of War and Peace, though quite unlike Tolstoy's.

A report in the *Spectator* magazine published[31] just four weeks before the Versailles Treaty was signed will start to explain the close link between the idea of equal pay for work of equal value and women's contribution to the war effort:

> attitudes and practices help to explain women's increasing job segregation and the fact that so much female labour was literally hidden. It is not surprising therefore that the unions of this period demonstrated a studied indifference if not downright hostility to women workers. Any attempts to organise women in this period came from outside the labour movement, often through the work of philanthropic women.' (footnotes omitted) See www.unionhistory.info/britainatwork/narrativedisplay .php?type=womenatwork.

[29] See chapter 1, in E. Boris, D. Hoehtker and S. Zimmerman (eds.), *Women's ILO, Transnational Networks, Global Labour Standards and Gender Equity 1919 to Present, Brill and the ILO* (Brill, 2018).

[30] Clementina Black is credited with first moving a motion for equal pay for work of equal value at a meeting of the Trades Union Congress (TUC) in 1888. Important though this motion is in historical terms, it was only a motion and not a legal right. See Janet Horowitz Murray and Myra Stark (eds.), *The Englishwoman's Review of Social and Industrial Questions: 1888* (Routledge, 2016).

[31] *The Spectator* 31 May 1919, at 20; see archive.spectator.co.uk/article/31st-may-1919/20/report-of-the-war-cabinet-committee-on-women-in-in.

> The War Cabinet Committee have issued a Report on Women's Industry, of which the scope and thoroughness will render it not only invaluable to the country at a moment when the whole question is urgently demanding attention, but historically important as evidence of the tremendous changes in the relation of women to labour which have occurred during the past four years. The opening chapters give an exhaustive survey of these relations before the war, and provide statistics dealing with the standard of wages then prevailing. Later sections are concerned with the position of women in occupations now recognized as open to either sex; and some very interesting pages are devoted to the results of inquiry into the causes of low rates of payment to women. The recommendations of the Committee with regard to the wage question are based, approximately, on the principle of 'equal pay for equal work' ...

The full title of the Report to which the Spectator referred was the 'Report of the War Cabinet Committee on Women in Industry'. We shall need to look a little closer at it, so I shall abbreviate this long title to the 'Women's Industry Report' or 'Report'.[32] In the Spectator's, very brief, summary of the Report, we can see the outline of many of the issues that were important then:

- the relatively low pay of women in the jobs that they did;
- justifications for the gender segregation of jobs based on stereotypic assumptions about the capabilities and needs of women and men;

---

[32] Cmd. 135 of 1919. This can be accessed online at https://babel .hathitrust.org/cgi/pt?id=njp.32101058837848;view=1up;seq=16.

- the erosion of those stereotypes in the face of women successfully proving their equal abilities;
- the consequent fears about men's role and value in the world of work; and
- growing pressure to reanalyse and confront the treatment of women in the light of enormous new social pressures.

Each of these points reappears time and again in the course of the story of the development of this principle over the following 99 years.

What was the background to the Women's Industry Report? Although the discussions within the labour movement both here and in other countries, such as France, Italy and the United States, had been going on for a long time, the contribution of women to the war effort had brought the issue of equal pay for equal work to the fore. This was for two principal reasons.

First, the extent of women's work during the period 1914–1918 was so great it simply could not be denied. Just as the *Spectator* noted, the statistics about women's contribution to the war effort on the home front in industry, commerce, agriculture and administration, were simply overwhelming. Our national war memorials say so much of the sacrifice of soldiers, but in doing so they rather hide the extent to which women gave themselves to the war effort. National Archives summarise the effect on women of the mass mobilisation of men for the war in this way:[33]

---

[33] See www.nationalarchives.gov.uk/education/britain1906to1918/g5/back ground.htm.

The shortage of workers was met by the recruitment of an extra 1 million women workers, doing traditionally men's jobs'. . . . They key point is that women filled the gaps in the labour market. About 950,000 went to work in munitions, and about 200,000 worked in other areas of engineering. They worked in many other areas like driving buses and taxis, and about 16,000 mostly young women joined the Women's Land Army.

Some figures from selected industries will emphasise the extraordinary proportionate increases this entailed through the war (see Table 2.1).[34]

Some of the consequences flowing from the upward acceleration of these figures were identified at an early stage in the war. Women who had previously only undertaken low

Table 2.1

Industry	1914	1915	1916	1917	1918	% increase over the period
Metals	170,000	203,000	370,000	523,000	594,000	249
Chemicals	40,000	48,000	87,000	109,000	104,000	160
Government establishments	2,000	6,000	72,000	205,000	225,000	11,150

[34] See A. Woollacott, *On Her Their Lives Depend: Munitions Workers in the Great War* (University of California Press, 1994), at p. 25. She attributes the table to the Public Record Office, MUN 5/71/324/34. Figures taken from diagrams based on Section C of the employment report prepared for the Board of Trade in January 1919.

paid or even unpaid 'women's work' were suddenly working alongside men or even taking over their jobs. How were they to be paid? There was much dispute.

On 19 March 1915, the trade unions entered into an agreement with the government, known as the 'Treasury Agreement for the acceleration of output on Government work'. One aim of this Agreement was to avoid what was called 'dilution'. The key clause proposed by the unions was that:

> Where semi-skilled or female labour is employed in place of skilled labour the rates paid shall be the usual rates of the district obtaining for the operations performed, and in case of any worker being unable to earn the usual rate of wages, the difference in earnings shall be made up to the rates paid prior to the innovation.

When the clause was finally agreed this had been altered because of the fear that this would lead to unskilled women new to the job *necessarily* being paid the same as skilled men. It said:

> Where under this arrangement semi-skilled men are employed owing to the war in place of labour of higher skill, the rates paid shall be the usual rates of the district for that class of work. The relaxation of existing demarcation restrictions or admission of semi-skilled or female labour shall not affect adversely the rates customarily paid for the job. In cases where men who ordinarily do the work are adversely affected thereby, the necessary readjustments shall be made so that they can maintain their previous earnings.

One aim of the unions was to secure that women were not paid less than men. That was desired both because it was right, and because men feared that their wages would be reduced as women entered the same workplaces as they had hitherto dominated. When the clause was finally agreed the latter point was clearly addressed.[35] It can also be seen that there was an assumption that the new female employees would often be of inferior skill to the males who they replaced. This issue of female skill in so-called male jobs bedevilled much of the later arguments in the last century. The assumptions behind it seem now to be incredibly sexist, but they were a frequent part of the argument about the value of women's work, in comparison to men's, when doing the same or similar jobs.

Although it is tolerably clear as to what was agreed, there were many complaints that the Agreement was breached by the government,[36] giving rise to a discourse between workers – in particular, women workers – and government. That discourse must be seen in the political context of the women's suffrage movement. This had been building its case for 50 years or more,[37] and by the start of the war was gaining real momentum. Most of us know a little more about this now we have rightly been celebrating the progress of

---

[35] See the Women's Industry Report, at pp. 203–204.

[36] See ibid. at p. 325 and ff. and passim.

[37] J.S. Mill had presented the Women's Petition to Parliament for universal suffrage on 7 June 1866.

that campaign to the first step to enfranchise women.[38] We have been reminded how in 1867 the first women's suffrage societies were formed, how the National Union of Women's Suffrage Societies came into existence in 1897, and how the Women's Suffrage and Political Union (WSPU) followed in 1903. The role of Millicent Garrett Fawcett and the Pankhursts has rightly been celebrated again with the unveiling of the statue to Millicent Garret Fawcett[39] in Parliament Square, in London, in 2018.

The righteousness of the demand for universal female suffrage seems so obvious now that we can hardly understand why it should have taken so long or stalled during the war. However, the call made on women to support the war effort had a direct effect on the women's suffrage movement. A clue to understanding this can be seen in a letter written on 15 August 1915 by Emmeline Pankhurst (the mother of Christabel, Sylvia and Adela) and sent to the WSPU's members:[40]

> It is obvious that even the most vigorous militancy of the WSPU is for the time being rendered less effective by contrast with the infinitely greater violence done in the

---

[38] For a good oversight see J.W. Grant, *In the Steps of Exceptional Women – The Story of the Fawcett Society 1866–2016* (Francis Boutle Publishers, 2016).

[39] www.theguardian.com/artanddesign/gallery/2018/apr/24/millicent-fawcett-statue-unveiled-in-parliament-square-in-pictures.

[40] See Grant, *Exceptional Women*, at p. 49; quoted from A. Rosen, *Rise Up Women!: The Militant Campaign of the Women's Social and Political Union* (Routledge Keegan and Paul, 1974), p. 248.

present war not merely to property and economic
prosperity alone, but to human life . . .

In short, her view was that while war was doing so much
violence to humanity, militancy at home was out of place. She,
like many others, advocated the postponement of the suffrage
campaign while the violence in Europe continued, and that
women should contribute to bringing about its end. Yet if
women were to contribute to the war effort, she would campaign to ensure that they were not going to suffer obvious
discrimination. It was hoped by the workers and the women's
representatives that the Treasury Agreement would underline
that women were not second-class workers.

Sylvia Pankhurst took this up in a letter[41] dated
25 March 1915 to Lloyd George, when the Agreement was
being negotiated, that was firmly premised on the right for
women to have equal pay for work of equal value:

> In the memorandum published in the press to-day, of
> the agreement arrived at by the Conference at the Treasury,
> the following sentences occur: —
>
> 'Where the custom of a shop is changed during the war by
> the introduction of semi-skilled men to perform work
> hitherto performed by a class of workmen of higher skill,
> the rates paid shall be the usual rates of the district for that
> class of work. A relaxation of existing demarcation
> restrictions, or admission of semi-skilled or female labour,
> shall not affect adversely the rates customarily paid for
> the job.'

---

[41] Ibid. at p. 205.

The wording of these sentences is ambiguous. Does it mean that in the case of women, as is clearly stated in the case of semi-skilled men, that if they are employed to do 'work hitherto performed by workmen of higher skill, the rates paid shall be the usual rates of the district for that class of work?'

Or are we to understand that this provision made in the case of the semi-skilled man is not made in the case of women?

This question is one viewed with the greatest anxiety by the members of the East London Federation of the Suffragettes, on whose behalf I write and by all women all over the country who keenly desire that there shall be equal pay for equal work for both men and women.

I ask you to reply at your earliest convenience, in order that our minds may be set at rest.

Yours, etc., Sylvia Pankhurst

The reply from Lloyd George the next day, indicates that he saw this principle as applying essentially to rates for piecework:

26th March, 1915.

Dear Miss Pankhurst,

The words which you quote would guarantee that women undertaking the work of men would get the same piece rates as men were receiving before the date of this agreement. That, of course, means that if the women turn out the same quantity of work as men employed on the same job, they will receive exactly the same pay.

Yours sincerely, D. Lloyd George

That, of course, left open the question of rates for time work. Were women to be paid the same rate per hour/day/ week/month? Arguments about the comparative value of men's and women's output per hour/day/week/month came more to the fore later in the war. In 1915, when Sylvia pressed her correspondence with Lloyd George, he did not reply.

In this correspondence we can see a theme that runs through the early debates on equal pay. When women really asserted the logic of their argument, the government was reluctant to engage. The women must have felt both deeply frustrated by this but also empowered. If the argument could not be answered, it must surely be unanswerable. Looked at the other way around, the refusal of the government to engage with such logical arguments evidenced the degree to which this gender discrimination was ingrained. This I think is a point that is no less important now.

1.2 Women's Strikes for Equal Pay

There were many occasions when women struggled to be paid equally with the men with whom they worked alongside. There were many jobs in which the skills argument had little or no relevance. Sometimes they were the clear victims of discrimination, and when that happened they sometimes took things into their own hands. One particularly important event occurred on 17 August 1918, just as the Second Battle of the Somme, in which my father fought, was raging.[42] Contrary to attempts to introduce war-time controls on industrial action, there was a wildcat strike of women bus workers in London, which was swiftly followed by similar action in Bath, Brighton, Bristol, Folkestone, Hastings and Weston-Super-Mare.[43]

I shall quote the report in the *Gazette* of the cause and effects of the strike because it is so expressive of the mood of the time on the home front:

> With startling suddenness Uxbridge and the whole of West Middlesex found itself tramless on Saturday through a strike of women workers.
>
> The cause of the trouble was that whereas the award of the Committee on Production gave five shillings to the men it declined a similar concession to the women employees. Those employed on several services of the London United Tramway Company including the Shepherds Bush, Uxbridge line refused to start work on Saturday morning.
>
> No intimation of their intentions was given and many early morning workers found themselves unable to get to business. The inconvenience increased during the day. People in the Hayes and Hillingdon districts who desired to get to Uxbridge or Southall to do their Saturday shopping were faced with the alternative of walking or going without provisions. There was no question of buying locally for many of the villages are rationed for meat, butter

---

[42] www.greatwar.co.uk/battles/somme/somme-battles.htm #secondsomme1918.

[43] See https://libcom.org/history/london-women-tram-workers-equal-pay -strike-1918.

etc at town shops and were therefore in an awkward position.

The stoppage came as a thunder-bolt to many of the men conductors and drivers who had heard nothing about it as it had been more or less secretly organised by the women. One conductress thus explained the situation, 'When we were taken on by the Company they promised to give us whatever rise the men had. We are doing just as much work as the men who realise the justice of our case and are supporting our strike.'

The strike was soon successful, at least in London. Mary Macarthur, General Secretary, National Federation of Women Workers, and founder of the First Trade Union of Women, writing about this strike just as it was being settled,[44] predicted it would lead to a deep discussion in the War Cabinet Committee. On this occasion, she was right and as the *Spectator* noted this did indeed happen. It was this strike that ultimately seems to have persuaded Lloyd George to set up the Cabinet Committee that produced the Women's Industry Report. Certainly, it was this strike that the Report discussed first.[45]

In her article, we can see some of the major concerns about the effects of equal pay that persist to today, in particular that a significant reason for the men's support for unequal treatment was a fear that equal treatment of women

---

[44] See *National News*, 25 August 1918, at www.unionhistory.info/britainat work/emuweb/objects/nofdigi/tuc/imagedisplay.php?irn=1123.

[45] See the discussion of the strike in Part 1 of the Women's Industry Report under the heading '1. Circumstances that led to appointment of Committee and first reference to it' at p. 1 and ff.

would undercut and drive down their wages. In addressing this she first asked rhetorically:[46]

> What is the secret of the opposition of the men to the entry of women into their trades and professions? They do not object to the women because they are women but because they are cheap – because they regard them as unscrupulous competitors in the labour market – instruments to degrade those standards of life and comfort which have so painfully been built up after years of struggle.

She added:

> If women are to win a permanent and honourable place in industry and commerce, they must play the game and they must convince their men colleagues and their employers that they do not intend to be used to degrade standards upon which their own happiness in the future, or what is more important the health and happiness of their children, may depend.

In short, for women to win equal pay they must persuade men at home and in power of their value. They had to change the terms of reference in a fundamental way to create a new framework altogether. She was well aware that if women secured equal pay for work of equal value, it would not necessarily mean more money all round. It could just as easily cause men's rates to fall, and, if so, that they – the men – would campaign for their protection. Two points of current relevance arise from this.

---

[46] See *National News*, footnote 44 above.

First, it is intriguing that she should be so aware that equal pay could be a zero-sum game for men and women – that more for women might well mean less for men. This concern, that equality in pay is a zero-sum issue, is one that is hardly talked about publicly in current discussions on equality. It is mostly answered on the macro level that a country that embraces equality is more likely to be successful than one that does not.[47] This is the point made by the World Economic Forum and McKinsey.

Yet I think it is a mistake not to engage more fully with it; it may or may not be true that securing equality will have this effect on the macro level, but it was obviously a real fear, then, at the level of the workshop or business. I am absolutely sure it remains a real fear, now, for many men at this same level. If so, it seems to me much better that its validity should be discussed than to ignore it. I shall return to this point below.

Secondly, it is also intriguing that this theme – the protection of men's rates in the face of claims by women to equal pay – is as contemporary an issue now as it was then. It is an issue that is still impeding progress to equal pay, because where the relative value of men's jobs and women's jobs show that men are overpaid and women underpaid, it is obvious to the men and to management that the future process of reconciliation of wage to value, will be bad news for the men.

---

[47] See, for instance, this article in the *Guardian* on 27 April 2017: Catherine Meyer, "'Let Women Eat Cake Too': Why Equality is not a Zero-sum Game', at www.theguardian.com/inequality/2017/apr/27/let-women-eat -cake-too-why-equality-is-not-a-zero-sum-game.

I recall being instructed in the early 2000s by a small council that had undergone a job evaluation study but not yet published the results. The study showed a consistent pattern of overpayment of men relative to women through bonuses and special premia. The council wanted to know if it was permissible to ignore the result and continue as before. When I explained that the answer was no,[48] the leading – male – officers and councillors were appalled and argued that it would lead to the deepest unrest in their workforce. They could not afford to bring the women up to the men's rates. They accepted my advice as right, but refused to consider implementing its consequences and did not instruct me further.

Other employers on discovering the degree of inequality have offered special payments to the men – known as 'pay protection' – as they attempt to transition to a fair non-discriminatory pay system. They are of course nothing more than a continuation of the discrimination and, save in very limited circumstances, unlawful. I first litigated the issue of 'pay protection' at length in the case known as *Redcar & Cleveland Borough Council* v. *Bainbridge & Ors*,[49] and it has been litigated several times since, including in front of our Chair in *Glasgow City Council* v. *Unison Claimants & Ors*,[50] just last year.

---

[48] See the judgment of the House of Lords in *O'Brien* v. *Sim-Chem Ltd* [1980] 1 WLR 1011, [1980] 3 All ER 132, [1980] ECC 411, [1980] ICR 573, [1980] IRLR 373, (1980) 124 SJ 560. Documents: Case Analysis [1980] 1 WLR 1011, [1980] ECC 411, [1980] ICR 573.

[49] [2008] IRLR 776, [2009] ICR 133, [2008] EWCA Civ 885; see in particular Part III of the judgment.

[50] [2017] CSIH 34, [2017] IRLR 739, [2017] ScotCS CSIH_34, 2017 GWD 19-300, 2017 SLT 729.

We can see some of these concerns also in a report presented – probably in about 1916[51] – to the 'Joint Committee on Labour Problems after the War' by the 'Standing Joint Committee of Industrial Women's Organisations' (of which Mary Macarthur was a member). The Joint Committee brought together Parliamentarians, members of the Labour Party, and trade unionists. It adopted the key conclusions of this Standing Joint Committee, including a passage in which the liberating effects of equal pay for women and for men were particularly noted, together with the problems that it was thought this might bring:

> The problem before women workers is, how are they to keep the improved industrial position they have won without the effect of their employment being the reduction of the wages of men? The fundamental need is to carry out the principle of equal pay for equal work, for the employment of women will always have a depressing effect on the wages of men as long as there is any economic sex distinction. It is important for women as well as for men to maintain the rate of wages at the highest possible level, for when they are not themselves wage-earners they are dependent on other wage-earners, usually men. During the war there have been two great changes in the position of women workers, both of which have been to their advantage. In the first place, women have found many new trades opened to them in which the wages are higher than they have been accustomed to get. In the second place,

---

[51] It is possible that this report was later. It is not clear from the document itself when it was published. See http://mrc-catalogue.warwick.ac.uk/records/MSX/1546.

> Trade Union organisation has been able to make use of the
> demand for women's labour to gain marked increases in
> the wages of women in many women's trades, as well as to
> succeed in getting their rates in men's trades approximated
> to those of men.

It intrigues me how in this passage the Joint Committee
sought to turn this point on its head and argue for higher
women's wages on the basis that low women's wages operated
to depress men's wages. The validity of this argument will
depend on the extent of the overall demand for labour and the
connected direction of pay rates generally. At this time in the
war, the demand was of course high; the validity would look
very different when the recession came, soon after the war
ended.

The second part of the argument is also intriguing,
acknowledging that keeping men's wages up was critical for
dependent women. This argument about the potentially
adverse effect of the principle of equal pay for work of equal
value on non-working dependent women was frequently
deployed at this time. It really took both the world wars and
the social changes that occurred as legislation that made
married women dependent on their husbands was
removed,[52] and as women were able to control their own
fertility, for it to disappear from general discourse on equal
pay, though there is little doubt in my mind that many men
still believe in the concept of the family wage. As we shall see,
the political condition for its disappearance was the

---

[52] There is a good synopsis of the range of such legislation in the Royal
Commission on Equal Pay 1944–1946, at [342] and ff., at p. 109 and ff.

introduction of compensatory allowances to those with dependants, through the tax system.

1.3 The Women's Industry Report 1919

The War Cabinet Committee's Women's Industry Report was published in April 1919, just a few weeks before the Versailles Treaty was finally agreed. Its work was undertaken in parallel with the preparatory work for that treaty, which was undertaken in what was known as the Paris Conference which ran from 18 January 1919.

Its Report is now largely forgotten, yet it is really very important for anyone who wants a deep understanding as to how the principle of equal pay for work of equal value has developed in the UK, since it tried to consider all these points I have made – and more – in a comprehensive way. In the result it has really laid the foundation for all the later work on this issue.

The Cabinet Committee charged with making the Report was appointed by the Prime Minister Lloyd George on 5 September 1918. Perhaps inevitably it contained four titled men and two untitled women.[53] The Chairman of the Committee was the then Atkin J, shortly to become Atkin LJ, and in due course, as Lord Atkin, to be the author of the main

---

[53] Sir James Richard Atkin, Kt (Chairman); Miss J.M. Campbell, MD; Sir Lynden Livingstone Macassey, KC, KBE; Sir William W. Mackenzie, KC, KBE; Lt-Col the Rt Hon. Sir Matthew Nathan, GCMG; and Mrs Sidney Webb. Later a further man was added to the Committee: Mr J.L. Hammond from the Ministry of Reconstruction, which had a special Women's Employment Committee.

judgment in that most famous of Scottish cases *M'Alister (or Donoghue) v. Stevenson.*[54] The two women were very distinguished in their own right. They were Dr Janet Campbell (later Dame Janet Campbell[55]), then Chief Woman Adviser to the Board of Education, and Mrs Sidney Webb (better known to history as Beatrice Webb) who, with her husband Sidney, are remembered as leading Fabians and co-founders of the London School of Economics.

All but one of the members of the committee (Beatrice Report) concluded in their report that the principle of equal pay for work of equal value should indeed be adopted. In effect there was therefore a Majority and a Minority Report. However, the way in which they expressed themselves was less than revolutionary.[56]

In the first place they were not prepared to consider the direct comparison in an analytic way of the value of quite different jobs, as is now required in an equal value claim or where a job evaluation exercise is carried out:[57]

Women and Men in different Occupations.

As regards . . . men and women do[ing] radically different work – it is not possible to lay down a relation between their wages. There is no way of making any comparison

---

[54] [1932] AC 562, 1932 SC (HL) 31, 1932 SLT 317.
[55] According to the Oxford Dictionary of National Biography, she had recently written 'a valuable and influential report for the Carnegie United Kingdom Trust on the physical welfare of mothers and children'.
[56] See [9] at 4–5, for the summary statement of the recommendations of the Majority of the Commission.
[57] See [210] at 184–185.

between the efforts and sacrifices of a coalminer and
a nursemaid on which theoretically their respective wages
might be based. Any relation that may be adopted in the
wages paid for similar or the same work will, however, have
its effect on the wages paid for dissimilar work by
encouraging or discouraging the selection by women of
one or the other.

If women's wages in occupations where men and
women are both employed on similar or the same work
approach the level of men's wages, these occupations (if it
is not made impossible to enter them) will attract women
and decrease the numbers of them competing in the
exclusively women's occupations and so raise their value in
the latter. To this interplay of industrial forces the
settlement of the relation in the case of dissimilar work
must be left, State intervention being confined to securing
the general raising of the women's level in the ways that
have already been indicated.

The first point about this is, of course, the casual
acceptance of a discriminatory recruitment policy as not
merely acceptable but a necessary condition for the economic
success of the policy.

We can also see that the Majority did not have the
same vision for the effect of this principle as we now do. They
did think that generally women's wages were too low but
thought that they would generally rise compared to those of
men as a result of women's greater access to, and payment for,
jobs that had been traditionally done by men. As we now
know, achieving that in peace time, when there was no driver

of necessity, requires clear laws against gender discrimination in recruitment, but they did not recommend such a change.

The Majority continued[58] in the next paragraph to show that they did not even think that the principle of equal pay for work of equal value went any further than women undertaking the same work or closely similar work:

Women and Men in same Occupations.

It is in connection with women ... doing similar or the same work as men that the formula 'equal pay for equal work' has been mainly used and the governing condition of its application is thus that women should be engaged on or introduced on to work of the same class as that on which men are employed or should be engaged in or introduced into an occupation or section of an occupation or job in which men are also employed, so that there is, as between the man and the woman, community of work or of calling as the case may be.

In such a case there may or may not be equality of efficiency. Both alternatives call for consideration, but before dealing with the arguments in favour of either, we desire to accept the principle involved by the general formula in so far as it is intended to prevent reduction of men's wages by the competition of women with lower standards and less organisation. We consider that it is not to the national advantage that women should be employed in preference to men at work in which they are less efficient than men in order to cheapen labour and increase profits.

The grant of equal pay to women for similar or the same work as that done by men without equality of efficiency has

---

[58] Ibid. at [211].

been expressed as 'the rate for the job' or 'equal time rates.' The grant of equal pay with equality of efficiency corresponds more closely to the formula 'equal pay for equal work.' It has also been described as 'equal pay for equal value,' the underlying idea being that pay should be in proportion to efficient output.

So the Majority were particularly fixated on the comparative output of men and women, but this approach begged many questions. One key point was whether equal pay was a general or personal issue? It was an obvious argument that the most productive woman is likely to exceed the output of the least productive man in most, if not all, situations in which there is time work. If so how can it be said that women are not entitled to the same time rate? The Majority made some progress in addressing this, and along the way developed some insights that are still relevant.

After considering the economic effects predicted to occur for both men and women if equal pay for work of equal value were adopted as a principle, the Majority concluded:[59]

Adoption of Principle and its Application to Industry.

For all these reasons the Committee adopt the principle of 'equal pay for equal work' in the sense that pay should be in proportion to efficient output. The difficulty will be to secure its adoption by employers and employed, and its

---

[59] Ibid. at [217] at 219–220.

reasonable application to the varying circumstances of the different industrial, commercial and professional occupations. *It is, of course, not to be applied individually, but as between women as a class and men as a class.* As in the case of men employed on time the women employed at the rate equivalent to their efficient output will have to come within certain limits of efficiency to justify their being taken on or continued in work. For the reasons already given, it cannot be expected that employers will take on women to do, under the formula, the work, or any part of the work, previously performed by men until under the natural pressure of economic or social forces some shortage of men has occurred. It is not contemplated that their introduction should then be arbitrarily effected by the employer or direction or management concerned, but that it should be negotiated or agreed with the men affected. *The difficulty of such negotiations has been represented to us, inasmuch as the employer alone has at his disposal the data to show whether the women's output is equal to the men's, or what, the true proportion should be.* We think this difficulty has been exaggerated ... (Italics added for emphasis)

I think few would now make normative statements that equal pay *ought* – as a matter of law justice or morality – to be *negotiated* between men and women, since we now recognise this as a right. Yet in fact that is what has been happening in many contexts ever since.

We can see in this passage both the concerns about the lack of transparency of wage systems that bedevil many workplaces still, and also, the realisation that the comparison had to be conducted on an objective basis that was not specifically focussed on the work of an individual woman or man.

Beatrice Webb not only wrote the very extensive Minority Report, but also followed that up with her own book entitled 'Wages of Men and Women: Should they be equal?'[60] It is not that she was against women being paid fairly, as compared with men, but she did come out strongly against the principle of equal pay for work of equal value as identified by the Majority as a guiding principle for wages. She was also highly critical of the approach being taken in the contemporaneous Paris Conference discussions leading to the formation of the ILO.

Her principal complaint was that the concept encapsulated in the phrase was too ambiguous to be useful, and so was potentially detrimental. While legal history has not sided with her in rejecting this principle, her analysis of some of its potential to cause trouble has been amply demonstrated, as we shall also see when discussing what has been happening here in Scotland.

She said:[61]

The Formula of 'Equal Pay for Equal Work' must be Rejected, but only because of its Ambiguity—
We have seen that this formula has no precise meaning and is diversely interpreted by the persons concerned as (1) equal pay for equal efforts and sacrifices; (2) equal pay for

---

[60] Published by the Fabian Society in 1919. This too can be read online at https://catalog.hathitrust.org/Record/000953039.

[61] See her Minority Report at [9] at p. 288 and ff.

equal product; (3) equal pay for equal value to the employer. Hence any adoption of the formula would lead to endless misunderstandings between employers and employed, and increased industrial friction.

The first interpretation of it – equal pay for equal efforts and sacrifices, measured by some convention of time or task – amounts, as we have seen, merely to what has been called the National Minimum, and the Occupational or Standard Rate upon a time-work basis.

The second interpretation – that of 'Equal Pay for Equal Product' – can only be put effectively into operation by the adoption of piecework or some equivalent method of payment per item of output . . .

The third interpretation – Equal Pay for Equal Value to the Employer – whether secured by lower time or piecework rates to any members of a staff engaged on similar work (usually the women), who are alleged not to be as profitable to the employer as some other members of that staff, or by making deductions from such rates in respect of the alleged individual shortcomings of such inferior portion (again usually the women), has been already sufficiently dealt with and shown to be inconsistent with the effective maintenance of any rates at all . . .

A similar criticism applies to the ideal which the Paris Conference is formulating for the guidance of the International Labour Conference of the League of Nations. To say that 'equal pay shall be given to women and to men for work of equal value in quantity and quality' is, unfortunately, to evade all the difficulties and encourage all the evasions. Is the 'equal value' – say of the piece of cloth produced – to be computed according to its value to the ultimate consumer, or to the profit-making employer, who has to consider differential overhead charges, or to the community, which needs to consider the relative efforts and sacrifices imposed on the producers?

I cannot but think that the phrases that my colleagues use in the Majority Report of this Committee are equally ambiguous. In their opening definition they declare 'that women doing similar or the same work as men should receive equal pay for equal work in the sense that pay should be in proportion to efficient output.' But does this refer to identical work only, or to work that is not identical; and is the efficiency to be tested by the quantity or quality of the product, or by the time taken, or by the amount of space and plant required? When I look for light . . . I find only confusion.

They declare, for instance, 'that in every case in which the employer maintains that a woman's work produces less than a man's, the burden of proof should rest on the employer, who should also have to produce evidence of the lower value of the woman's work, to which the fixed sum to be deducted from the man's rate for the particular job throughout the whole of the industry should strictly correspond.'

How can a deduction to be made throughout the whole of the industry correspond, strictly or otherwise, with evidence of the lower value of the work of one particular woman? I defy any Trade Union or any Employers' Association to work out a list of piece-work prices or time-rates according to this rule.

What can we take from all this? In the first place, I think that we must note how the ambiguity of the phrase was so much discussed. If it was not clear what 'equal pay for work of equal value' meant and entailed when it was first used in the UK, then perhaps we should be less critical of those who now find it difficult to get to grips with its implications. On the other hand, if it is to be a meaningful UN Sustainable Development Goal, we cannot now treat it as an empty vessel, into which we can pour whatever are our current ideas. The task of eliminating any ambiguity is one for all of us.

Secondly, it is fascinating that there was such a fear that employers would evade its application by tweaking the jobs that were done by men so as to seek to be able to argue that the women were not doing comparable work. This is a complaint that has been much made in modern times. As a prediction it was entirely correct. It has taken determined litigation and incisive judges to cut through the smoke and mirrors to see what has actually been happening.

Thirdly, in the Majority's conclusion that the principle should not be applied individually, but to classes of women and men, we see the first realisation that what is needed is an objective approach to the assessment of value. Within any such group of women there will necessarily be both the very hard working and the very competent and also the opposite. Any comparison that pitches the very hard working and most competent of one gender against the least hard working and least competent of the other gender will be distorted and useless as a means to establish any kind of equity. The Majority expressed the point differently but clearly saw it.

Fourthly, the Majority also saw that the burden of proving the non-application of the principle had to be on the employer. Reading this report in 2018, I am struck with how prescient this was. I can only think that it was a direct result of the promise in the Treasury Agreement, and the challenges that posed to the government every time there was an arguable failure to meet the promise. If women were to support the war effort on equal terms, then government had to explain every time it appeared that those terms were not equal. That discourse naturally placed the burden on the government, as national employer. The Majority approving that approach adopted it in their recommendations. We shall see this issue recurring in the debates that followed; the fact that the authors of the Report were so clear about it must have provided powerful encouragement to the activists who came later in the inter-war period to press and press again for explanations for apparently unequal pay systems.

Finally, we must note the realisation that the phrase's success as a principle to benefit women depended on there being economic circumstances that would enable the men to permit its application to succeed. Such circumstances could arise fortuitously, as in war time, or could be the subject of forced changes. As I discuss in Chapter 3, demographic change could also be a driver for greater demand for women to enter the labour market as the working-age population diminishes with diminished national fertility.

There is one further aspect of this Report which I must address. This is the Committee's analysis of the arguments used to justify lower pay for women. The Majority's

Report had specific sections[62] discussing the arguments that women were:

- less physically strong;
- less appreciated;
- less stable;
- less trained;
- less organised; and
- less in demand.

The Majority did not dismiss these arguments out of hand, but sought to explain them, and to consider how the developing economy might render them less significant. In reading the paragraphs of the report, three features, thought then to be typical of women's experience by the Majority, stand out.

First, that it was conventional for women to expect to be married and therefore either were, or were thought to be, less committed to a career. In 1919 the median age for women to marry in England and Wales was 25; it is now 31.[63] I have no reason to believe it will be much different in Scotland or Northern Ireland, so whether this change is cause or effect of the campaign for equal pay, its relevance is greatly diminished.

Secondly, it was a given that women and women alone were responsible for domestic chores. On this there

---

[62] See her Minority Report at [81]–[86] at p. 69 and ff.

[63] See the ONS Dataset, Marriages in England and Wales, at www
.ons.gov.uk/peoplepopulationandcommunity/birthsdeathsandmarria
ges/marriagecohabitationandcivilpartnerships/datasets/
marriagesinenglandandwales2013.

has been a great change in social attitudes and a rather less remarkable change in practice.[64]

These two factors were thought to supply the major reasons for the inferior position of women in the labour market. Above all else they implied a third point, which runs like a seam through the Committee's report as central to the men's arguments that their wages should be maintained and there was a justification for their take home pay being greater than women's. This was the stereotypical assumption, I have noted above, that men had dependants, while women were themselves dependent, and so, because men had dependants, they needed to earn enough to support them.

The Majority did understand well enough that, if equal pay was secured, any such need for women to depend on men would diminish or be eliminated. However, their capacity to imagine a world in which this might occur, was limited too much by the reality of the world in which they lived. I think it is hard in retrospect to be too critical of the Committee in this respect. I suspect most of us will be found wanting when our understanding of the future comes under scrutiny. Yet although the Committee did recognise that women too might have dependants, it took no significant note of this in its analysis.

What I do take from this is the fact that the ideas summarised in the Report remain potent for too many men, human resource departments and senior management. They

[64] See, for instance, the research into British Social Attitudes by the National Centre for Social Research at www.bsa.natcen.ac.uk/media/38 457/bsa30_gender_roles_final.pdf.

do not, of course, survive examination as to their universal and immutable truth. The failure to get to grips with this seems, in retrospect, to be a major – though perhaps understandable – failing of the Majority. There is now, and there was then, no pre-ordained reason why women cannot live any life they wish. In theory, if not always in practice, marriage is, and was, an option; dependence of one or the other spouse within marriage is, and was, an option; domesticity or the complete lack of it is, and was, an option. We see these points much more clearly now and can say these things because women have been more than merely enfranchised in the vote, but in their ability to seek their own destiny. Yet at the time the economic pressures then on women to have children and to manage homes was infinitely greater. The fact that, for the 4 years of the war, another way of living had been discovered by women was simply not fully understood by the predominantly male Majority.

The list of women's supposed handicaps in the labour market was important for another reason. By setting these out in this way, the scene was set for a later challenging response. Such a response – noted but not developed in the Report – identifies the skills in which women commonly excel and indeed outperform men. From this, when in due course job evaluation protocols came to be written and applied, it became possible to strive for a non-discriminatory balance in the factors by which jobs were to be valued and non-discriminatory weightings be ascribed to those factors.

The detail of this Report, with its qualified endorsement by the Majority of the principle of equal pay for work of equal value, has to be contrasted with the simplicity of the text in the contemporaneous provisions of the Versailles Treaty addressing the same subject. Of course, the former was concerned with the practicalities of domestic application of the principle, whereas the latter was an international legal instrument. Yet in the end we shall see that it was a good thing that the treaty did not define further what it meant, whether by accepting or rejecting what the Cabinet Committee had said in the Report. This is because in due course its simplicity enabled a deeper (if more difficult) concept of equal value to emerge.

1.4 Equal Pay in the Inter-war Years

With so much momentum towards achieving a right for equal pay for work of equal value, it would be nice to think that 1919 was a new dawn of a better world for women in which discrimination would be outlawed and their work would soon be truly valued. It was not to be, despite many attempts.

Possibly the first was the House of Commons resolution on 19 May 1920:

> That it is expedient that women should have equal opportunity of employment with men in all branches of the Civil Service within the United Kingdom and under all local authorities, . . . and should also receive equal pay.

The text of this simple resolution was not so far removed from that of the treaty and certainly in the spirit of the war-time discussions. It was not to be; on 17 June 1920, the Prime

Minister Lloyd George poured a dose of cold water on implementing it.[65]

There was no more luck with developing the ideas in the Versailles Treaty. Although the Versailles Treaty contained processes by which states could complain about the failures of other states in relation to the terms on which the ILO was set up, as far as I am aware no such complaint was made at this stage. No doubt this was because it was expected by the signatories at least that further international law would be made by the ILO to give effect to these principles. It was one thing to get agreement to the text set out above and quite another for it to be implemented in any material further provisions.

Only the softest of very 'soft' law emerged from the ILO, in this inter-war period, perhaps the most significant of which were:[66]

- the Labour Inspection Recommendation, 1923 (No. 20),[67] which provided that the labour inspectorate 'should include women as well as men inspectors ... [who] ... should in general have the same powers and duties and exercise the

---

[65] https://api.parliament.uk/historic-hansard/commons/1920/jun/17/civil-service-womens-pay.

[66] See G. Rodgers, E. Lee, L. Swepston and J. Van Daele, *The ILO and the Quest for Social Justice, 1919–2009* (ILO, 2009), at 57–58; see also the submission by Lin Lim Lean for the ILO Century Project, August 2007, and M. Gaudier, *The Development of the Women's Question at the ILO, 1919–1994 – 75 years of Progress towards Equality* (ILO, International Institute for Labour Studies, 1996).

[67] See now www.ilo.org/dyn/normlex/en/f?p=NORMLEXPUB:12100:0::NO::P12100_ILO_CODE:R020.

same authority as the men inspectors, . . . and should have equal opportunity of promotion to the higher ranks'; and

- the Minimum Wage-Fixing Machinery Recommendation, 1928 (No. 30) concluded by saying 'it [is] right to call the attention of Governments to the principle affirmed by . . . the Constitution of the International Labour Organisation that men and women should receive equal remuneration for work of equal value'.[68]

G.N. Barnes, who as a member of Lloyd George's cabinet responsible for much of the negotiation that led up to the Versailles Treaty, has described the contemporary understanding of the purpose of such recommendations, as being:[69]

> . . . general principles for the guidance of national Governments in drafting national legislation or in issuing administrative orders.

There is, as far as I am aware, no UK legislation, as such, in the inter-war period in which the principle was adopted.[70] There is only one case in the inter-war period[71] in which the work of the ILO was even mentioned. In this case, *Attorney-General for Canada* v. *Attorney-General for*

---

[68] See now www.ilo.org/dyn/normlex/en/f?p=NORMLEXPUB:12100:0:: NO::P12100_ILO_CODE:R030.

[69] See G.N. Barnes, *History of the International Labour Office* (Williams and Norgate Ltd, 1926), at p. 51.

[70] Some steps were taken elsewhere; some states of the USA, such as Michigan and Montana in 1919. See the Report of the Royal Commission on Equal Pay, 1944–46, Cmd 6937, at [283]–[285].

[71] That I can find on a search of the Westlaw database.

Ontario,[72] the Privy Council (with Lord Atkin in the chair) struck down as *ultra vires* various Acts of the Parliament of Canada, designed to outlaw exploitative working hours in accordance with draft ILO Conventions, and the Labour Part of the Treaty of Versailles, 1919, that had been ratified by the Dominion of Canada.[73] No doubt he supported the limitations, but, as the case showed, the dualist nature of the common law limited the reach of international law. It was only effective domestically to the extent it had been properly transposed. In a judicial capacity the future Lord Atkin never had to consider the principle of equal pay for work of equal value as set out in the ILO's constitution.

He did, however, have one opportunity – of which I am aware – to address an argument about equal pay in a judgment. In May 1924 the now notorious case of *Roberts* v. *Hopwood*[74] came before the Court of Appeal. The judges hearing the appeal were Lords Justices Bankes, Atkin and Scrutton. It may be recalled that the appeal concerned a decision by the auditor as to the lawfulness of expenditure by Poplar Council in London. The Council considered that as it wished to be a model employer, it should not pay any of its servants less than £4 a week. Those wages were considerably in excess of the rates fixed by awards of the Joint Industrial Council, and also of the pre-war rates of wages coupled with

[72] [1937] AC 326.
[73] Because the legislation related to matters coming within the class of subject 'Property and civil rights in the Province', which was assigned exclusively to the Legislatures of the Provinces by head 13 of s. 92 of the British North America Act, 1867.
[74] [1924] 2 KB 695.

the officially recognised decrease in the cost of living since the war. The district auditor disallowed the excess above what he considered would have been a reasonable payment and surcharged the councillors. Atkin and Scrutton LJJ disagreed and held that the payments were not unreasonable. Bankes LJ considered otherwise and when the case went to the House of Lords they agreed with him and the Auditor.[75]

One of the sub-plots in this battle between local government and the Auditor was the payment of women's wages. Atkin LJ said:

> The wages of all women seem to have been put up in May of 1920 from 50 shillings to 80 shillings, and to have been maintained at that rate. At the beginning of the period in question the maximum payable under awards of the Joint Industrial Council was 69s. 3d. The 20 shillings margin allowed by the auditor would make the allowable wage at the beginning of the period 75 shillings instead of the 80 shillings paid by the council, though the cost of living substantially declined on the whole during the period. The number of women employed is 44. Possibly the action of the council was based upon the view that women ought to receive equal pay with men for equal work. In any case I cannot think that the council acted so unreasonably as to be acting ultra vires in this respect.

Although the judgments of the majority were overturned in the House of Lords, the principle of equal pay for work of equal value was not directly challenged, and indeed was partially affirmed by Lord Buckmaster:[76]

[75] [1925] AC 578.   [76] Ibid. at p. 590.

[The Council] standardised men and women not according to the duties they performed, but according to the fact that they were adults. It is this that leads me to think that their action cannot be supported, and that in fact they have not determined the payment as wages, for they have eliminated the consideration both of the work to be done and of the purchasing power of the sums paid, which they themselves appear to regard as a relevant though not the dominant factor. *Had they stated that they determined as a borough council to pay the same wage for the same work without regard to the sex or condition of the person who performed it, I should have found it difficult to say that that was not a proper exercise of their discretion.* It was indeed argued that that is what they did, but I find it impossible to extract that from the statement contained in the affidavit. (Italics added for emphasis)

Lord Sumner agreed, but his judgment is interesting because it is, I believe, the first time in a UK judgment that the concept of comparable but different work was discussed as being in some way potentially equal in value. He said:[77]

The one definite thing is that the [councillors] contend [is] that no adult employee should in any circumstances have less than £4 a week, whether young or old, male or female, married or single, skilled or unskilled. *It is not shown that the women's work is the same as, or is comparable with, the men's, or that the women inter se or the men inter se are engaged in equivalent tasks.* . . . (Italics added)

[77] Ibid. at pp. 609–610.

These though were merely straws in the judicial wind, and had little, if any, impact on the government. Many historians have of course discussed the economic circumstances in the inter-war periods, the recession, the unemployment and deflation of wages. None of these facts made the arguments for legislation to secure equal pay for work of equal value any easier. If wages were being reduced, it was hard to argue that women's wages should be raised to those of men. However, the flame of this idea was not extinguished.[78] As a continuation of the campaign for equal suffrage, various organisations did continue to press for equal pay for equal work, particularly in the light of the 1920 resolution on equal pay in the Civil Service.[79]

One important context in which this argument could be put forward was the 1931 Royal Commission on the Civil Service (under Lord Tomlin). Harold Smith has described[80] what happened:

> The Royal Commission recommended that the civil service follow a policy of 'a fair field and no favour' toward female employees, but it was 'almost equally' divided on the equal pay issue and therefore made no recommendation on it.

[78] I must acknowledge my debt in the following paragraphs to the article by Harold Smith: Harold L. Smith, 'British Feminism and the Equal Pay Issue in the 1930s' (1996) 5.1 *Women's History Review*, 97–110. See www.tandfonline.com/doi/pdf/10.1080/09612029600200102.

[79] Harold Smith comments that 'Following the 1918 grant of partial suffrage, the [London Society for Women's Suffrage (LNSWS)] adopted a new programme focusing on the economic emancipation of women, and made equal pay its special concern ...' : see ibid. endnote [2].

[80] Ibid. at p. 100.

The commissioners endorsing equal pay maintained that the principle of fair relativity supported equal pay for women who did equal work. They pointed out that it was misleading for the Treasury to compare female civil servants with women in private industry in that when the latter received lower pay, they were usually not doing equal work since their jobs were sex segregated. The appropriate comparison would be to professional women and others who did equal work. Since the pay of professional workers in the private sector was generally set without regard for the employee's sex, the principle of fair relativity should lead to equal pay in the civil service. They noted that this was already the case for civil service medical women and for the female scientists at the National Physical Laboratory.

In fact, thereafter it seems that the government actually reduced the extent to which it operated a policy of equal pay to any women within the Civil Service.[81] And then the inevitable reaction came; campaigners motivated by this pusillanimous response moved to get the issue before Parliament. A motion for equal pay was raised and as Harold Smith states:[82]

> On 1 April 1936 the Government [which was against the issue] was defeated in the House of Commons by a vote of 156 to 148 on a motion to provide equal pay for women in the common classes of the civil service.[83]

[81] Ibid. passim. [82] Ibid. at p. 97.

[83] He states that, 'The common classes were those in which women and men were interchangeable.' Previous references to this vote have attributed it to trade union and Labour Party pressure for equal pay. See

The debate in the House of Commons[84] makes for compelling and fascinating reading. I wish I could share it all with you. There are two passages which a lecture of this kind cannot omit.

Katharine Stewart-Murray, the Duchess of Atholl, was then Scottish Unionist MP for Kinross and West Perthshire, and one of the seven women then in Parliament. She had been a member of the Tomlin Commission and was later known as the 'Red Duchess' for her left-wing views. This is how she saw the issue:[85]

> very little consideration has been given to a question which was very much before the Royal Commission, namely, the question of the bigger family responsibilities of the men. No one wishes to deny that there are many women who have a mother or perhaps a sister to support, but, taken by and large, I think nobody can deny that the family responsibilities of men are considerably larger than those of women, and it was very remarkable that in the evidence that was presented to us by the men's organisations, though several of these organisations said they favoured the principle of equal pay, many of them were very interested in pressing on us the need, as they saw it, of higher salaries for the men at the period in life at which the

Sheila Lewenhak, *Women and Trade Unions: An Outline History of Women in the British Trade Union Movement* (St Martin's Press, 1977), p. 229.

[84] See https://api.parliament.uk/historic-hansard/commons/1936/apr/01/civil-service-women-pay.

[85] See HC Deb 1 April 1936 vol 310 cc2017–96, https://api.parliament.uk/historic-hansard/commons/1936/apr/01/civil-service-women-pay.

family responsibilities of married men are greatest, that is to say, at the time when the family is being educated. That was a claim that we heard from many of the men's organisations, and, frankly, it did not seem to me to be consistent with the rather lukewarm support that some of the associations gave to the principle of equal pay.

I think we have to remember that though the women do not rise to the same final remuneration as the men [in the Civil Service], they do rise to three-quarters or four-fifths. They enter at the same level, but gradually the men outstrip them by a quarter or a fifth, that is, in those years in which for most men family responsibilities are increasing. Moreover, those of us on the Royal Commission who felt that we could not recommend equal pay, put on record that the relative pay of the sexes in the Civil Service was fully abreast of that in practice in the outside world. It was, I think, clearly set forth that the Civil Service ought to be in the position of a good employer, or of the best employer, but not out of step with what was happening in the world outside.

It also became clear that, just because there was this general recognition of the weight of family responsibilities resting on men, if equal pay were granted, inevitably it would be followed by a demand for family allowances? There was general recognition, not always vocal, but sometimes tacit, though often vocally expressed, that there are heavier family responsibilities resting on men than on women, and this is something fundamental, from which, we cannot get away. Therefore, it was made clear in the course of the evidence that if equal pay were granted, it would only be the prelude to a further demand for family allowances in order to remedy the injustice to the married men which they would feel if they found there was nothing to compensate them for their bigger responsibilities.

I therefore feel it my duty to point out that if equal pay is granted, that is only the beginning of a very much bigger salary bill in the Civil Service. I do not wish to argue the question of family allowances here. I only wish to point out that you are only at the beginning of a considerable addition to salary expenditure in the Civil Service if the principle of equal pay is adopted.

. . .

I am sure the working women in my constituency would feel it a grievance for women without family responsibilities to receive the same pay as married men. If this question is going to be looked at from the electoral point of view, that is how it appears to me, but I want to look at it from the point of view of justice. Because I think that, on the whole, in the vast majority of cases, there is a weight of family responsibility resting on the married man that does not rest on the unmarried woman, and because that fact came before me very clearly during the course of my work on the Royal Commission, I feel bound to vote against the [proposition] to-night.

We see here, yet again, three of the most important barriers that proponents of equal pay for work of equal value faced:

- the economic argument of a zero-sum gain. If equal pay was afforded, men's wages might have to be reduced, with the further consequence that the male primary earners would need financial support;

- this would set non-working dependent married women against and at a disadvantage to unmarried women;
- on the other hand, if women's pay was to be brought up to that of men, the pay budget would have to increase.

The barriers that the Red Duchess saw ignored the value of the work on any objective assessment of the skill, effort or stress of the job, but focussed on the utility of the wage in a general social sense. The Red Duchess' concept of society, with women and children dependent on men, must have seemed to her as real and determinative. Although she had considerable ideas about changing society elsewhere – she visited the Republicans in the Spanish Civil War[86] – in this passage she showed no understanding that equal pay for work of equal value could be transformative for women, liberating them to plan to live their lives in different ways.

On the other hand, there was an interesting and important aspect to this argument which must not be ignored in any assessment of what she said, in the context of the debates about the nature of equality that were being developed at the time. Did equality mean *from each according to their ability to each according to their need* or *to each according to their effort*? The former was what was expected of a truly Communist society, the latter was only a step on the way. The difference between the two concepts was discussed extensively in a book by a well-known intellectual and former MP, John Strachey,[87] published the same year by the Left

---

[86] See Duchess of Atholl, *Searchlight on Spain* (Penguin, 1938).

[87] She would almost certainly have known John Strachey as he was a leading intellectual, politician and member of the ubiquitous Strachey

Book Club.[88] We can see that the Red Duchess' arguments were closer to the former view.

Her views must be contrasted with a wonderful speech, based on the ILO's express terms, from the Conservative Lady Nancy Astor, the first female MP to take her seat in the House of Commons,[89] that demonstrates the depth of cross-party feeling:

> This is the day of treaty-keeping, and we are told that all countries must honour their treaties. I want to ask the Government to keep their treaty, for it must be remembered that in Part XIII of the Treaty of Versailles the following is incorporated: Among these methods and principles, the following seem to the High Contracting Parties to be of special and urgent importance: ... The principle that men and women should receive equal remuneration for work of equal value. That is one part of the Treaty of Versailles which has never been kept by any Government since the treaty was signed. The Government cannot get away with it on the ground of cost. After all, they set up a committee to inquire into the working of the sugar industry and there was an almost unanimous report that it was extravagant, that it was not on sound grounds and that it ought gradually to be done away with. The Government refused that report and went on to vote

family. He had been an MP from 1929 to 1931 at the same time as her and was later returned to Parliament in 1945, becoming ultimately Secretary of State for War in the Attlee Government.

[88] See *Chapter XI, Socialism and Communism Distinguished* in J. Strachey, *The Theory and Practice of Socialism* (Victor Gollancz Ltd, New Left Book Club, 1936).

[89] See footnote 85 above, cols 2047 and ff.

£7,000,000 for an industry which the report said would never be able to stand on its own feet. The Government cannot say they cannot afford to give the money, for if they gave equal remuneration to all grades and classes it would amount only to £1,000,000. But we are not asking so much, because we know the Government will not do that at once. As other hon. Members have said, we wish to be reasonable and to get what we can. If the Government say they cannot afford it, they will make the House look ridiculous, and hon. Members will look ridiculous if they go into the Lobby against this Amendment.

[HON. MEMBERS: 'Agreed!']

Well, we shall see when the Division comes. I am certain that there is hardly an hon. Member here who has not given a pledge on this question of equal pay for equal work, and now is the time for them to keep that pledge.

This question always seems to cause some amusement in the House. Some hon. Members seem to regard any question affecting women as a good joke, just as mothers-in-law used to be regarded as a joke. But I ask them to remember that this question is very far from being a joke. It is a serious matter and some hon. Members may find that it will be a serious matter for them, in view of the large number of women electors in the country. I would remind them that four out of five women in England to-day are at work. We are not living to-day in the kind of world described in 'Pride and Prejudice' which was quoted by the hon. Lady opposite, the kind of world in which a woman's only occupation was to get married. A great many women to-day find that it is too strenuous an occupation and even if they could marry, they do not wish to do so. They have a perfect right to remain single if they want to remain

single. As to the argument which has been advanced about
dependants, one could give many instances of women in
the Civil Service who have dependants. I have one friend
whose whole family is dependent on her work. (2049) She
is in the position, not only of doing equal work with men
but of seeing men who are under her more highly paid than
she is herself.

[HON. MEMBERS: 'Shame!']

It is a shame. It is really unfair that such a state of things
should be allowed to go on and we here have the power to
stop it.

Then we are told about the wastage caused by marriage.
The wastage caused by marriage is no higher than the
wastage caused by deaths among men. The death rate is
higher than the marriage rate in the Civil Service. We have
also been told that the incidence of sickness is higher
among women, but Lord Tomlin has shown that there is
very little difference between men and women in regard to
the rate of sickness. Therefore that argument cannot be put
forward any longer. Nor can the argument any longer be
advanced that the country is unable to afford it. The Prime
Minister recently paid a tremendous tribute to women and
in a very interesting speech pointed out how grateful men
ought to be to women. He spoke of the ability, loyalty and
capacity of women and added something about their
discretion. If women were not discreet where would men
be. I submit that on the ground of their discretion alone
they are entitled to equal pay with men.

Some of the best women in the country are in the Civil
Service and their demand is based on justice. We do not
make any extreme claim and we do not make any threats.
But we know that women would never have got the vote if

they had gone on behaving like perfect ladies. No one pays very much attention to a perfect lady, particularly when it comes to getting something done and women are not going to stand this kind of injustice for ever. The other day we had a meeting at the Caxton Hall at which 25 different organisations were represented and it was necessary to arrange for a huge overflow meeting. That gathering included many of the best women of the country who feel this injustice very strongly. I, myself, belonging to a great and powerful party, in a country which prides itself on setting an example to the rest of the world, feel that now is the time when we ought to meet the women's demand for equality in this respect.

I ask the Government not to seek for every possible excuse to avoid the issue. I beg the House to consider that equal pay for equal work is a matter of common justice if not indeed of common humanity. I do not say that in all branches of work women are as good as men but I would say to hon. Members who are listening to me: Give your daughters the same chances as you give your sons and see what will happen. Send them to college as you send your sons to college. I do not say that they will all take advantage of it. All the sons do not take advantage of their educational opportunities. But I say, give the young women an equal chance and you will find that it will not only pay you but will pay the State. There are some very fine young women to-day going into the Civil Service. They have a very high sense of service and of loyalty but they are discouraged when they find in the fairest country in the world, the country which is supposed to show an example of justice to the rest of the world, they are denied equal pay for equal work.

I appeal to hon. Members not to listen to the Whips on this occasion. A Government is no use if it has a lot of tame followers. I ask hon. Members also to bear in mind that it will not hurt their chances of promotion to take an independent line on these matters. Governments respect people with independence, especially when they have such a feeble Opposition. However the hon. Lady who moved this Motion said she did not want to be rude and I do not want to be rude either. I only say that, unless hon. Members on our side have the courage of their convictions on this matter and show the Government that they really mean it, there will be trouble, because there is great discontent and disappointment on this subject among the thousands of women throughout the country who backed the National Government, believing that it was for the national good. I would appeal to the young and rising Financial Secretary. Let him rise on justice and let him not be pulled down by Treasury officials who seem to have forgotten what justice is so far as women are concerned.

Things might have turned out very differently, had not the Prime Minister Stanley Baldwin made the issue a matter of confidence, and so persuaded the Commons to overturn this resolution the very next day. Yet Harold Smith notes[90] that:

Even though they did not gain equal pay, the feminists who had initiated the parliamentary campaign were privately very pleased with the extent of the House of Commons support for equal pay. Philippa Strachey, the [London Society for Women's Suffrage] secretary,[91] thought this

[90] Smith, 'British feminism' p. 105.
[91] I understand her to be John Strachey's first cousin.

reflected a 'great change' in public opinion since 1933, which the Government had badly underestimated.

I would like to think Lady Astor's speech was well known to the delegates at the ILO's International Labour Conference the following year. It unanimously adopted a resolution from the United States with various general principles of social policy concerning various aspects of the position of women workers. The ILO's governing body was requested to draw these principles to the attention of all governments 'with a view to their establishment in law and in custom by legislative and administrative action'. The principles included the proposition that:

> it is for the best interests of society that women should have full opportunity to work and should receive remuneration without discrimination because of sex.

1.5 Equal Pay in the Second World War

It was but a short period in this history from 1936–7 to the start of the Second World War when once again the demand for female labour increased hugely. A recent government paper[92] has summarised just how important was the role of women:

> With thousands of men away serving in the armed forces, British women took on a variety of jobs during the Second World War. They also played a vital role on the home front, running households and fighting a daily battle of

---

[92] See www.gov.uk/government/news/the-women-of-the-second-world-war.

rationing, recycling, reusing, and cultivating food in allotments and gardens. From 1941, women were called up for war work, in roles such as mechanics, engineers, munitions workers, air raid wardens, bus and fire engine drivers. At first, only single women, aged 20–30 were called up, but by mid-1943, almost 90 per cent of single women and 80 per cent of married women were working in factories, on the land or in the armed forces. There were over 640,000 women in the armed forces, including The Women's Royal Naval Service (WRNS), the Women's Auxiliary Air Force (WAAF) and the Auxiliary Territorial Service (ATS), plus many more who flew unarmed aircraft, drove ambulances, served as nurses and worked behind enemy lines in the European resistance in the Special Operations Executive.

All the same arguments as for the First World War were rolled out to both call for and deny them equal pay. The campaign that had been fought so hard but with so little success since the Treasury Agreement of 1915 continued with no less passion. There were several events that gave the campaign for equal pay a boost, even if not outright success. One concerned the provision of pensions and allowance to, or in respect of, civilians who were killed or injured as a result of actions by the enemy or in the performance of civil defence duties. Initially these were paid on a sex discriminatory basis. However, as the National Archives states:[93]

---

[93] See http://discovery.nationalarchives.gov.uk/details/r/c3b3e7cf-1cab-4f80-880a-a246b0ae2956.

This scheme was opposed by women's organisations and action was co-ordinated by the National Association of Women Civil servants and the British Federation of Business and Professional Women. A committee was instituted, firstly on an ad-hoc and then a permanent basis, with representatives from the Women Power Committee, The National Association of Women Civil Servants, the British Federation of Business and Professional Women, the National Council of Women, the Women's Publicity Planning Association and later the Women's Freedom League. The chair was Mavis Tate MP. A select committee was subsequently instituted which overturned the existing legislation and resulted in equal compensation rates being paid in 1943. With this achieved, attention was extending the work to equal pay more generally and a new committee was appointed under the title of the Equal Pay Campaign Committee, with a sister branch in Scotland and an attached advisory council.

Another of the key events was again a Parliamentary motion in favour of equal pay for equal value that was overturned as a motion of confidence. On 28 March 1944, Mrs Cazalet-Keir, a Conservative MP for Islington East, and later President of the Fawcett Society, moved an amendment to the Education Bill then before Parliament to establish that female teachers should get equal pay to that of males.[94]

---

[94] HC Deb 28 March 1944 vol 398 cc1355–96, see https://api.parliament.uk /historic-hansard/commons/1944/mar/28/clause-82-remuneration-of-teachers.

The case to be made was about as simple a case of equal pay for work of equal value as one could imagine; she argued:

The teaching profession seems to be a completely clear-cut case of equality between men and women, which scarcely needs arguing. Men and women enter the training colleges at the same age, with the same entrance qualifications. They take equivalent courses of training for exactly the same length of time; when they emerge from the training colleges, they receive the same certificates from the Board of Education or the university, and they enter their professional lives in exactly the same way by applying for teaching posts when vacancies occur. When they get into the schools they are confronted with the same problems, responsibilities and conditions of work. In a mixed school they are, as a rule, entirely interchangeable.

The Committee will see that everything is equal until they assume responsibility, and then they become unequal. I will give the Committee only one example. I will take a London school, a mixed central school, which many hon. Members have visited, where boys and girls, from 11 to 16, are taught side by side by a mixed staff – five men and eight women, with a headmistress in charge, all at their maximum salaries. The teachers specialise in all subjects. There is no difference in the work of the men and the women and all take equal shares in the exchange of duties, such as in the provision of meals and milk. The men receive £84 a year more than the women, and cases like this could be multiplied a hundredfold. It is difficult to see any grounds why women teachers should receive less pay for their responsibilities and work in schools than men. The argument always advanced – and I feel certain that it will be advanced here again – is that men as a rule have families to support. These arguments will be far less impressive when the Government scheme for family allowances is introduced. Let me assure the Committee that the effect of two successive wars has been to increase, by an amazing percentage, the number of women supporting dependants, and as the war proceeds, this number will be still further increased. From every possible point of view, I beg the Minister to look with favour on this Amendment. I am certain that public opinion is ready, anxious and waiting to accept the principle which it embodies.

Her motion was carried, the government were defeated, but the next day Churchill came to the House of Commons to say:[95]

At this very serious time in the progress of the war, there must be no doubt or question of the support which the Government enjoy in the House of Commons. Accordingly we have decided, as the first Business on the next Sitting Day, to resume the Committee stage of the Education Bill, and to delete Clause 82, as amended, entirely from the Measure. This act of deletion will be regarded as a Vote of Confidence in the present Administration. If the Government do not secure an adequate majority, it will entail the usual constitutional consequences.

[95] HC Deb 29 March 1944 vol 398 cc1452–7, see https://api.parliament.uk /historic-hansard/commons/1944/mar/29/education-bill-government-defeat.

History knows that the war-time government did not fall. The amendment was overturned. Equal pay for equal work as a legal right was postponed yet again. There may have been retribution, though. It has been argued that this decision by Churchill was one of the causes of his later defeat in the post-war election.[96]

We do not need to dwell further on the detail of the debates on equal pay at the time, apart from to say that eventually it led to another enquiry and report – the Royal Commission on Equal Pay 1944–1946,[97] but before considering the work of this Commission, I must mention two other steps of greater importance in establishing a comprehensive legal right to equal pay.

1.6 The Developing Idea of Job Evaluation

In 1944, the ILO held its 26th Conference in Philadelphia in the USA. This Conference adopted what has come to be known as the Philadelphia Declaration.[98] Section II of this Declaration stated:

> Believing that experience has fully demonstrated the truth of the statement in the Constitution of the International Labour Organisation that lasting peace can be established

---

[96] See www.historymatters.group.shef.ac.uk/the-men-turned-me-winston -churchill-gender-politics-1945-election/.

[97] Cmd 6937. See https://archive.org/stream/royalcommission 0033426mbp#page/n6/mode/1up.

[98] See www.ilo.org/legacy/english/inwork/cb-policy-guide/declarationof Philadelphia1944.pdf.

only if it is based on social justice, the Conference affirms that:

> (a) all human beings, irrespective of race, creed or sex, have the right to pursue both their material well-being and their spiritual development in conditions of freedom and dignity, of economic security and equal opportunity.

This statement marks a critical development towards the international law recognition of the principle of equal opportunity for women and it came with a Recommendation on Employment (Transition from War to Peace)[99] that set out eleven general principles and their suggested methods of application, including General Principle IX:

> The redistribution of women workers in each national economy should be carried out on the principle of complete equality of opportunity for men and women in respect of admission to employment on the basis of their individual merit, skill, and experience, and steps should be taken to encourage the establishment of wage rates on the basis of job content, without regard to sex.

---

[99] R071 – Employment (Transition from War to Peace) Recommendation, 1944 (No. 71). The Recommendation can be seen at www.ilo.org/dyn/normlex/en/f?p=1000:12100:2651399124926::NO::P12100_SHOW_TEXT:Y. It is now superseded by the Employment and Decent Work for Peace and Resilience Recommendation, 2017 (No. 205)], see www.ilo.org/dyn/normlex/en/f?p=1000:12100:2651399124926:12100:NO::P12100_INSTRUMENT_ID:3330503.

It is obvious that the ILO's focus on pay according to job content stood in deep contrast to the approach that pay should be based on need. The general statement of approach was fleshed out by paragraphs 37(1) and (2) of the 'Methods of Application':

> 37(1). In order to place women on a basis of equality with men in the employment market, and thus to prevent competition among the available workers prejudicial to the interests of both men and women workers, steps should be taken to encourage the establishment of wage rates based on job content, without regard to sex.
>
> (2) Investigation should be conducted, in co-operation with employers' and workers' organisations, for the purpose of establishing precise and objective standards for determining job content, irrespective of the sex of the worker, as a basis for determining wage rates.

In this Recommendation we see the most important step-change in a legal instrument on the approach taken to equal value. The idea that there should be such objective assessment of 'job content' as a basis for determining pay meant that a scheme for job evaluation was necessary. Unsurprisingly, given the intransigence on this issue that it had shown to date, the UK reserved its decision whether to adopt Principle No. IX and paragraph 37(1) until its Royal Commission reported.

The second event of importance that year was the decision by the state of New York to pass the New York Equal

Pay Act 1944.[100] Other states in the USA passed similar legislation soon after. This Act was passed in a context that would have
been well understood by the members of the first UK Royal
Commission. The driving force for the Act was a campaign to
protect men's wages as women became more involved in undertaking jobs hitherto done by men, just as much as it was
proposed to give women equal pay for work of equal value.[101]
It is intriguing to note how this context would have been well
understood by the members of the Cabinet Committee in 1918
and to wonder what they would have said, reflecting how little
progress had been made in a quarter of a century.

The New York Act used some methods to enforce
equal pay that are similar to those used in other equality
contexts in the UK, particularly in the first Race Relations
Acts,[102] and even now. Recognising the weakness of women's
bargaining power and the difficulties of addressing the
demands of returning male soldiers, an Industrial
Commissioner was given powers to investigate and to attempt
to adjust equitably controversies between employer and
employee in respect of wage claims. The Commissioner was
empowered to take assignment of wage claims in trust for the
assigning employee and to sue employers on wage claims made
under the law.[103] The Commissioner appointed a committee to
assist him in preparing the programme for the administration

---

[100] NY Laws 1944, c 793.
[101] See the discussion of the Act in NY Labor Law, s. 199-a, Equal Pay for
Equal Work, Columbia Law Review Vol. 46, No. 3 (May, 1946), pp.
442–452.
[102] Of 1965 and 1968.
[103] Powers of enforcement by criminal proceedings were also granted.

of the new provisions. That committee set about making an analysis of particular types of occupations for the purpose of establishing a standard of equalisation for the evaluation of wages. It also presciently proposed to formulate a programme of education whereby both employer and employee would be fully informed of all the elements and principles of equal pay and would additionally be provided with a comprehensive analysis of the law, its provisions and purposes.[104]

Mirroring the work of the ILO, the Act also made it clear that there had to be evaluation of jobs that were quite different. Job analysis as a means to determine pay had by now had a relatively long history, as complex industrial organisations had striven to work out how to establish pay differentials that could be seen to be internally justified.[105] The means to undertake this task had been described in the US War Manpower Commission's Information Manual on Industrial Job Evaluation Systems published the previous year.[106] It is interesting to note that there is a very close similarity between the content of the manual and the process of job evaluation now typically used.[107]

---

[104] New York State Department of Labor, Press Release, 1 June 1944.

[105] The process is generally considered to have been started with the work of Frederick W. Taylor starting in the late nineteenth century in the Midvale Steel Company: see F.W. Taylor, '*Shop Management, 1903*', in *Scientific Management* (Harper, 1947). For a short description of Taylor's work see www.bl.uk/people/frederick-winslow-taylor.

[106] This important text can be seen at https://babel.hathitrust.org/cgi/pt?id=uiug.30112106661819;page=root;view=plaintext;size=100;seq=3;num=i.

[107] The guide had sections on Planning, Collecting and Recording Job, Evaluation Systems, Ranking, Job Classification, Points, Factor

These were important first steps in taking the concept of equal pay for work of equal value away from merely a slogan – mostly applied to the same or closely analogous work – to work that could be very different. However, the New York Act also provided for material factor defences to be advanced in answer to claims for equal pay. The opacity of this concept when introduced into the UK's Equal Pay Act 1970 has possibly been the biggest barrier to success for women in the UK once litigation started.

The New York Act was well known to the UK's Royal Commission, but it does not seem to have made a very great impact on its conclusions, even if later the ideas in the legislation came to be developed here and more widely in Europe.

1.7 The Royal Commission on Equal Pay 1944–1946

The composition of the UK's Royal Commission on Equal Pay was slightly more balanced than for the Cabinet Committee set up 26 years earlier, with a ratio of five men to four women.[108] Once again, a High Court judge was chosen to

Comparison, Pricing the Job, and the Relationship to Occupational Analysis. It may be compared with, for instance, the guidance given by the Equality and Human Rights Commission (see www .equalityhumanrights.com/en/advice-and-guidance/job-evaluation-schemes) or the NHS Employers Job Evaluation Handbook (the 11th edition can be seen at www.nhsemployers.org/~/media/Employers/ Publications/NHS_Job_Evaluation_Handbook.pdf).

[108] Apart from Asquith, the other Commissioners were the Countess of Limerick, Jasper Nicholas Ridley, Dame Anne Loughlin, Dennis Holme Robertson, Charles Stanley Robinson, John Brown, Lucy Frances

chair the Commission, Asquith J, later Lord Asquith of Bishopstone. It is not clear to me whether the fact that Asquith was the son of Herbert Henry Asquith, the Liberal Prime Minister who had taken the country into the First World War, but had been replaced by Lloyd George, had any bearing on his selection. The other eight members were chosen for their balance of skills, and on the basis that none of them had, as of then, declared themselves for or against the principle.

This time the aim of the Commission was not to make recommendations,[109] but:

> to examine the existing relationship between the
> remuneration of men and women in the public services, in
> industry and in other fields of employment; to consider the
> social, economic and financial implications of the claim of
> equal pay for equal work; and to report.

The Commission's report was therefore intended to be less directive than that of the Cabinet Committee. The report is long and discursive, considering the situation in relation to equal pay for work of equal value across almost all areas of

Nettlefold and Janet Vaughan. As far as I am aware, none of them was a Scot. For interesting discussion of the basis for their selection as members of the Commission, see S. Evans, 'A Memorandum of Dissent: Divided Opinion within the 1944–46 Royal Commission on Equal Pay', a paper written for the Economic History Society available at www .ehs.org.uk/dotAsset/6f7e8e03-2d50-4178-9cfc-dbf744397d0f.docx.

[109] As the Commission's report expressly noted at [6]–[7], see p. 2. This has been explained as being because the Chancellor of the Exchequer considered that it was premature to reach a final conclusion until after the end of the war, see Evans, 'A Memorandum'.

employment in the UK as well as in the USA, Russia, Australia and France. This is useful to the historian, but also reflects the limited purpose of the Commission.

Before undertaking the task of examination, the Commission considered it was crucial for it to define what 'equal value' meant. The Commission had a very limited concept in mind, and ruled out consideration of evaluating job content, as in the approach taken in the New York legislation. Indeed it seems it was more concerned to identify the ambiguities it found in the concept than to focus on its practical application in the future. This is all evident in the following passage, which I think well summarises the difficulties women faced in persuading the establishment of the time to take the issue forward in the UK:

Meaning of 'equal pay for equal work'

11. 'Equal pay for equal work' is primarily a battle-cry and in a battle-cry it is proper to expect power rather than precision. Expectation is not disappointed in this instance; the ambiguities of the expression are admitted and deplored by all who attempt seriously to grapple with the issue as a problem for peaceful debate, irrespective of the party to which they belong. But before ourselves indicating the nature of these ambiguities one general observation must be made if our own attitude is not to be misunderstood.

12. The cry of ' equal pay for equal work ' is a demand for something which is thought to be required by simple justice. It might be supposed, therefore, that when from the various possible interpretations we select one as the primary meaning which the words are to bear throughout

our report, unless notice is anywhere given to the contrary, we are ourselves subscribing to the view that it would be proper that equality in this sense should be brought about. But this would be to misconceive our position. The interpretation we shall treat as basic will be chosen for no other reason than that it appears to be the interpretation dominant in the minds of those who put forward the claim. It is perfectly compatible with this choice that if the claim is justified at all it is justified, not in this but in one of its other feasible meanings.

13. The difficulties of the expression are concentrated in the words 'equal work', but even the conception of equal pay requires some elucidation. We do not allude to the question whether pay is to be understood in terms of what the employer makes over to his employee, or in terms of what standard of living the employee, having regard to the various personal responsibilities he sustains, can achieve in virtue of it. It is manifest that, as a matter of definition, the former of these alternatives is the only workable one. Nor are we concerned with the complexities of various forms of remuneration basic wage or salary, bonus of one sort or another, payment in kind, and the like. Although for particular purposes these may require separate consideration it is clear to us that, again as a matter of definition, ' pay ' must be understood to cover them all. But ' equal pay ' denotes only a certain relation between the remuneration of the two sexes; it leaves open the question of the absolute level at which that relation is to be exhibited. In theory equality might be established in the first instance either by reducing the man's rate to the level of the woman's, or conversely by raising the woman's rate

to the level of the man's, or by bringing the two together at some intermediate point. We are, however, satisfied that the most practical course is to understand by a policy of equal pay a policy of raising the women's rate to whatever is, at the relevant time, the male level of remuneration. This is unquestionably what the advocates of equal pay intend.

14. Our decision regarding the meaning to be attributed to the phrase 'equal work' is, we are conscious, more open to argument. The first problem that confronts us here is how widely we are called on to extend our purview. At one end of the scale we find employments so closely similar that it would be usual to say that men and women engaged on them are doing 'the same work' or 'identical work.' At the opposite extreme we have employments of utterly disparate natures employments, in some cases, confined in practice if not by law to one sex only, such as those of the nursemaid and the coalminer about which the question may be asked, but not, we think, answered, whether in some sense or other of the word the work which they involve is or is not equal. It may be asked, for instance, whether those engaged in these very diverse activities are or are not called on for equal effort and equal sacrifice. We doubt whether there is any standard of measurement by reference to which this might be decided, or any serious proposal that remuneration should be based on such a decision. We take it that, in the context of our enquiry, equality signifies at least some degree of similarity between employments: but we are unable to discover any general principle in the light of which to decide what degree of similarity is required in order that the work done in two employments may be described either as being unequal or

as being equal. For instance the teaching of infants and the teaching of grown boys are in some respects similar and in other respects dissimilar employments ; and the work of a weaver who does his own 'beaming-off' is in some respects closely similar and in other respects dissimilar to that of one who does not. The boundaries round an 'employment' can seldom be clearly and precisely drawn. In determining, therefore, the range of our discussion we have had to follow the guidance of common sense as best we can.

15. The next difficulty is that, even as applied to kinds of work so similar that they would commonly be spoken of as 'the same work,' the words 'equal work' remain ambiguous in several respects. On the one hand work may be defined simply in terms of the nature of the thing to be done, whether it be the filing and indexing of papers or cotton-weaving or the cleaning of railway carriages, without reference to the question whether one worker gives the employer a return of equal value to that given by another. On the other hand this disregarded factor may be treated as the essence of the matter and equality of work be understood to mean equality of the worker's value from the employer's point of view. Moreover, unequal value may exhibit itself in more than one way. In the first place workers engaged in similar work may execute it with different degrees of efficiency as measured by either the quantity or the quality of their product. For example one weaver may weave 25 per cent, more cloth of a given type and quality than can another weaver in the same time. Or we may take such an occupation as lens polishing; here two workers may be working at the same speed, as measured by

the number of 'pieces' finished in a given period, but one of them may be working to a higher standard of accuracy than the other. These are both instances of the first type of unequal value. But secondly, as we have already indicated in paragraph 10, it may be relatively unprofitable to an employer to employ some particular class of workers, not because while actually 'on the job' they are less efficient than their fellows, but either because the conditions under which he has to employ them involve him in special overhead charges or because for one reason or another they possess what we have termed a lower overall value.

16. We think that, if regard is to be had to the meaning attached to the claim of equal pay for equal work by most of those who urge it, it is convenient to understand by the expression the same thing as is expressed in the widely used phrase 'the rate for the job'. We propose therefore to leave inequality in respect of overall value out of account in deciding whether work should or should not be called equal and to this extent at least 'equal pay for equal work' will not, as used by us, have the same import as 'equal pay for equal value to the employer'.

17. The difference of import will, however, go further than this, and for the reason that, as reflection shows, the phrase 'the rate for the job' is unfortunately itself ambiguous. For apart from the difficulties, discussed in paragraph 14, of defining the boundaries of an employment or job, the phrase evidently carries different implications according to whether the method of payment actually in force is payment by time or payment by the piece. In both cases, indeed, the claim of the rate for the job means that all persons working at the job should be paid at the same rates: but this apparent similarity

conceals a fundamental diversity of principle as regards the
significance of the first type of inequality of value
distinguished in paragraph 15. For in the case of piece-work
the claim so expressed is, broadly speaking, compatible with
the principle that pay should be proportioned as closely as
possible to effective output, while in the case of time-work it
is not compatible with that principle and is indeed definitely
put forward in antithesis to it.

18. Our definition therefore does little more than rule out,
in conformity with what we believe to be in the minds of
most of those who put forward the claim to equal pay for
equal work, those considerations of special overheads,
overall value, etc., which have been alluded to in paragraphs
10 and 15. It does not attempt to take the further step of
identifying the claim with a single unambiguous principle.
Still less, we must repeat, does the adoption of any particular
definition prejudge in any way the question either of the
justice of the claim in the defined sense or of the probable
consequences of its being successfully pressed.

Although the Commission's Report was signed by all
the Commissioners, three of the female Commissioners
(Dame Anne Loughlin (who had recently been the first female
President of the Trades Union Congress (TUC)); Dr Janet
Vaughan (then Principal of Somerville College, Oxford); and
a businesswoman and lawyer, Lucy Frances Nettlefold[110])

---

[110] The career of Lucy Frances Nettlefold as a campaigner first for women's
admission to the legal profession and then later as business woman and
anti-apartheid campaigner can be seen at www.oxforddnb.com/view/10
.1093/ref:odnb/9780198614128.001.0001/odnb-9780198614128-e-101944#o
dnb-9780198614128-e-101944-headword-4.

appended a 'Memorandum of Dissent' to the chapters giving 'Explanations of the Prevailing Differences between the Remuneration of Men and Women and with the Economic and Social Consequences of Equal Pay in Private Industry and Commerce'.

This Memorandum is very important as marking a sea-change in the view that the extent to which physical strength in which men excelled over women justified a higher value and higher pay than that for women.[111] Again, the full relevant text of the Memorandum is too long to set out here in full, but there are some passages that seem to me to be too significant not to mention, where, with an almost sardonic sense of irony, they demolish the so-called 'natural factors' that were said to justify treating the value of men's work more highly:

> 4. We now turn to the 'natural' factors. Historically, the greater physical strength of men has obviously had a large influence in determining the demand for male labour, but its importance is being continuously reduced with the development of modern technique. This operates in two ways. Firstly, the newer industries such as plastics, radio, etc. are of a nature demanding manual deftness or machine operations rather than physical strength. Similarly modern developments of old industries, ... tend to cut out heavy manual work. Secondly, the war has greatly accelerated the use of mechanical devices and 'gadgets' to reduce the physical

---

[111] Evans, 'A Memorandum', also considers the Memorandum of Dissent to have been a far more powerful document in the long run.

effort demanded in numerous operations in nearly all industries. . . . The whole trend of modern production methods is towards the substitution of mechanical for muscular power a substitution greatly assisted by the availability of easily installed fractional horse-power power units.

5. No quantitative analysis of jobs has been made, but we find it hard to believe that at the present time more than three-quarters of all industrial jobs require physical strength beyond the capacity of women. The so-called 'heavy industries' employ only 4,000,000 men. Moreover we believe that, with a small expense of capital and of ingenuity, the amount of muscular effort required would be reduced in a large range of jobs, and that this would be of advantage to employers and to male workers as well as to women.

This Memorandum marks the moment in my researches into the development of this idea in the UK, in which the argument that dexterity – a facility which was obviously more common among women – was contrasted explicitly with muscle. It fascinates me that it should have been the Second World War, and in particular, the need the war engendered for greater efficiency, that enabled these women to make this point so well and so appositely. When the reduced need for muscle diminished, the justification for this particular male premium, it became possible to claim a counter-vailing value for those manual skills that women had in greater abundance. The possibilities for comparing the value of different jobs were beginning to be developed.

I think that these women would have been very pleased to see this submission 20 years later in 1986, when intervening in Case 237/85 *Rummler* v. *Dato-Druck GmbH*:[112]

> The United Kingdom considers that the principle of non-discrimination does not preclude the use of a criterion in relation to which one sex has greater natural ability than the other, so long as that criterion is representative of the range of activities involved in the job in question. A system based on the criterion of muscular effort is discriminatory only if it ignores movements of small muscle groups characteristic of manual dexterity.

Their next wry comment punctuates the sexism of the time in a way which must have made difficult reading for the other Commissioners:

> 6. The next alleged natural disadvantage of women is lack of adaptability and capacity to deal with 'surprise situations'. This appears to be based mainly upon war time experience, when large numbers of women with short training were called upon to perform a wide variety of jobs entirely new to them. It is certainly to be expected that experienced workers should show greater capacity to deal with emergencies than raw hands, but the view that women are inherently lacking in adaptability seems highly implausible in view of the 'surprise situations' which constantly arise in the natural and traditional sphere of women's work, housekeeping and the care of children even in normal times, not to mention the conditions 'a morning after a blitz'.

[112] ECLI:EU:C:1986:277 at [9].

7. The majority accept in part the view of many witnesses that the superior 'career value' of men contributes to their higher wage-rates. In this connection there seems to be a widespread confusion of thought. The fact that the majority of women workers stay in industry for a shorter time than the majority of men, and that most women are less eager than most men to acquire skill and to obtain promotion, would account for the fact that the average earnings of all women are less than the average of all men. We should certainly expect, under a regime of equal pay and equal opportunity, that more men than women would be found in the most highly skilled, responsible and highly paid posts. But this neither accounts for, nor justifies, sex-differentiation of rates of pay at any particular level of skill.

8. Finally, some importance is attached by the majority to the greater absence rates and poorer time-keeping of women than of men. . . . We dissent from the view that these factors justify lower rates of pay for women than for men on comparable jobs. It is both unfair and economically undesirable that an individual woman should be penalised, even if she is never absent, and an individual man benefited, even if his attendance is poor, because, on the average, men have a better record of attendance than women. Some incentive for good attendance, irrespective of sex, would be the appropriate way of dealing with this problem.

9. . . . We do not . . . follow the majority in their acceptance of Mr. Harrod's argument[113] that it is a fortunate dispensation that women earn less than men

---

[113] The Minority noted that he 'claim[ed] as one of the "social causes for unequal pay" "to secure that motherhood as a vocation is not too unattractive financially compared with work in the professions, industry

(for whatever reason) because this tends to drive women into matrimony. We should like to remark in passing that the majority here seem to have fallen into a major inconsistency. They hold that the introduction of equal pay would tend to exclude women from industry ; to be consistent, therefore, they should surely advocate equal pay, for total unemployment would be a more powerful incentive to marriage than mere low earnings.

. . .

23. We do not pretend that the enforcement of the rate for the job, taking a broad interpretation of the term, would by itself remove all restrictions on the sphere of women's work. Prejudice, convention and sectional privilege would remain to be combated. Fear of unemployment will persist, for some time at least, as the majority point out, even if a successful employment policy is put in hand. But we believe that the general acceptance of the principle of the rate for the job would make an important contribution to breaking down barriers to the employment of women, because it would remove one of the main elements in the objection of male workers to opening new jobs to women, i.e., fear of undercutting. Moreover, prejudice and convention would be weakened by the very fact of granting equal pay. As Mrs. Barbara Wootton wrote in evidence:

'Absence of discrimination between male and female wages might be an important secondary influence in undermining the convention of female inferiority. Lower pay is an obvious badge of inferiority, and without this

or trade'". (See paragraph 48(ii) of Appendix IX 2 to minutes of evidence.)

label candidates for jobs might be more likely to be considered on personal merits. The word 'secondary' in this context should, however, be stressed. Equalisation of pay will not of itself induce a different attitude towards the place of women in society. Its significance would be that it might reinforce a half-formed belief that the present method of discrimination is unscientific, and out of keeping with modern standards. But the roots of that belief must be independently formed.'

Public opinion has been continuously shifting away from traditional views of the economic position of women, and this movement has been much speeded up by experience in the recent war. It may be that we are at a psychological moment when the enunciation of the principle of equal pay would crystallise sentiments at present vague, and would have an important influence in breaking down the non-economic as well as the economic barriers which have hitherto restricted the sphere of employment of women.

... we do not share the fear of the majority that equal pay would work to the disadvantage of women.

In the light of the history of the discussions of equal pay for equal value it is easy to see how there was too much wisdom in this for the majority to accept.

The Report provides much evidence of the differential health of women and men and the time taken off work by women in order to look after children, husbands and others. Yet reading the report of the Royal Commission now, some 60 years after it was written, it is impossible not to be impressed by the progress women have made in the workplace over two generations.

On a more personal note, I should add that my copy of the Royal Commission's Report is *ex libris* the Girton College, Cambridge Library.[114] It is rather pleasing to speculate how the Report and in particular this copy must have played a part in advancing equality for women in a particular way. In 1946 Girton was not yet a full college of the university, but the then 'Mistress', Kathleen Teresa Blake Butler, was about to change all that. At the Vice-Chancellor's request, she postponed her retirement to pilot through the measure by which, in 1948, Cambridge finally conceded to women full membership of the university, enabling them to be admitted to degrees on equal terms to men.[115]

1.8 Post-War International Law Developments

From 1946 onwards, the principle was able to take several steps forward on the international stage quite quickly. First, it was incorporated into the United Nations Universal Declaration of Human Rights signed on 10 December 1948, again in Paris: see Article 23(1).[116]

---

[114] My copy, purchased through Abebooks, is stamped 'Hollond' and marked in pencil MTH and seems originally to have belonged to the College Bursar Marjorie Tappan Hollond, who was responsible for much of the work involved in ensuring equal access to the university for women: see the Oxford Dictionary of National Biography, at www .oxforddnb.com/view/10.1093/ref:odnb/9780198614128.001.0001/odnb-9 780198614128-e-65548?rskey=cko4Yl&result=1.

[115] See the Oxford Dictionary of National Biography, at www .oxforddnb.com/view/10.1093/ref:odnb/9780198614128.001.0001/odnb-9 780198614128-e-62108?rskey=lVk663&result=1.

[116] www.ohchr.org/EN/UDHR/Documents/UDHR_Translations/eng.pdf.

Secondly, and really much more significantly, the ILO decided at last to address the subject of equal pay by a Convention, thereby imposing a much greater obligation on States to take action to amend their domestic law accordingly. This Equal Remuneration Convention of 1951[117] addressed the issue in much greater detail than the Universal Declaration or indeed than any previous ILO measure. The formal concept of job evaluation by objective assessment of jobs on a non-discriminatory basis at last became an obligation on all states that ratified the Convention. That ultimately included the UK, though it did not ratify until 15 June 1971,[118] and, eventually, all the states that were shortly to sign the Treaty of Rome on 25 March 1957.

The key provisions are these:

Article 1
For the purpose of this Convention–

(a) the term remuneration includes the ordinary, basic or minimum wage or salary and any additional emoluments whatsoever payable directly or indirectly, whether in cash or in kind, by the employer to the worker and arising out of the worker's employment;

(b) the term equal remuneration for men and women workers for work of equal value refers to rates of remuneration established without discrimination based on sex.

---

[117] C100 – Equal Remuneration Convention, 1951 (No. 100). The Convention entered into force on 23 May 1953. See www.ilo.org/dyn/normlex/en/f?p= NORMLEXPUB:12100:0::NO::P12100_ILO_CODE:C100.

[118] www.ilo.org/dyn/normlex/en/f?p=1000:11200:0::NO:11200: P11200_COUNTRY_ID:102651.

Article 2

1. Each Member shall, by means appropriate to the methods in operation for determining rates of remuneration, promote and, in so far as is consistent with such methods, ensure the application to all workers of the principle of equal remuneration for men and women workers for work of equal value.

2. This principle may be applied by means of–

   (a) national laws or regulations;
   (b) legally established or recognised machinery for wage determination;
   (c) collective agreements between employers and workers; or
   (d) a combination of these various means.

Article 3

1. Where such action will assist in giving effect to the provisions of this Convention measures shall be taken to promote objective appraisal of jobs on the basis of the work to be performed.

2. The methods to be followed in this appraisal may be decided upon by the authorities responsible for the determination of rates of remuneration, or, where such rates are determined by collective agreements, by the parties thereto.

3. Differential rates between workers which correspond, without regard to sex, to differences, as determined by such objective appraisal, in the work to be performed shall not be considered as being contrary to the principle of equal remuneration for men and women workers for work of equal value.

There was much that has been later argued to be ambiguous about this Convention. Perhaps the most important issues concerned the degree to which job evaluation was mandatory at some level and, if so, on what basis. However, we should not be so critical of the Convention in retrospect. It very obviously built on the discussions I have sketched above in a progressive and material way. The focus was 'objective appraisal' of the 'work to be performed' and not, in the first place at least, on the output of the worker. This cut across the distinctions between piece and time work that had obfuscated much of the argument in 1919 and again in 1944–6. It also ignored the arguments that the Red Duchess (and others) had found so compelling that the key point was the use to which the wage was generally put. Her argument was that those men who had dependants were for that reason not in a comparable position to the working women. They had a greater need and so were justified in being paid more.

It had to be an objective system of assessment and had to be based in the first place on the ordinary remuneration, thereby removing the arguments about bonuses. On the other hand, the system had to be non-discriminatory, so of course discriminatory add-ons, by bonuses or other premia, were to be outlawed.

1.9 Post-War Politics

The way in which the campaign for equal pay played out in the UK's early post-war domestic politics is complicated but well discussed by others. As a generalisation, it is enough to say that initially, as a party, Labour's lack of energy on the issue was lamentable, and the work of some Conservative MPs, working in unison with female Labour MPs, truly remarkable.[119] The issue had become more and more bipartisan at the political level, even though the trade unions and the Ministry of Labour, almost exclusively led by men, were much too ambivalent still about promoting it because of the impact of equal pay on men's wages and on the economy more generally.

Yet 1954–5 saw the UK take another small step forward towards political acceptance of the principle of equal pay for work of equal value. The Labour Party discussions that year eventually committed the party to equal pay. Thus, the Manifesto the following year explicitly stated[120] under the heading 'Fair Shares':

> Labour re-affirms its belief in equal pay for equal work and will immediately extend it to industrial workers in Government service and so give a lead to industry.

So one important part of the framework for discussing equal pay issues – the political competition – was beginning to change. It is a measure of the increasing acceptance of the principle of equal pay as a matter of general fairness that the Conservative Chancellor of the Exchequer, R.A. Butler (later Home Secretary and finally Lord Butler of Saffron Walden) became frightened that

---

[119] For a deeper discussion of the political arguments see e.g. H.L. Smith, 'The Politics of Conservative Reform: The Equal Pay for Equal Work Issue, 1945–1955' (Jun., 1992) 35(2) *The Historical Journal*, 401–415.

[120] See www.labour-party.org.uk/manifestos/1955/1955-labour-manifesto.shtml.

the Labour Party's commitment had potential for political traction in the forthcoming election. This caused him to argue forcibly within his party for reform but on a gradual basis within limited parts of the Civil Service. And so, as a result, from 1955 limited steps to introduce equal pay were at last taken within those parts of the Civil Service where men and women did the same or very closely analogous work.

In the context of all that had gone before it was not much, and certainly did not involve legislation giving women individualised enforceable legal rights. They did not say generally their work should be compared with that of men's.

In retrospect, I think it is also noteworthy how the proposal from the Labour Party was concentrated on the Civil Service alone. This was one part of the economy where there was at least an argument that a greater wage bill might be sustained. The Labour Party did not propose legal rights for women in private industry where this would be much more difficult; it was merely hoped that change in the Civil Service might cause industry to put its own house in order. The obvious unlikelihood of this ambition ever being achieved without legislation, in the light of the history I have set out, reflected once again the fear that in the private economy equal pay would be a zero-sum issue for men and women. It was something to be hoped for as a magic wish, but not to be forced by legislating enforceable rights.

1.10 The Treaty of Rome 1957

As we now reflect on the UK's divided views about Brexit, I believe it is important to shout out loud how much more progressive were the founders of the European Union. The Equal Pay Convention having been written in language that could be more widely adopted by nations as a legislative base led them to incorporate the principle as a key component of the social bargain at the heart of the Treaty of Rome of 25 March 1957.[121] Chapter 1 Social Provisions, in Title VIII Social Policy, Education, Vocational Training and Youth,[122] contained a range of Articles designed to improve the working lives of citizens of the Member States.

In particular Article 119 of the Treaty Rome provided that:

> Each Member State shall during the first stage ensure and subsequently maintain the application of the principle that men and women should receive equal pay for equal work. For the purpose of this Article, 'pay' means the ordinary basic or minimum wage or salary and any other consideration, whether in cash or in kind, which the worker receives, directly or indirectly, in respect of his employment from his employer. Equal pay without discrimination based on sex means:

---

[121] See https://eur-lex.europa.eu/legal-content/EN/TXT/HTML/?uri=CELEX:11957E/AFI/CNF&qid=1532101770037&from=EN.

[122] These are found in Part 3 of the Treaty, 'Community Policies'.

> (a) that pay for the same work at piece rates shall be calculated on the basis of the same unit of measurement;
>
> (b) that pay for work at time rates shall be the same for the same job.

It will be seen that Article 119 did not expressly use the phrase 'equal value', referring instead to 'equal work'. Did the latter include the former? In the first *Defrenne* case, Case 80/70 *Gabrielle Defrenne* v. *Belgian State*,[123] Advocate General Dutheillet De Lamothe implied that he thought so when he explained the crucial role of ILO Convention 100 in persuading the drafters of the Treaty of Rome to incorporate its terms into Article 119:[124]

> Since it appears to be the first time that you have to interpret Article 119 of the Treaty, I should like first of all very briefly to recall its origin and scope. The debates which took place in certain parliaments on the ratification of the Treaty, in particular the explanations given by the Government of the Netherlands to the Second Chamber of the States General provide us with certain information on the origin of this provision. It appears to be France which took the initiative, but the article necessitated quite long negotiations. Although its adoption scarcely raised any difficulties for States which had already ratified Convention No 100 of the International Labour Organization (ILO) which, as the German Government

---

[123] For the judgment see ECLI:EU:C:1971:55; for Advocate General Dutheillet De Lamothe's Opinion see ECLI:EU:C:1971:43.

[124] Ibid. [I], at p. 455.

stressed in the Bundestag, had very much the same scope
and on certain points the same wording as the draft article
in question, three of the Member States, or rather future
Member States at the time, had not ratified this agreement,
because its application risked creating very serious
difficulties for them in internal law. It seems that the reason
for the State's finally succeeding in reaching agreement is
to be found in the double objective pursued by this article:
a social objective, it is true, since it leads all the countries of
the Community to accept the principle of a basically social
nature raised by the ILO Convention; but an economic
objective, too, for in creating an obstacle to any attempt at
'social dumping' by means of the use of female labour less
well paid than male labour, it helped to achieve one of the
fundamental objectives of the common market, the
establishment of a system ensuring that 'competition is not
distorted'. This explains perhaps why Article 119 of the
Treaty is of a different character from the articles which
precede it in the chapter of the Treaty devoted to social
provisions.

The UK was not a signatory to the Treaty of Rome and
did not become an established member of the European
Communities until after the first referendum on Europe in
1972 had confirmed the political move to join. So, Article 119,
whatever was thought about its potential, was not a material
legal text for the UK until the European Communities Act
1972 brought the effects of the UK's accession treaty into
domestic law. It is a moot point whether our equal pay laws
would have been more comprehensive and easier to access
had we joined earlier. Certainly, the fact that the UK started its

own domestic right to equal pay in 1970, before accession, has led to some complexity, as that legislation has had to be construed consistently with Article 119 and its successors once accession became a domestic law fact.[125]

1.11 Progress to the UK's Equal Pay Act 1970

I have already noted the importance of the Ford Dagenham Strike of 1968. It undoubtedly is a very significant milestone in the progress from the aspirations I have described to the first piece of legislation that actually conferred individual rights in the UK to equal pay for work of equal value. Barbara Castle introduced the Bill that became the Act into the House of Commons. This was not only a worthy fulfilment of her promises to the Dagenham strikers, but a personal fulfilment. A recent article by the House of Commons Hansard Writing Team records:[126]

> On 9 March 1954, four MPs put aside party political differences to present an 80,000-signature petition to Parliament demanding equal pay. Ulster Unionist Patricia Ford, Conservative Irene Ward and Labour MPs Edith Summerskill and Barbara Castle grabbed the attention of the press by arriving at Westminster with the petition on 8 March in horse-drawn carriages decorated in rosettes and streamers in suffragette green and white. Nothing was overlooked in planning this photo-opportunity: even their

---

[125] See e.g. the effect of the European equal pay provisions in causing words to be written into domestic legislation in *Redcar and Cleveland BC* v. *Bainbridge* [2007] EWCA Civ 929, [2008] ICR 238, [2007] IRLR 984.

[126] https://ukvote100.org/2017/11/09/women-demand-equal-pay/.

coachman, Dave Jacobs, was a veteran of feminist campaigns, having driven for Emmeline Pankhurst and Millicent Fawcett.

The Equal Pay Act that has been litigated is not the Act that Barbara Castle steered through Parliament in 1969–70. The Act was significantly amended by the Sex Discrimination Act of 1975 and it was included in a Schedule to that latter Act.[127] Before I discuss the concept of equal value as it has been developed in this Act, I must share some of Barbara Castle's speech to the House of Commons on introducing the Bill.

This is what she said on the second reading:[128]

[127] The Equal Pay Act 1971 was substantially amended by the Sex Discrimination Act 1975; see s. 8 of the Sex Discrimination Act 1975. The Equal Pay Act 1971 as re-written was then set out in its new form in Part II of Sch I to the Sex Discrimination Act 1975.

[128] HC Deb 09 February 1970, 1970 vol 795 cc 913–915, see https://api .parliament.uk/historic-hansard/commons/1970/feb/09/equal-pay-no-2 -bill. Her introduction to the passage cited in the main text is also worth reading: 'While other people have talked—lots of people have talked— we intend to make equal pay for equal work a reality, and, in doing so, to take women workers progressively out of the sweated labour class. We intend to do it, if the House will back us, in ways which will give a lead to other countries whose governments have left us behind in adopting the principle but who are still striving for effective ways of implementing it. The concept of equal pay for equal work is so self-evidently right and just that it has been part of our national thinking for a very long time. Here, as in other things, it was the Trade Union Movement which gave the lead. Indeed, as far back as 1888 the T.U.C. first endorsed the principle of the same wages for the same work—a very courageous avant garde thing to do in those days, long before Queen Victoria's Diamond Jubilee, when women who worked in industry were certainly not considered respectable, even if they were regarded as human beings at

Up to now, the extension of equal pay in industry has always foundered on three arguments: how should we define equal pay for equal work? How can we enforce it? And: 'The economic situation is not right.' It is a tremendous credit to this Government that they have found the answer to all three.

First, let me take the question of definition as we have embodied it in the Bill. When my predecessor in this job, the right hon. Gentleman the Member for Southwark (Mr. Gunter), first started his discussions with both sides of industry on the implementation of equal pay in fulfilment of our election promise, it seemed as if this problem of definition might prove insoluble.

The C.B.I. was all in favour of the definition embodied in the Treaty of Rome: Equal pay for the same work but the T.U.C. emphatically rejected this as inadequate. The T.U.C. wanted the [ILO] Convention definition: Equal pay for work of equal value which the C.B.I., in turn, rejected as being far too open ended and indefinite. I think that they

all. Since then the struggle against discrimination against women in rates of pay has had a chequered course. There was that great moment during the war when Mrs. Thelma Cazalet Keir, with strong Labour support, led a successful revolt against the Government on the issue of sex discrimination in teachers' pay, and the great man himself, Winston Churchill, had to come down to the House the next day to make the re-imposition of sex discrimination a vote of confidence. (915) Since then, the cause of equal pay has had its partial victories: the non-industrial Civil Service, non-manual local authority workers and teachers all got the first of seven instalments towards equal pay in 1955, and full equality in 1961. But its extension to that far greater number of women in industry for whom the T.U.C. fought so long ago has so far eluded us. The trade union movement has realised that this can be done only by legislation, and previous Governments have refused to legislate.'

were both right: 'Equal pay for the same work' is so restrictive that it would merely impinge on those women, very much in the minority, who work side by side with men on identical work, while, equally, the [ILO] definition is far from satisfactory.

What does one mean by 'work of equal value'? What does one mean by 'equal value' in that context? The Convention is not very helpful on this matter, but merely says that its phrase refers to rates of remuneration established without discrimination based on sex. That is fine. This is what we are seeking to achieve. But how does one establish whether and in what forms discrimination has taken place?

The phrase 'Equal pay for work of equal value' is too abstract a concept to embody in legislation without further interpretation. Is it suggested that some one should set a value on every job a woman does? Even if that were practicable it would not solve the problem, because what we are concerned with is the relationship between men's pay and women's pay, and men, of course, have never had equal pay for work of equal value. One could only establish the relative value of men's and women's work by evaluating the work, not only of all women but of all men in the population, which is something we have never attempted in our wildest dreams of prices and incomes policies.

The [ILO] Convention does not require anything remotely like this. Indeed, it is pretty off-hand about this whole approach to job evaluation. All it says is: Where such action will assist in giving effect to the provisions of this Convention, measures shall be taken to promote objective appraisal of jobs on the basis of the work to be performed. So the [ILO] definition does not make job evaluation mandatory. Besides, the Convention leaves open whether the principle of equal pay shall be applied by legislation or through collective bargaining.

In this passage we can see Barbara Castle identifying many of the issues that would have to be worked through after the equal pay legislation came into effect:

- She identified three problems for the extension of the principle of equal pay for work of equal value: the problems of legal definition, enforcement and the effect on the economy.
- She pointed out that men do not get equal pay for work of equal value, and muses on the possibility of a national evaluation before rejecting it.
- She saw a contrast between the ILO Convention's approach and that taken in the Treaty of Rome in that the latter did not expressly refer to work of equal value.
- She sees the trade unions as a source of power for the women and contemplates achieving equal pay for work of equal value through collective bargaining.

1.12 The Equal Pay Act's Failings

As the Bill was presented to Parliament, and indeed as it was enacted for many years, there was no possibility for a woman to make her own claim to equal pay for work of equal value unless there was already a job evaluation scheme in place. A woman still could not require such a comparison. That had to be done by the employer; she had no right to initiate such an evaluation.

This obvious defect was raised explicitly by Labour MP Renée Short, but Barbara Castle dodged the question:[129]

> MRS. RENÉE SHORT ... Can my right hon. friend say how the woman would be able to take her case to a tribunal if a job evaluation exercise had not been carried out? I understand that it is one of the basic provisos that a job evaluation exercise must have been carried out. What happens if the firm concerned refuses to do this?

> MRS. CASTLE It is not only in the case of a job evaluation exercise having been carried out, but in a case where the woman claims to be doing a job equivalent to the men concerned, but where we are trying to measure the value of work done, it must be through job evaluation. This is why it is important to realise that 30 per cent. of the population are covered by job evaluation schemes. There is nothing to prevent unions asking for their extension, which would be very much in keeping with all that is best in the development of pay structures at present ...

Perhaps this evasion was the price of political support; perhaps it was because Barbara Castle did not think much of the process of job evaluation; perhaps more likely the transitional cost would have been too great for the Treasury or Ministry of Labour to have contemplated. As it was, Barbara Castle told the House of Commons that it was expected that the national wage bill was expected to rise by 3½ per cent and accordingly it was proposed to take up to the end of 1975 before the law came fully into effect giving individual rights of action. So I think, in the end, the premise for this failure to address the deficit, that Renée Short so clearly saw,

---

[129] See Hansard ibid.

was that it would have undermined her argument that the economic situation was right.

Barbara Castle also explained the nature of the defence to a claim on the basis of material factors:[130]

> Clause 2 also contains a concept which is crucial to the whole intention of the Bill. This is the concept of 'a material difference' between a woman's case and that of comparable male workers. The intention of the Bill is not to prohibit differences in pay between a woman and comparable male workers which arise because of genuine differences other than sex between her case and theirs. If an employer wishes to make additional payment to people employed on like work, in respect of matters such as length of service, merit, level of output and so on, the Bill will do nothing to hinder him, provided that the payments are available to any person who qualifies regardless of sex. But such payments must be related to actual differences in performance of service. It will not be permissible for an employer to discriminate between men as a class and women as a class, because he believes that in some way women generally are of less value to him as workers than men.

The significance of those last two sentences has probably still not been taken on board by all human resource departments: a difference in pay must reflect a difference in the performance of the service provided by the individual, and not be merely because the employer considers the man more valuable.

---

[130] Hansard, ibid.

1.13 Three Extraordinary Women

I must now return to the developments in Europe. At first it had been thought that the provisions of Title VIII of the Treaty of Rome were programmatic and did not give rise to individual rights. However, a group of lawyers who had worked in, or close to, the European Commission, began to argue that the Treaty conferred real rights. Eliane Vogel-Polsky, who has been described as one of the founding mothers of Europe,[131] and Marie-Thérèse Cuvelliez, working with Gabrielle Defrenne, started the *Defrenne* series of test cases. It is no exaggeration to say that in doing so these three women, Mesdames Vogel-Polsky, Cuvelliez and Defrenne, achieved the most important changes to the prospects of all European women seeking to be equally valued in all that they do at work.

In the first *Defrenne* case[132] they challenged pension differentials for men and women and in the process had asked whether Madame Defrenne, who was an air hostess, did the same work as an air steward. This was not the first question in the case, but it was designed to test what were the factors that determined when work was equal. I have already noted how Advocate General Dutheillet De Lamothe linked Article 119's naissance to the ILO Recommendation which did indeed refer to equal value. However, the European Court of Justice, giving

---

[131] Among the many extraordinary jurists I have met, I consider her to be in the very first rank, because of her imagination of a different world, her determination to achieve it, her tenacity despite initial setbacks and her personal humility.

[132] See Case 80/70 *Defrenne* v. *Belgium* ECLI:EU:C:1971:55.

judgment on 25 May 1971, declined to answer this specific question because it had already concluded that the issue in the case concerning state pensions was not within the scope of Article 119.

Yet the first *Defrenne* case having raised the question of deciding what was 'equal work' prompted further debate within the European Commission. The Commission, seeing the importance of alignment with the ILO Convention, eventually proposed an Equal Pay Directive,[133] and this was finally agreed by the Council on 10 February 1975. This definitively explained that Article 119 applied to work of 'equal value'. It also required Member States to provide mechanisms to establish whether the value of one job and another was equal:

> Article 1 – The principle of equal pay for men and women outlined in Article 119 of the Treaty, hereinafter called 'principle of equal pay', means, for the same work or for work to which equal value is attributed, the elimination of all discrimination on grounds of sex with regard to all aspects and conditions of remuneration.
>
> In particular, where a job classification system is used for determining pay, it must be based on the same criteria for both men and women and so drawn up as to exclude any discrimination on grounds of sex.

---

[133] Council Directive 75/117/EEC of 10 February 1975 on the approximation of the laws of the Member States relating to the application of the principle of equal pay for men and women. This Directive was repealed from 15 August 2009 by the Equal Treatment Directive (Recast) (2006/54/EC), which came into force on 15 August 2008.

> Article 2 – Member States shall introduce into their
> national legal systems such measures as are necessary to
> enable all employees who consider themselves wronged by
> failure to apply the principle of equal pay to pursue their
> claims by judicial process after possible recourse to other
> competent authorities.

Although the UK was a member of the European
Council that agreed this Directive, the Equal Pay Act 1970
was not immediately amended. It still did not permit women
to initiate their own equal value claim unless there was a pre-
existing job evaluation system. In her speech on the second
reading, Barbara Castle had told the House of Commons
that:[134]

> There will be no obligation on employers to carry out job
> evaluation, but where it has been done or is done in the
> future discrimination in pay on grounds of sex between
> jobs of equivalent value will be prohibited. Job evaluation
> schemes cover probably 30 per cent. of the working
> population

I suspect that this was a generous estimate. What really
mattered was that at least 70 per cent of the working population of women in the UK had no effective right to equal pay
for work of equal value and the 1970 Act was not designed to
help them. Did the Equal Pay Directive? The problem was that
a directive did not normally confer rights on women directly
but only required Member States to transpose its requirements into domestic law. So, until the Equal Pay Directive

---

[134] HC Deb 09 February 1970 vol 795 col 918.

was transposed, 70 per cent of working women were unable to make real progress. All employers had to do to avoid undesirable consequences to their pay bill arising from the 1970 Act was to make sure that there was a difference in the work content of jobs and refuse to undertake an evaluation.

This is where the second *Defrenne* case became a game changer. Every employment lawyer (and most lawyers and law students) now knows that on 8 April 1976 in the second *Defrenne* case the European Court of Justice held that Article 119 could be relied on horizontally.[135] It gave real rights to all European women to sue their employers for equal pay in accordance with Article 119 without the problem of construing difficult domestic legislation. If they could do that, then they ought to be able to sue on the basis that Article 119 provided them with a right to equal pay for work of equal value. In short, the true power of the Equal Pay Directive was in its interpretation of Article 119 as including 'equal value' in the concept of 'equal work'.

Yet how, and by whom, was the comparative value of two jobs to be determined if there was no job evaluation system in place? No national system of job evaluation existed in the United Kingdom.

I was acutely aware of this deficit. On 10 February 1978, I argued an equal pay case on appeal for the first time in *Dance and Others* v. *Dorothy Perkins Ltd*.[136] The Employment Appeal Tribunal concluded on 17 March

---

[135] See Case 43/75 *Defrenne* v. *Société Anonyme Belge De Navigation Aérienne Sabena* ECLI:EU:C:1976:56.

[136] [1978] ICR 760; [1977] IRLR 226.

that my client Ms Dance was not undertaking like work to that of her chosen comparator. The tribunal, having dismissed my argument, concluded by saying:[137]

> the differential in pay [between the men and women] was very marked. Unfortunately there is nothing we can do about this except to say that the women ought to have been upgraded as a matter of job evaluation.

So they ought! I was outraged by the law's inadequacy and I have regretted for a long time that I did not think to advise her that, following the second *Defrenne* case and the Equal Pay Directive, Ms Dance had Article 119 rights to initiate a judicial evaluation of her work compared with other men employed at Dorothy Perkins![138] Still, as most trial advocates know, losing a bad case is one thing, losing one where the merits are entirely on your client's side is a great spur to hard work and deeper thought. I have remembered her misfortune every time I have been instructed to act for women in an equal pay case.

Whatever the judgment in the second *Defrenne* case meant, the domestic law in the Equal Pay Act 1971 still did not permit individual legal actions to secure a ruling on equal value. The domestic legislation obviously had a chilling effect on progress on this front.

Noting this, the next year the European Commission wrote to the United Kingdom on 3 April 1979, stating that in its opinion Article 1 of the Equal Pay Directive had been incorrectly

---

[137] Ibid. see 764H–765A.

[138] I can only say that I was only just out of Pupillage, having been called to the Bar of England and Wales in November 1974.

applied in the United Kingdom. Correspondence followed, the Commission giving the United Kingdom a period of two months to adopt the measures needed to comply with the Equal Pay Directive by ensuring women could bring their own equal value proceedings even if there was no job evaluation system in place. The UK did not respond and so on 18 March 1981 the Commission started enforcement proceedings against the UK.

On 6 July 1982 in Case 61/81 *Commission of The European Communities* v. *United Kingdom of Great Britain and Northern Ireland*[139] the European Court of Justice held that the UK was in default and was required to make the legislative changes necessary.

This judgment ends the first Part of this lecture. From here on the discussion will look at how the UK has responded to this obligation.

PART 2 WORKING THE EQUAL VALUE RIGHT

2.1 Baby Steps to Equal Value

At last women were – in theory – to be able to litigate to claim equal pay for work of equal value. The UK was required to ensure that they were to be able to go to court and seek a judicial determination of relative value of their work. However, despite having in Margaret Thatcher a female Prime Minister, many Tories in power had a visceral dislike of women's rights. No longer was the electoral advantage, that R.A. Butler had seen, the issue. Any new right to sue business

---

[139] EU:C:1982:258.

was a deeply unwelcome burden to be avoided if possible, and to be made as difficult as possible, if not.

It could not be avoided, short of leaving the European Communities. Compliance with the judgment in Case 61/81 *Commission of The European Communities* v. *United Kingdom of Great Britain and Northern Ireland* required the UK to introduce regulations to amend the Equal Pay Act 1970 to give women the necessary rights. But the Tories had no intention to make those rights easy to exercise. Several drafts of amending legislation were sent around, and they were duly criticised by the Equal Opportunities Commission for their opacity. Ultimately amendments to the Equal Pay Act 1970 to permit individual claims were made by the Equal Pay (Amendment) Regulations 1983.[140] These were drafted in the Department of Employment, and on 24 July 1983, Alan Clark MP, then Under-Secretary of State for Employment, laid the draft before the House of Commons.[141]

He was called out by the newly elected Claire Short MP for being drunk at the time, and there is no doubt he was; he has admitted as much in his diaries. Much admired by men and misogynists for his 'wit' during his lifetime, we must see him now for exactly what he was: an unpleasant relic of a bygone age. Churchill at his worst might have approved of his approach to stultifying women's campaign for their work to be given equal value; we should not. Instead of simply saying that a woman can apply to an employment tribunal for determination of the question whether or not her work is of equal value to that of an identified man, the Regulations he introduced had one

---

[140] SI 1983/1794. [141] See HC Deb 20 July 1983 vol 46 cc479–500.

complete bar to such a step where there was already a job evaluation scheme, and procedural rules that presupposed that there would be an argument in most cases that such a complaint was vacuous and irrational. As a further blow to women, the amendments made to the Equal Pay Act 1970 did not come into effect until 18 months after the European Court's judgment that the UK was in default on 1 January 1984. These Regulations were an insult to women, but they were on a par with the intransigence and obfuscation I have described in Part 1.

Probably the second of these was the more important for its chilling effect on equal value litigation. Thus the Amendment Regulations introduced a new section 2A into the Equal Pay Act 1970 that said:

Procedure before tribunal in certain cases

2A. – (1) Where on a complaint or reference made to an industrial tribunal . . . a dispute arises as to whether any work is of equal value as mentioned in section 1(2)(c) above the tribunal shall not determine that question unless—

(a) it is satisfied that there are no reasonable grounds for determining that the work is of equal value as so mentioned; or

(b) it has required a member of the panel of independent experts to prepare a report with respect to that question and has received that report.

. . .

Note the double negative: this was clearly intentional. On its face it seems obvious that the provision was designed to encourage employers to mount a challenge to any claim *in limine*. Given the proportion of women in the workforce who had never had the chance to argue that their work was of equal value, and thus the lack of any established national framework of consistent assessment free of discrimination, the brazenness of the procedural hurdle in the new section 2A(1)(a) was breathtaking then and still seems so now.[142]

This new section of the Equal Pay Act 1970 introduced a further control on a woman succeeding that was not entirely obvious from reading this text. The tribunal had to have requisitioned and received an expert's report. The Regulations further provided that the requisition could only go 'to a member of the panel of independent experts for the time being designated by the Advisory, Conciliation and Arbitration Service [ACAS]'.[143] I have no quarrel with this requirement in principle. The judicial member of an employment (or as they were then called industrial) tribunal would have no idea as to how to conduct an evaluation of this sort without guidance. However, we shall see that this procedure has produced its own problems.

At the outset these amendments provided little more than an illusion of equality. As was entirely predictable,

---

[142] In fairness, though, it should also be noted that when the draft regulations amending the Equal Pay Act 1970 were considered in the House of Lords, unlike Alan Clark, Lord Gowrie had said that only the most hopeless cases should not go to an independent expert. His statement was cited to the industrial tribunal with effect by David Pannick (as he then was) on 10 April 1984 in *Hayward* v. *Cammell Laird Shipbuilders Ltd* [1985] ICR 71, [1984] IRLR 463 at [7].

[143] See s. 2A(4) as introduced into the Equal Pay Act 1970 by the new Regulations.

employers took every point to argue that an expert should not be appointed.[144] This was very effective. In the first 17 years, there were only about 200 cases in which a tribunal appointed an independent expert.[145] These figures seem extraordinary given that only a minority of workplaces had job evaluations systems already in place, which would have ruled out equal value claims, and given the pent up anger I have described above. Up to 2002, only about eleven cases a year were made complaining that work was undervalued of such strength that the tribunal considered that it should ask for the view of an independent expert.

The pace of application was not constant. By the late 1990s that figure was rising, but the delays were also increasing. A bottleneck was emerging that once again had a chilling effect on women coming forward, once they were told how long a case would go on for.[146]

Thus, an assessment undertaken in 2000 showed that the average time taken from a tribunal's decision to refer a case to an independent expert to the tribunal's ruling was

---

[144] The litigation in the multiparty equal value case *Brierley* v. *Asda Stores Ltd* would seem to be a recent example.

[145] In its annual report for the period 2001–2, ACAS reports that: 'Since the Equal Value Regulations were introduced, the tribunals have appointed experts in 227 cases (Up to 31 March 2002); 21 of those arose in the period 1 April 2001 to 31 March 2002.' See p. 34. The Report can be found at www.acas.org.uk/media/pdf/d/o/acas_02_ar_1.pdf.

[146] The bottleneck could also have dire effects for employers if the women's case was established, since interest had to be paid at judgment rate on the arrears.

just under 20 months, with the time ranging from 5 months to over 4 years.[147]

One reason for the lack of real progress was the hideous complexity of the rules of procedure that applied to such cases. Because the independent expert had to make an objective assessment of the value of the work, consideration had to be given to identifying the job that was actually being done by the complainant and her comparator. This could take a great deal of time and require hearings, disclosure and further directions from the tribunal.[148] Even after the independent expert had reported his or her assessment, the conclusion could be challenged by experts called by either side.

All of this was a million miles away from Barbara Castle's wish when introducing the Equal Pay Act 1970 that the procedure should be swift and simple.[149] In one case that reached the House of Lords, Lord Bridge was driven to note how the process of claiming that a woman's work was of equal value to that of a man was 'lengthy, elaborate and ... expensive'.[150]

---

[147] See the Full Regulatory Impact Assessment attached to the Explanatory Memorandum to the Employment Tribunals (Constitution and Rules of Procedure) (Amendment) Regulations 2004, SI 2004/2351, see www .legislation.gov.uk/uksi/2004/2351/pdfs/uksiem_20042351_en.pdf.

[148] See the Industrial Tribunals (Rules of Procedure) (Equal Value Amendment) Regulations 1983, SI 1983/1807, Industrial Tribunals (Rules of Procedure) Regulations 1985, SI 1985/16, and later the Employment Tribunals (Constitution and Rules of Procedure) Regulations 1993, SI 1993/2687. Similar regulations applied in Scotland and Northern Ireland.

[149] As she had explained when introducing the Bill that became the Equal Pay Act 1970 back in 1969.

[150] See *Leverton* v. *Clwyd County Council* [1989] AC 706, [1989] 2 WLR 47, [1989] 1 All ER 78, [1989] 1 CMLR 574, [1989] ICR 33, [1989] IRLR 28.

The logic of these difficulties had a perverse outcome. It made sense to make sure that any litigation that was started had the best possible chance of success. That meant making comparisons on a range of bases with various different men's jobs. As a result the complexity was multiplied, and the difficulties Lord Bridge noted were compounded.

For their part, employers sought to take advantage of the hurdles that the Amendment Regulations and concomitant tribunal rules had created. Employers sought to stop the appointment of an equal pay expert by alleging that they had such a good material factor defence to the claim that the expert's opinion would have no relevance to the ultimate outcome.

This practice was approved by the Employment Appeal Tribunal in a judgment given by Wood J when he was President in *Reed Packaging Ltd* v. *Boozer*.[151] It always seemed to me that this was to put the cart before the horse. How could it be argued that there was a material factor defence on an assumed or hypothetical basis in advance of the report of the expert? The materiality of any factor had to be assessed by reference to the issue of equal value, surely? Nonetheless, it was approved as a way forward and continues to have some judicial approval.[152] Encouraged by the willingness of tribunals to listen to such arguments, and deploying the increasing delays in getting an expert's report, employers deployed the greatest ingenuity that they could muster to argue their defence at the outset.

---

[151] [1988] ICR 391, [1988] IRLR 333.
[152] See e.g. *Wood* v. *William Ball Ltd* [1999] IRLR 773, and *Calmac Ferries Ltd* v. *Wallace* [2014] ICR 453, at para [7].

The right for individual women did not merely have to contend with Alan Clark's drunken malevolence, but also an increasingly deregulated labour market, where outsourcing was encouraged as a means of depressing wages. Sue Hastings, one of the country's leading pay experts, committed to achieving equal pay on a fair and proper basis, writing in 1999 concluded that these complex changes had actually had a negative effect on women's wages.[153] She pointed out how the changes brought a greater focus on separate pay bargaining for men and women's roles, the greater use of carefully constructed job evaluation studies that focussed overly on men's jobs, and the overall complexity of the legislation. Over time these points have had to be addressed.

The Tory employment policy, of deregulation and compulsory competitive tendering, encouraged the contracting out of service jobs (predominantly undertaken by women) by both the state and private sectors. Women increasingly found that the pay bargaining systems that they had enjoyed in their previous employment were no longer relevant to the new employer. Moreover the new contracted out entity might have few if any male employees with whom the women could compare themselves. This was a new and brutal form of gender job segregation. It probably would have happened even without the amendments to the Equal Pay Act 1970, since the aim was to drive down wage costs and disempower

---

[153] See S. Hastings, *Negative (Pay) Equity – an Analysis of Some (Side-) Effects of the Equal Pay Act*, Chapter 10 in *Women, Work and Inequality – The Challenge of Equal Pay in a Deregulated Labour Market* (eds. J. Gregory, R. Sales and A. Hegewisch, Macmillan Press Ltd, 1999).

trade unions, but it certainly helped in industry's fight back against women's empowerment by Article 119.

2.2 The Comparison Problem

Could contracted out women continue to compare their work with that of employees of the former employer? It took some time for the answer to emerge that in limited circumstances they could where there was a single source for the pay systems that applied.[154]

The first important case was C-320/00 *Lawrence* v. *Regent Office Care Ltd*.[155] Until 1990, North Yorkshire County Council had been responsible for providing its own cleaning and catering services to the schools and educational establishments under its control. Following compulsory competitive tendering, the responsibility was transferred to Regent Office Care Ltd.

During the tendering period, female employees brought a successful action against the council for equal pay without discrimination based on sex under the Equal Pay Act 1970. The work of the female applicants in those proceedings had been found to be of equal value to male council employees working in gardening, refuse collection and sewage treatment.

What would happen after the women were transferred? Some left and Regent Office Care thought it could re-

---

[154] See e.g. Case C-320/00 *Lawrence* v. *Regent Office Care Ltd* EU: C:2002:498; Case C-256/01 *Allonby* v. *Accrington and Rossendale College* EU:C:2004:18; and *North Cumbria Acute Hospitals NHS Trust* v. *Potter* [2009] IRLR 176.

[155] Ibid.

employ the women on rates of pay lower than those paid by the council prior to the transfer. New female employees, who had never been employed by the council, were also paid at rates below those paid to female council employees prior to the transfer.

All these women, understandably, complained, relying on their European law rights. They failed. The European Court of Justice did hold that if there was a single source from which pay decisions were made then a comparison could be made across businesses; that was not the case here.

There was another point employers took to avoid comparisons being made between men and women's work and so avoid a reference to the Independent Expert. This was based on the requirement in the Equal Pay Act 1970 that comparators had common terms and conditions with the women making the claim.

The last throw of the dice occurred in the most recent case I argued in the Supreme Court, on an intervention for the Equality and Human Rights Commission (EHRC), *North & Ors* v. *Dumfries and Galloway Council*.[156] The apparently restrictive conditions of the domestic legislation had to give way to the European law requirement that the sole condition for an apt comparison was that the men and women's pay was controlled by a single source.

A good deal of damage, though, had been done on the way, particularly for civil servants. In one case, which in my

---

[156] [2013] ELR 536, [2013] IRLR 737, 2013 SCLR 609, [2013] WLR(D) 264, 2013 GWD 23-439, [2013] 4 All ER 413, [2013] Eq LR 817, 2013 SC (UKSC) 298, [2013] UKSC 45, 2013 SLT 769, [2013] ICR 993.

view was undoubtedly incorrectly decided, the Court of
Appeal of England and Wales concluded that comparison of
men's and women's wages across departments was not permitted: *Robertson* v. *Department for the Environment, Food
and Rural Affairs*.[157] I cannot believe that before it made its
decision in this case the Court of Appeal had been informed of
the history which I have related.

2.3 The Enderby Litigation

The separate pay bargaining of different classes of jobs became
a particular means of avoiding equal pay, since it was argued
that any differences in pay that arose between jobs that might
be considered to be of equal value were not because of sex.
Fortunately, in Case C-127/92 *Enderby* v. *Frenchay Health
Authority*,[158] the European Court of Justice ruled that where
significant statistics disclosed an appreciable difference in pay
between two jobs of equal value, one of which is carried out
almost exclusively by women and the other predominantly by
men, Article 119 required the employer to show that that
difference in pay was based on objectively justified factors
unrelated to any discrimination on grounds of sex. It was not
enough to argue that the pay rates had been reached by separate pay bargaining systems.

This case probably has done more to see through the
mask that employers sought to draw over women's pay claims
by arguing that the pay differences were not due to sex but to

---

[157] [2005] EWCA Civ 138, [2005] ICR 750, [2005] IRLR 363.
[158] EU:C:1993:859.

segregated pay bargaining. The case did not completely stop employers from running arguments that different pay bargaining systems were a justification for unequal pay, but it did mean that they were usually not successful. The focus now was on the degree to which there was gender segregation. It should have been no surprise that within local authorities and the health service it was rampant. We are now discovering the extent to which this is also true in major areas of industry, such as supermarket staff and warehouse operatives.[159]

2.4 Procedural Changes

As a result of the increasing realisation by politicians of the difficulties, delays and complexity the Labour Government consulted on what could be done to improve the efficacy of the law. There was a concerted effort to address the obfuscation that women who brought equal value cases faced. As a result, in 2004 the relevant substantive and procedural legislation and rules were changed.[160] It was no longer possible to stop a case on the grounds of no reasonable prospect of success and the new procedural rules set out procedural timetables and made other relatively minor changes.

These procedural changes, though entirely welcome, have probably been more effective normatively: the

[159] The ongoing equal pay litigation against Asda and Tesco seems likely to provide good examples of this kind of segregation in the private sector.
[160] See the Equal Pay Act 1970 (Amendment) Regulations 2004, SI 2004/2352 and the Employment Tribunals (Constitution and Rules of Procedure) (Amendment) Regulations 2004, SI 2004/2351.

timetables have rarely been kept to, in my experience. The next problem was the insufficient numbers of independent experts to address the increased number of requests being made for their opinion. I well recall litigating equal pay cases in the 2000s and being told that it might take up to 2 years for an expert to report. By 2010, that is 25 full years after the right to bring a claim for equal pay for work of equal value, the number of references to the independent experts had risen to 718 cases in total, that is some 500+ more over the previous 8 years.[161] Between 2002 and 2010, the rate had increased to about 64 cases referred to independent experts each year.

This sharp increase was noted by ACAS in its 2010–11 Annual Report, where it stated that it had insufficient experts to whom it could refer cases.[162] It pithily summarised what it believed to be the cause of this bottleneck:[163]

> Local authority equal pay cases have put considerable demands on the independent experts on the panel. The cases are often complex and feature large numbers of claimants and comparators.

2.5 Multiparty Equal Value Cases

By the turn of the century the local authority equal value cases were indeed multiplying fast, but they had not been the

---

[161] See the ACAS Annual Report for 2010–11, see http://m.acas.org.uk/media/pdf/p/o/Acas_Annual_Report_Accounts_2010-11_colour.pdf.
[162] Ibid. [163] Ibid.

pathfinders. The new impetus to take very large equal value cases was seen first in the health service. Much credit must go to Unison, and above all to their representative Peter Doyle,[164] for bringing what were known as the Carlisle Hospitals equal pay claim.

There were some extraordinary differences in the pay of women and men in jobs which were very closely aligned, though not the same. The *Guardian* reported examples on 15 July 2001:[165]

- A domestic, who washes floors, who earns £7,505 a year, working a 39-hour week. 'Wall-washers', who are all men, earn £9,995 for a 37-hour week.

- A D-grade nurse earns £13,900 after completing degree-level qualifications and five years in the job, and can supervise up to 15 staff in clinical situations that can mean life or death for patients. A craftsman supervisor, who has a joinery apprenticeship, will earn £19,100 after three years' work, and will supervise a maximum of two people. The nurse is offered time off in lieu in return for overtime, while the craftsman supervisor is paid time and a half.

- A cook, who needs the same level of qualifications and serves the same length apprenticeship as a plumber, earns £172.62 for a 39-hour week. An NHS plumber earns £272.11 for a 37-hour week.

- A female ancillary worker in the clinical sterile services department will need up to NVQ level 3 qualification

---

[164] To read more about his critical role see www.theguardian.com/society/2006/feb/18/health.genderissues.

[165] See www.theguardian.com/society/2001/jul/15/equality.nhsstaff.

and will be paid £580 a month for a 39-hour week. A craft worker, such as a joiner, needs the same level of training, and will earn £996 a month for a 37-hour week. The female ancillary workers are more crucial to the working of the hospital, because without them all operations have to be cancelled, whereas joinery repairs can be done any time.

I acted on the instructions of Unison for the women in that case. I can still recall the palpable sense of shock to my sense of fairness on reading the first of these examples and then discussing it with the women concerned. Until then I could not believe the mendacity of those who had made such distinctions. The other examples were somewhat more complicated factually, but they too seemed all wrong. How could it be that such a gross unfairness was permitted and by our precious National Health Service? Where had all the fight and energy of the last 90 years gone? Had the lessons not been learnt?

The more I delved into the case, the clearer it became that these pay rates were the result of differential energy being applied in the negotiating process. I do not say that the relevant unions were explicitly discriminating in their approach, but the degree to which there was obvious inequality between predominantly male and predominantly female jobs was palpable. My brief, of course, was to try to resolve the issue in the here and now, and I confess I was not then aware of the whole of the story I have set out above.

Yet looking back now at this case, I can imagine all too clearly what the Pankhursts, Mary Macarthur, Lady Astor, the Minority members of the 1944–1946 Royal Commission,

Mrs Cazalet-Keir, the Dagenham women, and Barbara Castle (and the many other campaigners along the way) would have said. This time, though, it was different because the women were entitled to 6 years of back pay and interest on top. The sums involved began to look enormous. I cannot reveal exactly how much the Carlisle Hospitals case settled for, but I can say that the *Guardian*'s estimate that it was in the region of £300 million was not in the wrong area.[166]

2.6 The Local Authority Cases

The Health Service tried to address the disparities that were everywhere in the pay of women and men doing comparable work of equal value in an ambitious and very important programme called 'Agenda for Change'. Although its outcome was challenged as being discriminatory, it has largely stood the test of litigation. Sue Hastings, who had been retained with others to ensure that the job evaluation that lay behind Agenda for Change really worked, had done a good job. Indeed, it has been relied on as evidence to secure back payments prior to its implementation.[167]

The potential for claims to be brought by women in local authorities on a similar basis to those brought by the staff of the Carlisle Hospitals was appreciated by Stefan Cross. He had worked at the solicitors' firm Thompsons favoured by many unions, but became disenchanted with the way in which

---

[166] See www.theguardian.com/society/2006/feb/18/health.genderissues.

[167] See *Hovell* v. *Ashford and St Peter's Hospitals NHS Trust* [2009] EWCA Civ 670, [2009] ICR 1545.

women's right to equal pay for work of equal value was being promoted, and set up his own firm. There was really a single basic forensic insight that he had at the beginning, which was that the move to a unified pay bargaining across local government – the so-called single status agreements – like Agenda for Change in the NHS, provided huge opportunities to challenge the pay differentials that had applied as between men's and women's jobs. It is no exaggeration to say that cases brought by his firm have changed the perspective within local government and won many thousands of women large payments.

Stefan Cross' mother had been a low-paid local authority worker and so he had some personal insight from his family background of the way in which women's work was seen as second class. No doubt this was one reason he was motivated to try to do something about it. His second major contribution was to work out how to fund this litigation. For women – like his mother – to litigate on their own would have been a near impossibility. No legal aid was available and the Equality Commissions both in Great Britain and Northern Ireland did not have the resources to support these cases. Stefan Cross, however, worked out how to fund the cases by taking a percentage of their value.

Much has already been written about this litigation, so it is not necessary to discuss every aspect of it in this lecture. Yet some further reflections are apt.

One really important aspect of this litigation has been the development at last of judicial skills to undertake long, complex equal value cases. Some judges in the employment tribunal began to specialise in them. For a while, the Newcastle

Regional Office began to run the majority of the local authority cases.

The awards to be made or agreed in these local authority cases have also been calculated to be in the hundreds of millions. However, as these are public authorities with limited reserves and heavy statutory controls on their capabilities to deploy revenue, the sheer size of the claims has been a limiting factor on the path to conclusion of these cases. For instance, on 5 March 2014 the *Guardian* reported that:

> Birmingham city council is to sell off one of its landmark assets, the National Exhibition Centre (NEC), to help pay a £1bn bill to settle thousands of equal pay cases. The Labour-led city council has agreed settlements with female staff including home care workers and school cooks who were paid less than men for work of equal value. Some men have also been included in the payouts and claims are still being submitted. The council has borrowed money to help fund the settlements but the Department for Communities and Local Government (DCLG) will not allow it to take on any more loans.

Birmingham was one of the largest local authority employers in the UK, but other councils have had to take similar steps. It seems likely that Glasgow will have to take similar steps.

The complexities of making such arrangements can cause employers to try to stave off the final day of reckoning by taking points that are of little or no merit or to otherwise delay. This may be good for the lawyers they instruct and pay, but it is not obviously good in the long run for the public weal or the women whose rights have been in issue.

2.7 The Limited Role for Trade Unions

Stefan Cross was not afraid to identify the role that trade unions had sometimes played in causing unequal pay in local government. This is an uncomfortable truth that understandably many union officials have found very difficult to accept. There is not the slightest doubt that the major public service unions wanted throughout this period to have women members and wanted to look after their interests. They subscribed to the principle of equal pay for work of equal value in their national literature and conference resolutions.

However, in their day-to-day negotiations, there was no doubt that some of these unions sometimes underperformed in securing wage rises for women or overperformed for the men. In some cases they victimised local officials who supported applications by female members for equal pay for work of equal value.[168] The litigation brought by Stefan Cross on behalf of women at Middlesbrough and Redcar showed how this was true. He even sued a union for its part in causing unequal pay in *GMB* v. *Allen*.[169] The similarity between the facts that lay behind this case and the limited role of the trade

---

[168] For instance, in 2004, Peter Hamilton, who had been the GMB branch secretary at South Tyneside Council for 14 years, successfully brought proceedings against his previous union for victimising him in relation to advice that he had given to female members.

[169] [2008] EWCA Civ 810, [2008] ICR 1407, [2008] IRLR 690.

unions in securing equality for women before the Equal Pay Act 1970 came into being will appear all too obvious.

What had happened was that the GMB Union had entered into the national 'Single Status' collective agreement between trade unions and local authority employers with an objective of eradicating historical gender-based inequalities. It negotiated new terms and conditions of employment on behalf of its members with Middlesbrough Borough Council. In the process it secured some compensation for employees, including some women, who had suffered past pay inequalities. However, Stefan Cross' female clients who worked for Middlesbrough argued that the GMB had discriminated against them in the process by prioritising pay protection, which mostly benefited men, and future pay over compensation for past inequalities. The employment tribunal upheld the women's claim, finding that, by agreeing to a low settlement for past pay inequalities in order to release more money for future pay protection, the union had engaged in a potentially discriminatory practice that disadvantaged a group that was predominantly women. In response the Union argued that they were only doing their best to get a settlement of the claims that could be brought in relation to the old pay systems. However, the tribunal held that the Union's means for securing agreement, including mis-selling and manipulation, were unjustified, and on appeal the Court of Appeal agreed.

Leaving aside the Union's tactics in securing the women's agreement, which were deplorable, the conflict that the Union faced in doing its best to maintain the men's wages in the face of rising demands from the women is all too evident and to a very limited degree worthy of some sympathy. Its problem was how to square the competing interests of their male and female members.

2.8 The Zero-sum Problem

At the micro level there really cannot be any doubt that often, even usually, securing equal pay for women undertaking work of equal value to men is a zero-sum gain. It is hardly ever the case that the ratio of pay budget to head count is increasing in real terms. In most parts of the public sector, this has not been so for many years. In the private sector, this will depend both on growth in the business' profits and, no less importantly, the demands made on those profits by its creditors, bond holders and shareholders. In truth, this means almost always that more pay for the women = less for the men.

So a union negotiating on behalf of both men and women when there is an equal pay issue is going to get itself into trouble unless it is exceptionally careful. This has to be recognised as a basic fact of all equal pay issues. Ignore it and there will be trouble somewhere along the line.

As the UK faces up to the obligations to meet the UN's Sustainable Development Goal, the limitations to the role of trade unions in securing equal pay for a mixed workforce has to be addressed. In particular, this means that while trade unions have a role to play, that role is limited.

Women simply cannot rely on unions *alone* to secure their interests. That is the lesson of Part 1 and it is the lesson of

Part 2 as well. The unions have a major role to play in pointing up women's poor treatment, in developing common policies and promoting the principle of equal pay for work of equal value, but when it comes to the detail of delivery, there is a point at which they cannot proceed further.

I have seen this at first hand from both sides. The increasing reluctance of the unions to promote the success of the Carlisle Hospitals litigation has been discussed above. I have also seen this from the point of view of employers. I have advised in some very complex situations where local authorities have been committed to righting wrongs and delivering true equality. Women have pointed up that their jobs are not being given equal pay though they seem to be of equal or greater value. They have called for a comprehensive job evaluation. Sometimes, as in the field of local authorities, this has been agreed by collective agreement. This is by no means the end of the hurdles facing women on the way to true equality though, because where job evaluations are undertaken with a view to avoiding individualised litigation about equal value and references to the independent expert, equal value issues can come back into the picture. This takes some explaining, but it is very important to understand this problem if progress is to be made.

2.9 Implementing Job Evaluation Results

Even after a non-discriminatory job evaluation has comprehensively established the relativities of all the jobs in the undertaking, there is much work to be done to establish what pay will be attributed to each level of value, because job evaluation does not itself determine what wages are to be paid.

What has to happen next is to work out how the total available pay budget is to be shared out. At some levels established by the job evaluation there may be many jobs, while at others there will be fewer. Obviously those jobs evaluated as being higher than others must be paid more to avoid litigation. The undertaking has to model a so-called 'pay line', being the different steps in pay from lowest to highest valued jobs. Crudely,[170] the task is then to take the proposed rate of pay at each level in the pay line and multiply it by the number of jobs at that level. If the outcome exceeds budget then, while still maintaining relativities, proportionate adjustments need to be made to each pay level within the pay line.

Given infinite resources, it would be possible to have a pay line, stepped through the different jobs, that ensured that after the job evaluation was concluded and each job valued and ranked in order, there were no losers, each job had the same as before or more. However, that is never reality. There are never infinite resources and indeed since the crash in 2008, most public authorities have had diminishing resources. So as jobs are fitted to the pay line, in accordance with their ranking on the job evaluation, there will be losers. That almost always means men and indeed where it is not just men, it has consistently been my experience that it is predominantly men. This is the reality of

---

[170] Of course adjustments need to be made for part-time working, or if pay is based on output on the expected output of the individuals. Other assumptions about matters such as sickness and parental leave will also be relevant.

equal pay for work of equal value. So the degree to which a union having both male and female members can engage with this has to be limited. It can support job evaluation and even secure that it occurs by collective agreement; however, it will then come under huge pressure from those whose jobs seem to be overpaid according to the newly established relativities. It is too obvious to need much development that, in a world in which consumer spending is driven by increasing amounts of debt, it will often be catastrophic to reduce the pay of a worker.

When job evaluation leads to losers, the unions are bound to argue on behalf of their members for a transition from the old pay rate to the new. They could be expected to do no less, since it is likely to have been their argument that there be such a job evaluation in the first place. How otherwise are they to explain the result of the evaluation to their members? In practice, then, the unions will always argue for a temporary period of so-called 'pay protection'. Yet this brings further problems for the union and for the undertaking.

Let us assume – as is typical – that a man M and a woman W are both working in the undertaking. Their jobs are evaluated as being equal. Accordingly, they should be paid the same. However, M was paid previous to the job evaluation at £10 per hour more than the woman. After the evaluation, the undertaking, having modelled the pay line against the available budget, concludes that the wage for M's job should be reduced by £8 per hour and that for W's job should increase by £2 per hour, so that the wages for the two jobs are equal. Applying this outcome to M and W is fiendishly difficult.

M may wish to keep his job at the undertaking, but he is unlikely to accept an £8 per hour pay cut just like that. He would claim it was a breach of contract and probably resign. He may be persuaded to stay if his pay is protected at the old rate for some years, but even then he may resign during that period. He may claim unfair dismissal, even if he is given proper notice, though he may not succeed if the employer can establish that the dismissal was a result of his refusing to accept new terms and conditions to meet a business re-organisation need.

Secondly, the outcome of the job evaluations does not determine, but it certainly provides very compelling evidence, that W has been underpaid vis-à-vis M prior to the evaluation. So, she is provided with a very good argument to say 'I should have been paid £10 an hour more in the past'. She will have a relatively risk-free claim for arrears of pay based on the pay that M previously had. If she has been in the workplace for long enough she can claim up to 6 years arrears of pay in England and Northern Ireland and up to 5 years arrears in Scotland.[171] She, too, can argue that she wishes to be paid pay protection into the future at the same rate as M and for the same period as him.

Immediately, the undertaking has an anomaly. Both M and W are being paid more than the evaluation and the pay line says that their jobs should be paid. Removing that anomaly not only takes time, it is also fraught, since it may lead to resignations if implemented too swiftly,[172] and to an unsustainable pay bill if implemented too slowly. So, if supporting equal value cases in the tribunal was fraught with future risks for trade unions, the alternative for both them and the undertaking is in many ways even worse.

---

[171] The difference lies in the different periods of limitation and prescription.
[172] Also bringing the risk of unfair dismissal litigation.

What interests me now is how little these difficulties have really been discussed in the open. There are many different commercial organisations that offer job evaluation schemes, such as Korn Ferry using the Hay Method,[173] Mercer,[174] Towers Watson,[175] and even PWC.[176] Their commercial advertising hardly ever discusses the problems in implementing such schemes. Both the EHRC[177] and ACAS[178] have published detailed 'how to' guides to job evaluation, but again these do not really begin to address these problems. Yet I well know from discussions trying to settle large multiparty equal pay cases just how often consideration of these problems arises.

Moreover, when an undertaking has been persuaded to undertake a job evaluation process, and then later begins to understand the true costs involved in moving to the new system, there can be a temptation to take steps to overcome such an outcome by, for instance, so-called 'job enrichment', seeking to add responsibilities (which may be more or less

---

[173] See www.kornferry.com/solutions/rewards-and-benefits/work-measurement/job-evaluation.

[174] See www.mercer.com/about-mercer/lines-of-business/talent/job-analysis-and-job-evaluation.html.

[175] See www.willistowerswatson.com.

[176] See www.pwc.co.uk/services/human-resource-services/rewarding-your-people.html.

[177] See www.equalityhumanrights.com/en/advice-and-guidance/job-evaluation-schemes.

[178] See http://m.acas.org.uk/media/pdf/3/d/Job-evaluation-considerations-and-risks-advisory-booklet.pdf.

real[179]) to the men's jobs,[180] or by creating yet new job evaluation systems that might be more likely to weigh factors associated with typically male jobs higher.[181]

2.10 Equal Value in the 2010s

By 2012–13, the numbers of cases referred by the tribunals to independent experts were falling back again. Only ten cases were referred to the independent experts in 2012–13.[182] The next year ACAS' Annual Report for 2013–14 did not mention the number referred at all,[183] and by the following year, when the requirement for early conciliation of tribunal cases had come on track, ACAS' Annual Report 2014–15 barely

---

[179] See the judgment of the Employment Tribunal (EJ Rennie, Ms Menton, Mr Watson) 31 January 2012, in Case No. 250329/06, *Brennan* v. *Council of the City of Sunderland*, for an example of a case where job enrichment was held to be spurious.

[180] Another good example of this can be seen in the judgment of the Employment Tribunal (EJ Frances Eccles, James Burke and Peter O'Hagan) 18 June 2012 in Case No. S/107667/05 & Others, Case No. S/122698/06, and Case No. S/103308/07 2012, WL 12296504, *Equal Pay Claims* v. *South Lanarkshire Council.*

[181] This is the basic argument in the Glasgow equal pay litigation, where Glasgow sought to rely on a combination of two different evaluation systems. For a discussion of the two different systems, see *HBJ Claimants* v. *Glasgow City Council, Unison Claimants* v. *Glasgow City Council*, [2017] CSIH 56, 2017 SLT 1135, [2017] IRLR 993, 2017 GWD 27-439. I was involved in a stage of this litigation together with Jonathan Mitchell QC instructed by Stefan Cross.

[182] See https://archive.acas.org.uk/media/3730/Annual-Report-2012—2013/pdf/Acas-Annual-Report-2012-2013.pdf.

[183] See https://archive.acas.org.uk/media/4054/Annual-Report-2013–2014/pdf/Acas-Annual_Report-2013-14.pdf.

mentioned equal pay, and had no references to equal value or the panel of experts.[184]

The Annual Reports for the following years are no more illuminating. For a while it was not even possible to find a list of the current independent experts on the web,[185] notwithstanding ACAS' obligation to hold a list as set out in section 131 of the Equality Act 2010.[186]

There are, I believe, several reasons for this. One at least can be traced to the reluctance of employees to challenge their employers in the context of a general depression. The pay cap brought in by the emergency budget of the Coalition Government certainly had a strong persuasive effect on workers, convincing many that there was a very determined government that would fight pay claims to the last. Another reason may well be that the very large number of local authority equal pay cases that had started before 2010 began slowly to be settled without a reference to the independent expert, often because the job evaluation exercises under the single status process that had been adopted generally across local government indicated what the expert was likely to say or by pathfinding judgments that had wider implications. However, this may change as the current crop of equal pay cases against supermarkets proceeds.

---

[184] See https://archive.acas.org.uk/media/4356/Annual-Report-2014–2015/pdf/Acas-Annual-Report-2014-2015.pdf.

[185] I have been informed that ACAS intends to revert to disclosing the names of such experts and also the numbers of references.

[186] The list can now be seen at www.acas.org.uk/index.aspx?articleid=6576.

The Equality Act 2010 consolidated and updated much of equality law. Regrettably the one area it did not address very deeply was equal pay law. I was much involved in advising the EHRC and the government as to what might be done in other areas, but when it came to equal pay the message was loud and clear that this was not going to be the subject of a root and branch review. The main problem was that the legislation had to be completed before Parliament was prorogued and the election called. In the event there was only just enough time for the Bill to become a new Act. Some changes did occur, though.

First, the Equality Act 2010 contained a provision designed to protect women (and for that matter men) who had conversations about their pay. By section 77, any restriction in the terms on which a person works that purports to prevent or restrict them from disclosing is unenforceable, and it is an act of victimisation to penalise someone who makes or tries to make or to seek such a disclosure. As far as I am aware, there has never been a case in which this section has been relied upon. The wording of the section has been criticised for being too restricted.[187] However, I do not say it is unimportant. I am very aware that many contracts of employment, particularly those for workers in the financial services, where bonuses provide in important part of the total pay, had such clauses; I have read many of them and I know that they had a major chilling effect on women bringing equal value cases in

[187] See, for instance, the Handbook on Equal Pay, Income Data Services, 2011, ISBN: 9780414029873, at [9.64].

comparison with male colleagues.[188] They are now much rarer. Nonetheless, in my experience there remains a general reluctance among many workers to discuss the pay they receive.

A further section of the Equality Act 2010 took a different line in addressing this problem. In 2013 the Equality Act 2010 was amended to include a new section 139A, by which regulations could be made to empower an employment tribunal to direct that an employer undertake an equal pay audit (EPA) designed to identify action to be taken to avoid equal pay breaches occurring or continuing. However, first a material equal pay breach had to be established. Many had argued that the law should require all employers to carry out EPAs, even where no breach yet had been established. There is indeed something perverse about a provision that requires the breach to be established first before the tribunal before it can order an audit. In forensic terms, it makes much more sense to do the EPA first. However, this amendment to the Equality Act 2010 came in the Enterprise and Regulatory Reform Act 2013, the long title of which stated its aim as being[189] 'to make provision for the reduction of legislative burdens'. It is therefore hardly surprising that to date no tribunal has ordered this to happen.

Nonetheless, it does raise the ante in equal value cases. An employer who loses even one single case always

---

[188] A typical case I was instructed in was *Barton* v. *Investec Henderson Crosthwaite Securities Ltd* [2003] ICR 1205, [2003] IRLR 332, where the difference between the bonus paid to the male colleague of Ms Barton was £1m whereas she 'only' received £300k. Employers frequently sought to hide such differentials by clauses of the kind that this clause sought to outlaw.

[189] Inter alia.

runs the risk of such an order being made. This provides a useful encouragement to consider a settlement in advance of a judgment. Committed claimants' lawyers can still seek to include such an obligation in any settlement. Moreover, the EHRC has set out at length that carrying out such an audit is good practice.[190] The problem remains that an audit may – just as a job evaluation certainly can – provoke equal value claims which disrupt existing pay systems and can involve claims going back many years. In short, most competent employers' legal advisers will warn of the risks involved in undertaking such an audit.

2.11 Gender Pay Gap Reporting

And so this brings me back to gender pay gap reporting. The obligations in relation to this came on stream as a result of the Equality Act 2010 (Gender Pay Gap Information) Regulations 2017,[191] and, for public authorities, the Equality Act 2010 (Specific Duties and Public Authorities) Regulations 2017.[192]

This is the big news story now, but will it change the way in which women's work is valued? I do not doubt that it is a positive step to force larger companies to explain exactly how the pay budget is spent between men and women, but I am very sceptical that it will make much real change to the

---

[190] See, for instance, its guide 'Equal pay audit for larger organisations'; see www.equalityhumanrights.com/en/multipage-guide/equal-pay-audit-larger-organisations.

[191] SI 2017/172. [192] SI 2017/353.

value attributable to women's work, or, in the few cases where men are underpaid vis-à-vis women, to their pay. I have never heard of any company deciding to increase its pay budget so as to give the women more than previously in order to address the gap, yet as I have shown above, without increasing the budget to allow for this, closing the gap will be a zero-sum game. Why should men give up their better pay just for the public relations advantage of a better report on the gap in the firm?

Moreover, in every case where an official document has discussed gender pay gap reporting, it is emphasised that a pay gap does not necessarily mean that women lack equal pay for work of equal value. The distinction between the right to equal pay for work of equal value is constantly stated to be something quite different, though it may be one of many causes for any pay gap. For instance, see how Carolyn Fairbairn, the CEO of the Confederation of British Industry (CBI) commented on the requirement for gender pay gap reporting on 4 April 2018:[193]

> Gender pay gap reporting is an opportunity for businesses to drive change in their workplaces. For the first time, every larger firm will know the average pay difference between men and women in their company. What gets measured gets changed – helping to develop more inclusive workplaces and support more women into senior roles.
>
> There's nothing more important for firms than attracting and retaining the best possible people. Companies want to

---

[193] www.cbi.org.uk/news/gender-pay-gap-reporting-is-an-opportunity-for -businesses-to-drive-change-in-their-workplaces/.

close the gender pay gap. They have plenty of good practice to draw on – from great flexible working policies, to widening recruitment and engaging with schools to inspire young women into STEM subjects.

It's important that the gender pay gap is not confused with unequal pay, which is already illegal.

Firms have had plenty of warning and have no excuse for failing to submit their gender pay gap data accurately and on time. But businesses can't close the gap by themselves. Many of the causes of the gender pay gap lie outside the workplace and will require a partnership between companies and Government if we are to deliver long-term, lasting change.

The emphasis is not on considering whether women's work is undervalued, but on increasing access for women to the workplace.

Even the EHRC is somewhat guilty of this omission;[194] thus it states in its guidance on 'What is the difference between the gender pay gap and equal pay?':

The difference in pay
Whilst both equal pay and the gender gap deal with the difference (disparity) in pay women receive in the workplace, they are two different issues:

Equal pay:
Means that men and women in the same employment performing equal work must receive equal pay, as set out in the Equality Act 2010.

---

[194] It does of course have other excellent guides on equal pay issues.

Gender pay gap:
Is a measure of the difference between men's and women's average earnings across an organisation or the labour market. It is expressed as a percentage of men's earnings. In Britain, there is an overall gender pay gap of 18.1%.

Causes of the gender pay gap
The causes of the gender pay gap are complex and can be overlapping. Factors include:

Highest paid sectors are male-dominated
Girls often do well at school, but tend to end up concentrated in employment sectors that offer narrower scope for financial reward. On the other hand, many of the highest paying sectors are disproportionately made up of male employees.

The effect of part-time work
The difference in years of experience of full-time work, or the negative effect on wages of having previously worked part-time or of having taken time out of the labour market to look after family.

Stereotyping
Unconscious stereotyping, with assumptions about women not wanting to accept promotion, or not being in a position to do so, particularly where they have caring responsibilities. Women make up 47% of the workforce, but only 35% of managers, directors and senior officials.

It is not that any of the EHRC's or the CBI's prescriptions for change are wrong. The point is that they downplay the basic right that women have in relation to pay. Of course, discriminatory decisions in relation to promotion or arising from working part-time must stop, but surely the key point about such reporting ought to be that wherever a gap is found to exist, there should be an equal pay audit. This is the point made at the start of this lecture, when I quoted the Scottish Accounts Commission advising that a failure to provide equal pay for work of equal value was likely to be a cause of any gender pay gap in any company. It is also the first recommendation by the ILO to address a gender pay gap in its recent publication 'Pay Equity: A Key Driver of Gender Equality'.[195] If women really were paid the same as men, then there would be little point in segregating them or relying on outmoded stereotypes.

The role of the Commission is of course important, but that of the Government Equalities Office (GEO) in relation to these reports is even more so. The GEO receives them. So, it is also very significant what a company finds, having reported its gender pay gap to the GEO, by way of advice on the GEO's website. It will soon land on a page entitled 'Reducing the gender pay gap and improving gender equality in organisations: Evidence-based actions for employers'.[196] Does this say anything relevant to equal pay? No, this document mentions neither 'equal value', nor 'equal pay audit' nor 'job evaluation' anywhere.

I regret having to say this, but the only conclusion that one can reach from this is that the government is still not remotely serious about the core right which I have discussed. A hundred years have passed, but still government has not shown a commitment to supporting this most fundamental of

[195] See www.ilo.org/wcmsp5/groups/public/@dgreports/@gender/documents/briefingnote/wcms_410196.pdf.

[196] See https://assets.publishing.service.gov.uk/government/uploads/system/uploads/attachment_data/file/731288/Gender-Pay-Gap-actions_.pdf.

women's rights. The omission cannot be seen in isolation. The obfuscation and denial, the special pleading and long history of delay, relayed above at such length, cannot be ignored. It stands in support of the accusation that, in placing this emphasis on gender pay gap reporting while refusing to make pay audits mandatory, this government is no more serious about equal pay than its predecessors.

PART 3 THE SUSTAINABLE DEVELOPMENT GOAL

There is much training available to nations as to how to reach the SDG. The ILO has set up the Equal Pay International Coalition (EPIC), together with the Organisation of Economic Co-operation and Development (OECD) and the Women's section of the United Nations to help all countries to score.[197] Yet I am very pessimistic about achieving the UN's SDG within the UK; who would not be, given the history I have reported?

No doubt the information publicised by gender pay gap reports will be a source of encouragement to women to demand more of their workplaces. No doubt the greater focus on developing policies of shared parental leave will enable a more equal distribution of work time within families. No doubt making it easier for women to work part-time will assist them to remain at work. I do not quarrel with any of these points.

---

[197] See www.ilo.org/global/topics/equality-and-discrimination/epic/lang--en/index.htm.

My issue is that the basic economic problem has not been addressed. The history I have set out shows that despite arguments starting more than a hundred years ago, first enunciated by the ILO in 1919, and given greater detail in the ILO Equal Remuneration Convention of 1951, the UK has repeatedly (though I grant not in a consistent manner) made it difficult for women to secure their rights to equal pay for work of equal value, quickly and efficiently.

The economic costs, whether for private or public undertakings, in moving to a pay system where women are afforded equal pay for equal value are seen as being too great. The immediate cost of change may seem small against huge expected national gain in GDP modelled by the World Economic Forum and McKinsey,[198] but it is counted within the undertaking[199] or within the immediate annual fiscal constraints imposed by the Treasury; in either place it has seemed too large. Yet I am not without hope that more can be done.

On 26 September 2018, EPIC held a 'Pledging Event' in the UN's Headquarters in New York, 'Demonstrating commitment and leadership on equal pay'.[200] The flyer announcing the event includes examples of the kinds of pledges that governments and others can make to securing

---

[198] See footnotes 17 and 20 above.

[199] Where the undertaking is a quoted company, it must justify its pay bill to the market as well.

[200] See www.ilo.org/global/topics/equality-and-discrimination/epic/WC MS_635707/lang--en/index.htm.

that this SDG is achieved. I shall set them out here since they build on the themes that I have developed about equal pay audits and the connection to ILO norms:

Governments can commit to:

- Ratification of relevant international labour standards: e.g. C. 100, C. 111 by X date;
- Drafting or amending legislation governing equal pay, in consultation with social partners, and in line with relevant international labour standards by X date;
- Establishment of an equal pay commission by X date.

Any stakeholder can commit towards taking action to address implementation gaps with regard to ratified international labour standards, and to reducing the gender pay gap such as:

- Adoption or updating of a policy on equal pay by X date;
- Adoption of an action plan on equal pay by X date;
- Use of free online tools to evaluate whether pay gaps exist within an organization;
- Annual reporting on the jobs held by men and by women and their respective remuneration;
- Establishment of a minimum wage in female dominated sectors by X date;
- Promotion of awareness-raising, advocacy campaigns or initiatives on equal pay by X date;
- Financial support for evidence based research, data or statistical studies on equal pay in female dominated sectors with a view to informing policy or practice;
- Undertake a gender neutral job evaluation within an organization by X date;

- Implement results of a gender neutral job evaluation with an organization by X date.

The steering committee of EPIC is drawn from Australia, Canada, Germany, Iceland, Jordan, New Zealand, Panama, Republic of Korea, South Africa and Switzerland, the International Organisation of Employers (IOE) and the International Trade Union Confederation (ITUC). So the pledges that can be expected on or after this date ought to be imaginative and proactive and to provide a basis for change here too. Twelve countries have now made pledges,[201] as have a number of international companies and also NGOs; some are very proactive and exciting.[202] The UK has not unfortunately joined in making a pledge.

3.1 The Campaign for Equal Pay Audits

Above all else, there has to be logical system requiring mandatory equal pay audits. The current approach, that an audit only is required after a wrong has been established, is a nonsense and must be re-ordered. Perhaps the reporting of gender pay gaps over time will lead to more pressure for change, as the CBI seems to think will happen. Perhaps too, that will lead to a deeper realisation that women need to be

---

[201] Australia, Canada, Costa Rica, Ecuador, Iceland, Jordan, Lithuania, Mexico, Panama, Peru, Philippines and Switzerland.

[202] See www.ilo.org/global/topics/equality-and-discrimination/epic/lang--en/index.htm.

empowered by the knowledge of the pay relativities and job contents of their male colleagues that would flow from a mandatory pay audit.

3.2 Enforcement Help for Women

The history of the campaign for equal pay for work of equal value demonstrates time and again that it requires concerted effort by women and their supporters. I know of no case in which a woman acting alone without legal representation has succeeded in securing equal pay through litigation.

At present there is no question of legal aid being provided on a general basis for women to bring an equal value claim anywhere in the UK. So, it is inevitable that if they are to be brought, such cases will need the support of trade unions or lawyers willing to act on the basis of a cut of the pay awarded. This is of itself a further hurdle for women, though. Multi-party litigation is notorious for giving rise to conflicts between the different members of the group. Not everyone has the same interest in every aspect of such litigation. Moreover, as costs are not normally awarded in the tribunals where these cases are litigated, it means inevitably that the women will not get full recompense for past defaults.

It is time that the Equality and Human Rights Commission in Great Britain and the Equality Commission of Northern Ireland were fully funded to take test cases for selected individuals. I am glad to see that the House of Commons' Women and Equalities Committee have called for a greater engagement in equal pay issues by the Equality and Human Rights Commission.[203]

[203] See House of Commons Women and Equalities Committee, 'Enforcing the Equality Act: the law and the role of the Equality and Human Rights Commission', Tenth Report of Session 2017–19, HC 1470, 30 July 2019; see https://publications.parliament.uk/pa/cm201719/cmselect/cmwomeq/1470/1470.pdf.

Chapter 3

Comparing Across the Ages

Introduction: One Shot at Life

When will be your 'mid-life'? It struck me hard on my 45th birthday that I had become nearer to 90 than 0: would life treat me as well in the next 45 years, should I be spared? As I approached my 50th birthday,[1] my mid-life crisis began to make me think even harder about age equality. I began to raise it in various lectures on equality law in order to try and get my thoughts clear. I would ask 'All thgose in the room, if you are over 50, please put your hands up', and then 'All those who wish to live beyond 50, please do likewise'. The result was always a full house, because, of course, who does not want to live a long and healthy life?

Once we examine our own mortality like this, it is a short step to thinking generally about the implication of only getting one shot at life.[2] It's only another to listing our *needs* during that life, and making our 'bucket list' of *wants* – the adventures, experiences and achievements – that we

---

[1] 13 February 2001.

[2] Even if you base your life's beliefs on the Buddhist concept of Saṃsāra, and expect to return again to earth after death in some other form, you will want your current life to be as fulfilled and fulfilling as possible so that you will be rewarded in the next.

desire. And so, prompted to identify the constraints and hurdles lying ahead, we review our resources to meet them. Of these, our useful time left – a function of our age and health – will surely be the most important. We don't want to be impeded by our age, or the age category in which we fall, any more than is fair and unavoidable.

This is true for all of us: in an entirely fair world we would each have an entirely equal amount of time on earth; we could plan our time accordingly and compare our place in life's journey in a relatively easy way. Yet we know we don't and for the foreseeable future we will not. So how is age equality to be achieved? Is it through giving us legal rights, or by administrative or political fiat? What age-related aspects of our particular life-stories should, and should not, be taken into account in providing age equality? Can we really be protected from age discrimination?

These questions all go to the heart of the comparisons that can be made between us in the context of age.

There is not much of a legal framework within which to address them. In 2017 the United Nations High Commissioner for Human Rights assessed:[3]

> Very few countries provide explicit guarantees of equality
> and non-discrimination on the basis of age ... Most of
> them do not make explicit reference to age as a ground for
> discrimination to be prohibited, or guarantee equality

---

[3] Presented in 2017 to the 8th Session of the United Nations Open Ended Working Group on Ageing, see https://social.un.org/ageing-working-group/documents/eighth/Background%20analytical%20papers/Analysis_Equality.pdf.

explicitly for older persons. Where such explicit reference to age or older persons exist, the scope of coverage tends to be limited to employment and does not extend to other spheres of life.

However . . . there has been a steady progress in the adoption of legal provisions prohibiting discrimination on the basis of age. Notwithstanding this, the scope and coverage are uneven compared to guarantees against discrimination on other grounds. Many inconsistencies and gaps exist in terms of specificity, legal and material scope, protection from both direct and indirect discrimination, extent of special measures, differential treatment and exceptions, as well as monitoring and access to remedies.

His comments concern the world at large, but they are specifically relevant to the UK; here we have only limited rights to age equality, and these are very new and undeveloped. That is why, in my first Hamlyn lecture, I wanted to address what I saw as *'the newest problem'* in equality law, *'Making a fair comparison across all ages'*.[4]

---

[4] I do recognise there is some competition for the title of 'the newest problem' in equality law, and some might argue that equality for transgendered persons – rightly much discussed at present – is a still newer concept. There is indeed much to be done to promote those rights, as the House of Commons Women and Equalities Committee have shown in their recent report (See 'Transgender Equality' the First Report of Session 2015–16 of the House of Commons Women and Equalities Committee, see https://publications.parliament.uk/pa/cm201516/cm select/cmwomeq/390/390.pdf. See also the campaign for improved trans rights advanced by Stonewall, www.stonewall.org.uk/gender-recognition -act), but the Gender Recognition Act 2004 ante-dates our first domestic

The problem, as I explained in Chapter 1, is that no principle provides guidance as to when situations are to be considered comparable. We – not just jurists but society at large – have to work that out. This is not an easy task for age, because discussions about this have only just started, whereas by contrast the discussions about comparing men and women have taken place for much more than a century.

So far for age we have established very few baselines from which to identify with certainty what are apt and inapt comparisons. Yet although this is a new problem for jurists, politicians and the public, there are social forces afoot that are beginning to compel us to confront this task with greater energy and urgency. These are the changes in demography and in particular life expectancy, which are every bit as demanding of a response as those arising from climate change. They will force us to rethink our right to determine what we do with our lives at any point where our wants and needs must be contrasted with others of a different age. In short, the need to address age equality increases as lives lengthen.

In Northern Ireland the demographic is changing as rapidly as anywhere in the UK. Edel Quinn pithily summarised[5] these changes for AGE NI in 2014 as follows:

age equality laws made in 2006 by a margin of 12 years. And as long ago as 1996, the European Court of Justice determined in Case C-13/94 *P* v. *S and Cornwall County Council* that a person was entitled to protection from sex discrimination based on their changed gender following re-assignment.

[5] See E. Quinn, 'Stop Age Discrimination: Delivering the Programme for Government Commitment to Extend Age Discrimination Legislation to

> Northern Ireland has the fastest growing population in the United Kingdom and it is an ageing population ... There are approximately 366,300 older people over the age of 60 living in Northern Ireland today making up 20% of the population. Northern Ireland Statistics and Research Agency ... statistics revealed that in 2012, 15% of the population in NI was aged 65 and over (272,800), including 32,700 who are over 85. Between 2012 and 2017 the number of persons aged 85 and over in NI is projected to increase by 19.6%, from 32,700 to 39,100, and more than double between 2012 and 2032 to 75,800.

The claim that it is the fastest depends on the period over which the growth is measured. Certainly the latest figures show that it has grown at 6.2 per cent over the last 10 years to 2017, less than England (which has seen the bulk of immigration), but more than Scotland and Wales.[6] Moreover Northern Ireland has the lowest median age of the four countries and is therefore more likely to grow through natural change than the other countries.[7]

The most recent figures published by the Northern Ireland Statistics and Research Agency show how fast the number of those aged 85+ is growing. See Table 3.1.

the Provision of Goods, Facilities and Services' (2014) Age Sector Position Paper, AGE NI, at [3] (footnotes omitted), available at www .ageuk.org.uk/Documents/EN-GB-NI/policy/gfs/Stop_Age_Discrimin ation_Age_Sector_Position_Paper_July_2014.pdf?mc_cid=62f050 e303%3Fdtrk%3Dtrue.

[6] See www.ons.gov.uk/peoplepopulationandcommunity/populationand migration/populationestimates/bulletins/annualmidyearpopulation estimates/mid2017#growth-varies-less-across-the-uk-london-no-longer-growing-fastest.

[7] Ibid.

Table 3.1

	2007	2017	Increase
Females	19,700	24,600	24.8%
Males	8,200	12,500	52.6%

One reason for this lecture having been given in Northern Ireland is that it is a little behind the game in only having protection from age discrimination in the field of employment. Age rights go no further.

Rather than rush to follow legislation in Great Britain, Northern Ireland has debated the issue at greater length, but sooner or later it must decide if and how it will legislate, and whether to match or exceed[8] Great Britain, or indeed, the Irish Equal Status Act of 2000.[9]

Quite rightly the Commissioner for Older People for Northern Ireland (COPNI) has made this one of his priorities for policy development.[10] The office of the Northern Ireland Commissioner for Children and Young Persons (NICCY) has also been much involved in the discussion around extending

---

[8] Office of the First Minister Deputy First Minister (OFMdFM) published a consultation on proposals to extend age discrimination legislation in Northern Ireland into the fields of a goods, facilities and services on 3 July 2015 (see www.executiveoffice-ni.gov.uk/consultations/proposals-extend-age-discrimination-legislation-age-goods-facilities-and-services). That consultation has now closed and the initiative now lies with the politicians to take this issue forward. For the Equality Commission for Northern Ireland's response to the consultation and its position, see www.equalityni.org/Age.

[9] See www.irishstatutebook.ie/eli/2000/act/8/enacted/en/print#sec5.

[10] See www.copni.org/about-us/priorities-for-action.

protecting under-18s from age discrimination;[11] and the Equality Commission for Northern Ireland (ECNI) (with whom I have been privileged to work on many occasions) have also been very active in this field.[12]

This chapter is in four further Parts.

- Part 1 aims to provide the context from which the rest of the chapter flows by summarising some of the key points about demographic change.
- In Part 2 I shall try to identify some of the most important stereotypes about age that affect our current consideration of age equality. This is important if we are to widen the range of issues where we permit comparison to be made.
- Part 3 explains how age equality legislation has been developed to date. From this it is possible to see what are the limits and deficits that need to be addressed.
- A concluding section aims to draw out the threads of this discussion.

PART 1 DEMOGRAPHIC CHANGE AND ITS EFFECTS

First, we must get to grips with those statistics and deepen our understanding of those social forces unleashed by demographic change. Most people know that we are living longer, but few really understand what that means in terms of the strains it is putting on society. In part this is because it is

---

[11] See, for instance, www.equalityni.org/ECNI/media/ECNI/Publications/ Delivering%20Equality/Age-children-and-young-people-summary.pdf.
[12] Ibid.

a dynamic issue, and in part because the predicted changes are so huge they seem almost incomprehensible. We will see that there are some truly enormous social forces at work.

The statistics that Edel Quinn quoted provide some context for Northern Ireland, but since Miss Hamlyn, in endowing this lecture series, was concerned with the *whole* of the United Kingdom, they need extending. And whatever Brexit may bring, this is a European problem as well, so it is sensible to look wider still.

1.1 Europe

A Green Paper[13] published 13 years ago by the European Commission, showed what were then the actual and expected changes in the numbers of people across Europe in what were described as the first and last cohorts of working life. It showed the degree to which the old have depended, and were predicted to depend in the future, on the young.

The graph in Figure 3.1 showed how across Europe older persons are increasingly depending, economically, but also socially, on the labour of the young. Note that 2009 was the year of crossover. We are now some 9 years beyond that transition year, when the numbers in the last cohort exceeded the first.

The Green Paper put some of the numbers into text that:

> In 2050 there are expected to be 66 million persons of 55–64 and only 48 million of 15–24. This means that the working

[13] 'Confronting Demographic Change: A New Solidarity between the Generations', Brussels, 16.3.2005 COM(2005) 94 final.

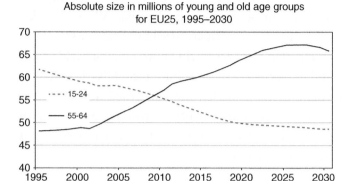

Figure 3.1 Size in millions of young and old age groups for EU25, 1995–2030
Source: Eurostat; 2004 onwards: 2004 Demographic Projections (Baseline scenario)

age population will start declining soon after 2010 and that the labour market will increasingly have to rely on older workers.

The graph also showed, though perhaps less obviously, how the young are likely to have to depend on the savings and capital of the old. Each of these phenomena have been growing and will do so more and more. So in a simple but compelling way, the graph highlighted how quickly significant changes were taking place in the capacity to exercise self-determination wherever your age placed you on this graph.

This graph has been very significant in encouraging me to think about age equality, but it is now quite old. In 2017, the European Commission updated its information, stating its review of Employment and Social Developments in Europe,[14] that:

> In addition to continuously increasing longevity, fertility was on the decline in the EU from the end of the 1960s until the beginning of the 2000s and recovered only very slightly afterwards. As a result, the EU's working-age population (those aged 20 – 64) peaked in 2009 and is projected to decline significantly over the next decades ...
>
> With total population further increasing, counting more elderly and fewer younger people in all Member States, it will be more difficult to distribute societal income fairly

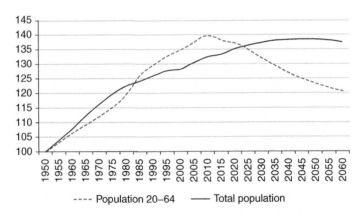

---- Population 20–64   ⎯⎯ Total population

Figure 3.2 Projections for total population and working age population, EU-28
Source: Eurostat 2015 population projections and UN 2015 World Population Prospects

[14] See https://ec.europa.eu/commission/presscorner/api/files/document/print/nl/memo_17_1987/MEMO_17_1987_EN.pdf.

among generations. An ageing Europe may thus face new challenges to all generations' welfare, but there are policy responses that could mitigate and prepare for these evolutions, among which:

- The impact of a shrinking working-age population on economic growth is cushioned by helping a higher percentage of potential workers into employment and extending the length of working lives;
- Increased net immigration and higher fertility help sustain population growth
- Enhance productivity of people in employment.

The rising scarcities resulting from population ageing thus put even stronger emphasis on the need to invest in all generations' employability. Also productivity needs to rise to uphold economic growth.

Demographic Change and Intergenerational Fairness?
The current demographic change implies a growing number of older people dependent on pension systems combined with a shrinking working age population generating society's income. In other words, dependency ratios are set to increase which will put a strain on pension systems.

Today's young workers and future generations face a double burden that stems from demographic change. On the one hand, they are likely to be confronted with rising contribution rates that will be necessary to fund future spending on the increasing number of pensioners. On the other hand, compared with today's pensioners they are likely to face lower pensions, relative to wages. This is because cost-containing measures in the pension systems seem inevitable in response to population ageing.

Due to past reform efforts, progress has already been made in improving pension systems' long-term sustainability but many reforms are phased in over a long period. That is, many of these reforms affect future contributors and future pensioners, not today's pensioners. Further efforts may be needed to improve adequacy and intergenerational fairness, and secure a positive perspective for younger generations.

1.2 The United Kingdom

If we focus down onto the UK by looking at recent figures[15] from the Office of National Statistics (ONS), in Table 3.2 we can see how the UK population currently divides between those under 16, those between 16 and 64, and those 65+, and how dramatically it has changed – so far – over my working lifetime.

Of course, the main proportion of the population remains in the working age group identified by the ONS, but using these figures we can compare the percentages of population in the pre-work and post-work groups graphically as seen in Figure 3.3.

It can readily be seen that we are at the point at which, on current projections, the lines cross and diverge. This is where we are now!

---

[15] See ONS Overview of the UK population: July 2017, Table 1, www.ons.gov.uk/peoplepopulationandcommunity/populationandmigration/populationestimates/articles/overviewoftheukpopulation/july2017/pdf.

Table 3.2

	0 to 15 years (%)	16 to 64 years (%)	65 and over (%)	UK population
	Age distribution of the UK population, 1976 to 2046 (projected)			
1976	24.5	61.2	14.2	56,216,121
1986	20.5	64.1	15.4	56,683,835
1996	20.7	63.5	15.9	58,164,374
2006	19.2	64.9	15.9	60,827,067
2016	18.9	63.1	18	65,648,054
2026	18.8	60.7	20.5	69,843,515
2036	18	58.2	23.9	73,360,907
2046	17.7	57.7	24.7	76,342,235

Source: Office for National Statistics

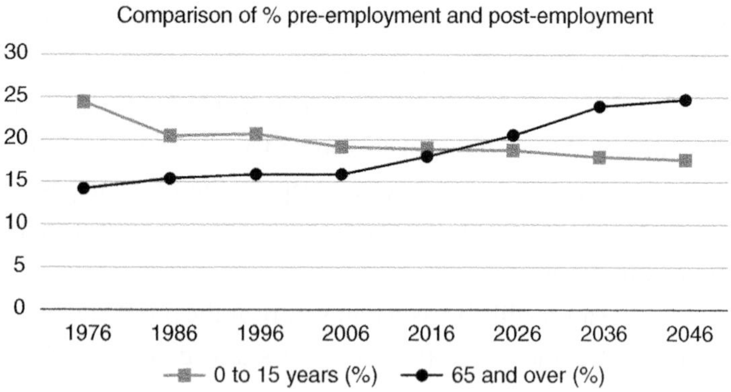

Figure 3.3 Comparison of % pre-employment and post-employment

Another way to understand demographic change is to look at centenarians. On some recent predictions, getting on for one in every three babies born today can expect to live to 100.[16] Allowing for outliers, that means that among this new generation there will be a non-negligible number who will live to 120 or so, perhaps two or three in a typical primary school class of thirty. That of course that will be in 2118, but how does that compare to where we are now and how soon will this change come about?

On 30 December 2010 the Department of Work and Pensions (DWP) – not a department prone to overstatement – issued a press statement under the rather terrifying[17] title 'Over ten million people to live to 100'. The DWP was head-lining the publication of a report by the ONS[18] showing that, already in 2010, there were 878,000 people living in the UK in the 65 to 99 age bracket, who were expected to live to 100.

The paper was updated the next year showing that in total 17.6 per cent of the current population currently aged under 100 would reach that big number. Analysed by age cohorts, 9.6 per cent of those aged 65 to 99 were expected to reach that age, and 26.8 per cent of those 16 and under.[19]

---

[16] See www.ons.gov.uk/ons/rel/lifetables/historic-and-projected-data-from-the-period-and-cohort-life-tables/2012-based/sty-babies-living-to-100.html.

[17] As a 67-year-old myself, I hope those in this cohort will forgive the irony.

[18] See http://research.dwp.gov.uk/asd/index.php?page=adhoc_analysis and http://research.dwp.gov.uk/asd/asd1/adhoc_analysis/2010/Centenarians.pdf.

[19] See also the DWP paper 'Number of Future Centenarians by Age Group', April 2011, https://assets.publishing.service.gov.uk/government/uploads/system/uploads/attachment_data/file/223173/centenarians_by_age_groups.pdf.

How aware of this are we? Hardly at all, I suggest; because this huge growth in centenarians has yet to begin. The current orthodoxy, which will of course have to be reviewed as facts replace predictions,[20] is that there will be an acceleration in the number of centenarians very soon.[21] The DWP paper contained the graph shown in Figure 3.4, based on inductive

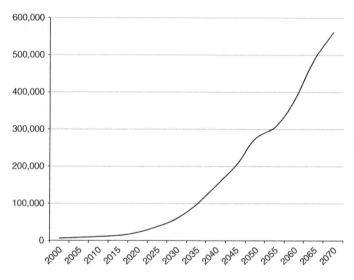

Figure 3.4 Population projections UK

[20] However, a different view is emerging that suggests that we have recently reached a plateau in this growth. See Chris White, 'Grinding to a Halt. Is the Growth in Life Expectancy Coming to an End?' ONS Blog. See https://blog.ons.gov.uk/2018/06/18/grinding-to -a-halt-is-life-expectancy-coming-to-an-end/.

[21] See www.ons.gov.uk/peoplepopulationandcommunity/birthsdeaths andmarriages/ageing/bulletins/estimatesoftheveryoldincludingcente narians/2002to2016.

reasoning from the speed by which average mortality had been increasing up to then.

This graph should probably now be approached with a little caution. There seems little doubt that there will be a large uptick in the near future, but revised figures from the ONS published in August 2018[22] (ONS August Report) suggest that it may not be quite so sharp as this graph shows. The main points in this latest paper are:

> Until 2011, life expectancy in the UK had been increasing for a number of decades; however, in the second decade of the 21st century, the UK along with several other countries has seen a notable slowdown in these improvements in both male and female mortality. Between 2011 and 2016, the UK experienced one of the largest slowdowns in improvements in life expectancy at birth and at age 65 years for both males and females out of the countries analysed.

There has been a degree of misreporting of this effect in the press suggesting that average mortality has gone into reverse, yet it should be emphasised that this is *not* what the ONS' latest report said. Rather, there has been a decline in the rate of increase; moreover there is probably reason to believe that

---

[22] See ONS, 'Changing Trends in Mortality: An International Comparison: 2000 to 2016', published 7 August 2018; see www.ons.gov.uk/people populationandcommunity/birthsdeathsandmarriages/lifeexpectancies /articles/changingtrendsinmortalityaninternationalcomparison/2000 to2016/previous/v1.

it will increase again when special factors have been taken into account.

The ONS noted that this is what has happened in Japan.[23] The King's Fund has also noted that the austerity measures that have been taken in the UK since 2008 may well be very significant,[24] particularly when our mortality rates are compared with other countries of a similar degree of economic development.

Another way of looking at demographic change is to consider the change in domestic projected life expectancy of a male aged 65 over time. These figures were very important in developing my ideas about age, as in the late 1990s I became aware of the speed of change taking place. Each year the new Ogden tables[25] were circulated in my chambers. I soon began to notice an accelerating trend.[26] A few years ago I prepared a table covering data from 1998 to 2010 showing the changes for a case I was to argue

---

[23] Ibid.

[24] See V. Raleigh, 'What is Happening to Life Expectancy in the UK?' (King's Fund, 2018), see www.kingsfund.org.uk/publications/whats-happening-life-expectancy-uk?gclid=EAIaIQobChMInpW_057W3QIV woTVChoz8wx2EAAYASAAEgKujvD_BwE.

[25] The 'Ogden' tables help actuaries, lawyers and others calculate the lump sum compensation due in personal injury and fatal accident cases; see www.gov.uk/government/publications/ogden-tables-actuarial-compensation-tables-for-injury-and-death.

[26] It contributed to my first attempt at litigating age quality issues as a variant on equal pay: *Rutherford and Bentley* v. *Secretary of State for Trade and Industry* [2006] UKHL 19, [2006] 4 All ER 577, [2006] ICR 785, [2006] IRLR 551.

in the Supreme Court.[27] This showed that the life expectancy of a British male at 65 had increased from about 17.4 years in 1998 to 21.4 years in 2010 – an increase of four years (23 per cent) over a mere 12-year period.[28] The figures for females, who already had a higher average life expectancy, have also moved up, though not by so much.

The ONS August Report noted this, too, when looking at life expectancy at birth. It stated that the improvements in the life expectancy at birth of males in the UK were running at 17.3 weeks per year from 2006 to 2011, but from 2011 to 2016 this had slowed to 4.2 weeks per year. Put another way between 2006 and 2011, if two siblings were born three years apart, the younger one could expect to live on average a year longer than his elder brother, whereas between 2006 and now, a second child could expect to live only a quarter of a year longer.

There is currently much discussion about the causes of the previous high rate and the current slowdown in the rate of increase. We do not need to explore those now. It is enough to note that medical care is constantly improving in its capacity to address ill-health. There is no reason at present to predict a reversal in average mortality and every reason to suppose that they will increase again in time.

[27] See my Case for the Appellant in *Seldon* v. *Clarkson Wright & Jakes* [2012] UKSC 16, [2012] 3 All ER 1301, [2012] 2 CMLR 50, [2012] ICR 716, [2012] IRLR 590, [2012] Eq LR 579. The detail was provided by William Latimer-Sayer QC in my chambers.

[28] The data was sourced from the Ogden tables, facts and figures, and the ONS website.

To show how this trend had proceeded, I can quote from the current ONS Decennial Life Tables for England:[29]

> Over the last 100 years life expectancy at birth has increased by nearly 3 years per decade For males, life expectancy at birth increased from 51 years in 1910–1912 to 79 years in 2010–12, while for females it increased from 55 to 83 years. Much of this increase is due to improvements in infant and child mortality in the first half of the 20th century, while gains in life expectancy at older ages have mainly occurred in the last 50 years. People aged 60 could expect to live around 9 years longer in 2010–2012 than 100 years earlier

There is nothing particularly unique to the different parts of the UK about these figures.[30] You will find similar figures in many economically advanced countries. Ms Rosa Kornfeld-Matte, the UN's Independent Expert on the Enjoyment of all human rights by older persons (The UN Age Expert) recently noted:[31]

> Older persons represent a large, and the fastest growing, segment of the global population. By 2050, for the first time there will be more older persons than children under the age of 15 worldwide, and it is projected that the number of

---

[29] See https://cy.ons.gov.uk/peoplepopulationandcommunity/birthsdeaths andmarriages/lifeexpectancies/bulletins/englishlifetablesno17/2015-09-0 1/pdf.

[30] The ONS August Report, ibid., contains an international comparison.

[31] UN Human Rights Council, *Report of the Independent Expert on the enjoyment of all human rights by older persons*, 8 July 2016, A/HRC/33/44, at [III A.] p. 5, see www.refworld.org/docid/57cd7e4d4.html.

older persons will more than double from 900 million currently to nearly 2 billion.[32]

These changing demographics represent advances in knowledge about medicine and diet, and the reduction in the degree to which the passage through life is physically strenuous. These are benefits that you and your children, and their children, will soon really notice, because the change is unlike anything that the world has seen before.

In order to help us predict how these forces may affect us, it is sensible to ask if there has been comparable demographic change. Yet history provides little past experience of so rapid a demographic change. The closest comparable degree of demographic change of which I am aware is the change caused by the decrease in infant mortality. This has indeed been huge, but the change occurred over a longer period.

The ONS' Decennial Life Tables, shown in Figure 3.5, describe how life expectancy at birth has almost doubled over 170 years.

The change in fact occurred over a longer period than this graph shows. Before the late 1700s, child mortality was desperately high; it had begun to decline from the end of that century but was still high in the late 1800s. A big fall took place in the early part of the nineteenth century and the early part of the twentieth; it is generally considered to be still declining.[33]

---

[32] See www.un.org/en/development/desa/population/publications/pdf/pop facts/PopFacts_2014-4Rev1.pdf.

[33] See www.ncbi.nlm.nih.gov/pmc/articles/PMC1633559/, though it is possible it was under-reported, see www.localpopulationstudies.org.uk/PDF/LPS87/ LPS%2087%20Razzell.pdf. The really steep decline only occurred from about

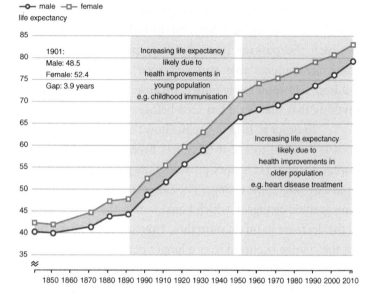

Figure 3.5 Life expectancy at birth, England and Wales, 1841–2011

Sociologists and public health officials have noted a close connection between high infant mortality and large families.[34] We can therefore say that the graph reflects the impact of better ideas about hygiene, housing and medicine, and

1935. Infant mortality continues to decline: www.ons.gov.uk/peoplepopula tionandcommunity/birthsdeathsandmarriages/livebirths/articles/trendsin birthsanddeathsoverthelastcentury/2015-07-15.

[34] There are many works that have discussed this issue; most reference, as one of the most important early assessments, G. Newman, *Infant Mortality, A Social Problem* (Methuen, 1906).

210

increased economic wealth. As it developed, the decrease in child mortality has been hugely liberating for women. The human, and family, pain of high child mortality had been borne by women, who were not in control of their own fertility until effective contraception became available,[35] and who were subject to economic pressures to have such large families. It is well understood that as child mortality decreased in line with economic and social improvements, birth control – long desired – not only became possible but made economic sense for families.

In tandem, women's claims for greater equality and for a greater right to self-determination grew and seemed more attainable.[36] It is not necessary to argue which is chicken and which is egg in this development. It is enough to note that the success of the campaign for proper gender equality laws, whether in relation to equal pay or in relation to all other

---

[35] It had been very difficult even to talk about the issue. On 18 of June 1877, Annie Besant and Charles Bradlaugh were indicted for publishing an obscene pamphlet called 'Fruits of Philosophy', describing and recommending various forms of birth control. They were convicted when the jury found that the book was calculated to deprave the public morals, but were exonerated from any corrupt motives in publishing it. Annie Besant and Charles Bradlaugh afterwards moved the Queen's Bench Division in arrest of judgment on the ground that the indictment did not set out the passages which were charged as being obscene, and the judgment was eventually set aside on that ground: see *R* v. *Bradlaugh*, 2 QBD 569, 3 QBD 607; see also the awful consequences of this criminal process for Annie Besant, who lost custody of her child as a result: *Re Besant* (1879) 11 Ch D 508. The first clinic offering contraception is generally considered to have been opened by Marie Stopes in 1921: see https://mariestopes.org/about-us/our-history/.

[36] Some of this development I discuss in my second Hamlyn Lecture.

aspects of life, has developed in parallel with the only other major demographic change of modern times.

I think that we can make several reasonable inferences about the effects of the demographic changes I have noted and from this comparison. Among them, the following seem to me to be the most important and obvious:

- there will be many more four-generation families;
- these will have new and different kinds of caring responsibilities, both at the beginning and end of life;
- there is likely to be delayed family formation;
- there will be pressure for longer working lives to address the economic dependency issues;
- there is bound to be a different relationship to leisure and consumption than anything we have seen before; and
- above all else we can expect that the demand for better and fuller age equality will build over time as change takes place and individuals have to reassess their expectations about the length of, and fuller enjoyment of, a modern life.

This will not affect people equally or at the same time. Each of these points will cause people to draw comparisons between the treatment they and others receive as they proceed through life. Some of these effects are already becoming visible, but they will become more and more obvious, and, as they do, they will lead to new pressures and constraints on that precious right to do what we want with our lives. The ONS has also recently tried to summarise the issues that arise:[37]

---

[37] See ONS, 'Living Longer – How our Population is Changing and Why it Matters – Overview of Population Ageing in the UK and Some of the

What are the implications of an ageing population?
Ageing is a cross-cutting issue with multiple economic, public service and societal impacts, for example, on pensions, social care, housing and well-being. It can also present opportunities both at a societal and individual level, for example, emergence of new markets, increased involvement in volunteering and community activism, longer working lives, spending more time with family and friends, and possibly providing care for family members.

In considering the implications of an ageing population it is important also to be mindful of the relationships and trade-offs between policy areas, for example, if people work for longer, does that mean that they will have less time to provide informal social care to elderly family members or to care for their grandchildren? How do older people contribute in other non-monetary ways, such as volunteering? If the availability of people to provide informal care declines, how might this impact on the demand for formal social care?

So how should the law respond to these demographic changes, happening now, and predicted to occur? Of course, much of the legal response will be piecemeal, reflecting particular social concerns. That certainly happened as child mortality fell, and women's demands for greater rights over their bodies and their lives increased.

Implications for the Economy, Public Services, Society and the Individual', 13 August 2018, see www.ons.gov.uk/peoplepopulationand community/birthsdeathsandmarriages/ageing/articles/livinglongerhow ourpopulationischangingandwhyitmatters/2018-08-13#what-are-the-implications-of-an-ageing-population.

However, I am concerned with a bigger picture. I do not think that considering these issues piecemeal will be enough anymore than thinking piecemeal about the implications of the decrease in child mortality and improved health and increased prosperity was enough to establish and entrench women's rights. If we see the campaigns for the principle of gender equality and concomitant sex discrimination law as both a response to those changes, and the basis of women's right to self-determination, surely we should expect to see something similar in relation to age.

We can already make a few key points about this. Whether here, or anywhere in the UK, or for that matter Europe, any discussion about providing age equality laws will have to:

- look much more deeply at the concept of 'age', because we cannot proceed on the historic basis that anyone aged 65 suddenly becomes 'old' and so different from those under that age;
- identify whether ideas such as 'young' and 'old', as used now in everyday language, need further examination, definition, or replacement; and
- consider if there are points in life where special protection from age discrimination is necessary or, for that matter, no longer necessary.

It also involves looking at the international extent of these protections because the changes in the dependency ratio that I have described also bring into focus our country's and Europe's approach to migration and, for that matter, encouragement to increase fertility.

This point was brought home to me after a workshop I attended at an international conference on ageing emphasised the extent to which ageing gave rise to North–South issues. The full discussion of those issues is outside the reach of this book, but we should realise that the social stresses that arise from changes in demography are happening elsewhere in the world as well as in Europe. With those stresses come pressure to migrate or seek immigration, with consequent questions about national identity and personal status.

Some countries in Europe – particularly Italy, Portugal, Spain, Greece and Germany – currently have a low birth-rate, well below replacement levels.[38] The issues I have identified are becoming more and more significant there. Some argue that immigrant labour is necessary to fill the dependency gap; others say this cannot occur without a major impact on ideas of national identity. Politicians use these arguments to seek political advantage by frightening the population and causing disharmony.[39] Fortunately, neither in the Republic of Ireland nor the UK are we in the same place as – for instance – Italy, but what is happening there needs to inform our approach to age equality now. Early thinking about how to do that can only be of the greatest benefit as these changes occur.

---

[38] www.worldatlas.com/articles/countries-with-the-lowest-birth-rates-in-the-world.html.

[39] For instance, Italian Interior Minister Matteo Salvini was reported to have said in an interview in *The Times* of London on 29 July 2018, that he looked to babies to 'save Italy's identity' – and that Italy's low birth-rate was being used as an excuse to 'import immigrants'.

So it is my view that these statistics demand hard thinking about how protections from age discrimination and the promotion of age equality can help our society as it transitions. In the process we shall discover that there are some features of this right that differentiate it from the other equality law protections. We shall need to think whether these are important or should be changed, and, if so, how they might be addressed.

On this, I shall argue that the differences between the different equality protections reflect some basic – but deeply held – political viewpoints (shared by many in the population at large), that somehow age equality *is* important, *but* also that there is a lack of certainty about how it is to be addressed. This may sound like a paradox; if it is, then there may be lessons to be learnt from the development of other equality rights, which in their time also came to be seen to be important, even before it was quite understood why, or what their full implications might be.

PART 2 PROBLEMATIC AGE STEREOTYPES

In any detailed discussion of what we need in a modern age equality law, it is necessary to identify, so that we can critically examine, and where appropriate discard, common prejudices and stereotypes about age issues. Of these, the most important stereotypes are based on the view that State Pension Age (SPa) rightly marks the transition in adult life from just an ordinary person to someone having a special protected status that rightly commands other benefits and entitlements. We can reduce this stereotype to the proposition that someone of, or over, SPa is 'old'.

SPa has changed over time, but quite literally – at whatever age it has been set – it has discriminated by dividing the population into those who receive the state's bounty and those who do not. In the process it has defined the moment a fundamental change occurs in society's expectations of its adult citizens; it is the moment when we tend to see ourselves, and are seen, as moving from contributor to the common-wealth, to deserving beneficiary of the state. For many years this assumption was reinforced by the close association between SPa and workplace retirement ages, and by the fact that, until 2006, the standard protection from unfair dismissal ended at SPa.[40]

Though the connection between SPa and work-place retirement ages and unfair dismissal protection ceasing has ended, the stereotypical assumption that the status of being 'old' starts at pension age when a new and generalised entitlement vis-à-vis the 'young' then arises, is still being reinforced by the political consensus that there should be a 'triple lock' on pensions.[41] That promise, highly generous in itself, has immunised those over SPa from many of the vicissitudes and limitations that workers have faced since the 2008 crash. It continues to do so, and

---

[40] The extent to which this was lawful was extensively discussed in the process of the litigation leading up to *Rutherford and Bentley* v. *Secretary of State for Trade and Industry*, footnote 26 above.

[41] The 'triple lock' states that the basic state pension (BSP) should be up-rated annually by the highest of: price inflation, measured by the Consumer Price Index (CPI); average earnings growth; or 2.5 per cent.

in doing so it imposes burdens on those under that age. It was at least one reason why in the emergency budget of the Coalition budget of 22 June 2010 there was to be a public spending pay freeze.

Given the size of the burden imposed, particularly on public sector workers, it may be asked why this stereotype has not been eroded. It is probably that workers, although knowing that until they reach SPa they bear its costs for others, have allowed this imbalance to continue because they believe in due course, if they live long enough, they too will reap those benefits for themselves. For those that do, that could be true, but for those that do not, it won't be; in any event it will only be true for those that do if the economy can bear the cost. Here the key point is that the wealth of the nation is increasingly in the hands of those over SPa.

The ONS recently noted the following:[42]

> As might be expected, wealth increases with age
> (Figure [3.6]), however, younger generations have less
> wealth at the same age than previous generations.
> A typical adult born during the early 1980s had half as
> much total net wealth at age 30 years compared with
> a typical adult born five years earlier when they turned
> 30 years old. Much of this is related to the housing
> market, with property wealth of those in their early 30s
> having steadily decreased over the last decade.
> (Footnotes omitted)

[42] ONS, 'Living Longer'.

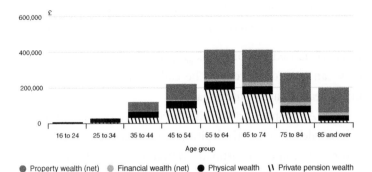

Figure 3.6 Median household wealth by age and wealth component by age of household reference person, July 2014 to June 2016, Great Britain.
Source: Wealth and Assets survey, Office for National Statistics

2.1 Are The Retired 'Old'?

It is therefore understandable that those of, and over, SPa have not historically been treated as being in a comparable situation to those under that age. Yet we are slowly breaking free from these perceptions about the SPa as more and more people work beyond that age. The statistics on demographic change, I have noted above, are challenging these norms head-on. The ONS states:[43]

> The proportion of those aged 65 and over who work has almost doubled since records were first collected. There were 10.4% (1.19 million) aged 65 and over in employment

---

[43] See www.ons.gov.uk/employmentandlabourmarket/peopleinwork/ employmentandemployeetypes/articles/fivefactsaboutolderpeopleatwork /2016-10-01.

in the period for May to July 2016. In the same period for 2006, 6.6% (609,000) of the 65+ population had a job.

It has visualised this progress graphically; see Figure 3.7.[44] So how can someone properly be called 'old' if they still have many years of active life ahead?

As people start working beyond SPa in such numbers, a fiercer debate about the legitimacy of forced (so-called 'mandatory' or 'employer justified') retirement ages also emerged. These forced retirements, though diminishing, are still in place in many workplaces, and are being increasingly scrutinised and challenged. For instance – just looking at the field of law – in 2012 the House of Lords Constitution Committee proposed

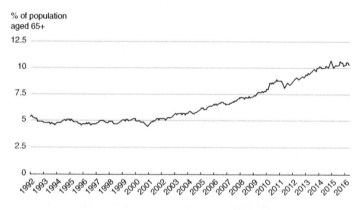

Figure 3.7 Change over time in the % of population of the UK aged 65 or over

---

[44] Ibid. See the chart entitled 'Employment rate for people in the UK aged 65+, March to May 1992 to May to July 2016'.

a reconsideration of the forced retirement for Court of Appeal and Supreme Court judges,[45] and in 2017, giving evidence to the Committee, Lord Neuberger said,[46] when still President of that Court but about to retire, that it was:

> a bit quaint that the retirement age used to be 75 and has been reduced to 70 at a time when retirement ages everywhere else are generally going up, or there are no retirement ages ... To have a sensible judicial career, one would therefore be well-advised to increase the retirement age to 75. I have been in favour of that for some time.

If we are to establish a concept of age equality fully fit to meet the challenges of demographic change, we need to be able to discuss these issues in a legal framework. One problem to be faced in developing this discussion is that the public discourse on demographic change is remarkably poor. What interests me now is how little the public discuss it, and how little the government has done to really get our population engaged with what it means for them. We don't talk about it with the same interest and intensity that we do the weather or Brexit.

---

[45] See the 25th Report published on 7 March 2012 at [188]–[197]: see https://publications.parliament.uk/pa/ld201012/ldselect/ldconst/272/27210.htm#a48.

[46] However, in *Hampton* v. *Lord Chancellor* [2008] IRLR 258, an employment tribunal held that the compulsory retirement of a part-time Recorder at the age of 65 was not justified, rejecting the argument of the Ministry of Justice that such a rule was necessary in order to make room for new appointments. The Ministry of Justice decided not to appeal, and subsequently announced an increase in the retirement age to 70 for all Recorders, Deputy High Court Judges, Deputy District Judges, Deputy Masters and Registrars.

Maybe we should! Until we have fully separated the idea of SPa as a marker for entitlement in general terms – as an 'old' person – there will be a difficulty about making those comparisons across the ages that will be necessary as work beyond that age rises. This is quite a problem; it is noticeable that, when the media discusses issues of age equality, almost always it does so in a very simplistic way. It is probably not that the media fail to recognise that demographic change is important; it seems to be that it is thought – probably rightly – that a typical audience of ordinary lay people can scarcely begin to understand what is happening.[47] This can make for very amusing, and sensational, but scarcely reliable, copy. For instance, on 13 June 2018 the BBC announced that 'Adults in Japan are getting younger'.[48] Of course they weren't; it was merely that Japan was redefining the age of full capacity – when parental permission was no longer needed – for various matters such as marriage and getting passports.

Closer to home, every kind of variation on the theme of 'Work till you drop' greeted the announcement of a review of the SPa by former Confederation of British Industry chief John Cridland on 2 March 2015.[49] The press avidly competed to frighten their readers the most, by saying that we shall all be required to work well into our 70s, to 75, or even to 81.[50]

---

[47] Headlines such as this www.telegraph.co.uk/news/2018/01/11/pensioner-incomes-rise-graduate-starting-salaries-first-time/amp/?__twitter_impression=true are becoming ever more common.

[48] www.bbc.co.uk/news/world-asia-44465196.

[49] For the terms of reference to the Report, see www.gov.uk/government/publications/state-pension-age-review-terms-of-reference.

[50] See www.techknow.org.uk/cms/1343-work-until-you-drop.html.

We won't; there is no limit on the choice of the age to which we wish to work.

The public's disengagement with the deeper issues of demographic change is exemplified also by the reaction to Cridland's ultimate report. When it was published in March 2017 it had a more serious tone,[51] highly relevant for the proper approach to making comparisons across the ages. It attempted, among other things, to address the key equality issue of intergenerational fairness in a time of increasing average longevity. Its focus was on domestic social policy and, above all else, a fair and equal approach to its development. It recalled that to its credit, the government is already engaged in much good policy work.[52] Yet it was not widely discussed even in the broadsheets.

Many of you will know that since the seminal decision of the European Court of Justice (CJEU)[53] in *Marshall v. Southampton Area Health Authority*,[54] there has been

---

[51] See www.gov.uk/government/uploads/system/uploads/attachment_ data/file/611461/print-ready-independent-review-of-the-state-pension-age-smoothing-the-transition.pdf.

[52] Such as the report of the Government Office for Science 'Future of an Ageing Population' (2016), see www.ageing.ox.ac.uk/files/Future_of_Ag eing_Report.pdf, and see more generally the work of the government's Foresight 'Future of an Ageing Population' project at www.gov.uk/ government/collections/future-of-ageing.

[53] For brevity, I shall refer throughout to the European Court that has considered preliminary references from domestic courts as the Court of Justice of the European Union or CJEU, although of course at the time of Mrs Marshall's case being referred it was known as the European Court of Justice or ECJ.

[54] Case C-152/84 *Marshall* v. *Southampton and South-West Hampshire Area Health Authority* EU:C:1986:84, [1986] QB 401, [1986] 2 WLR 780, [1986] 2

a programme of change to SPa, first of gender equalisation, and now leading on to increasing beyond 65 to 67. The current framework for this programme is found in the new Pensions Act 2014, which required[55] the government to publish its views on 7 May 2017, very shortly before the general election that year, as to whether and when the SPa should change. The government broke the law and did not do so.

The Pensions Act required the government to respond to advice from the Government Actuary (GA), Martin Clarke FIA, as to how a change in the pension age might alter the proportion of an average adult's life that would be spent in retirement. His advice had been given the previous March, in response to the government's stated aspiration that as much as one-third of an average adult life should be spent in retirement.[56] Inevitably the GA had pointed out in his advice that achieving the one-third aspiration would be costly, requiring SPa to increase and increase and thus for future generations to work longer and longer before achieving that magic milestone marking this transition.[57] The Cridland report had come out at roughly the same time, so there was

---

All ER 584, [1986] ECR 723, [1986] 1 CMLR 688, [1986] ICR 335, [1986] IRLR 140.

[55] See s. 27 of the Pensions Act 2014.

[56] See www.gov.uk/government/uploads/system/uploads/attachment_ data/file/263660/spa-background-note-051213_tpf_final.pdf.

[57] This had been presented to Parliament on 24 March 2017: https://assets .publishing.service.gov.uk/government/uploads/system/uploads/attach ment_data/file/603139/print-ready-periodic-review-of-rules-about-state -pension-age-gad-report.pdf.

much to discuss, in particular: would the effort necessary to achieve the government's aspirations be acceptable?

That seems to me to be a pretty important democratic issue, involving, as it does, deep questions about our social and economic relationships, one to another, both within our own age cohort, and across the generations. It interests me, and I suspect that most members of the public – if the issue was fully explained – would also have views on it. Notwithstanding, our then government consciously decided to ignore its legal obligations, claiming it would be inappropriate to explain its views in the middle of a national election campaign.[58] So, we were all denied an opportunity to vote on one of the most critical issues of intergenerational fairness of our time. Yet no one seems to have minded much, and the public did not object.[59] The Cridland scare story was news, the detailed report was something else.

In a way, this incident exemplifies many of the aspects of the difficulties in making comparisons across the ages. The 2014 Act recognised that getting such an important age-related issue as SPa right requires technical insight into the

---

[58] Contemporary correspondence seen by the author between the Good Law Project and the government pointing out the government's obligations and the government's response. To be fair to the government, the date of 7 May 2017 had been chosen by legislators enacting the Pensions Act 2014 as the first reporting date so that it might fall roughly mid-term of a fixed five-year Parliament: see [126]–[129] of the Explanatory Memorandum to the Pensions Act 2014 at www.legislation.gov.uk/ukpga/2014/19/notes/division/6/3/2.

[59] There will, however, be more chances as the SPa must be kept under regular review. The Act requires periodic review of this issue: see s. 27 and the 2014 Act more generally.

implications of demographic change as they appear to be from time to time. It recognised these implications affect us all, whatever our current age, because they are dynamic. The implications of the government's decisions will affect us both as workers and as consumers, and that is why the government's views have to be published widely and reviewed regularly.

Yet they just are not easy to address in the public discourse typical of a general election, or indeed at all. This is so, even though it is obvious that they involve questions about what is fair, what is reasonable, and what is possible. These questions are at the centre of any discussion about the framing and utility of equality law. So if we accept that the implications of demographic change are so important for all of us, we must also ask: why has the level of public discussion about them been so relatively muted?

I think that this is because the public actually have no idea as to how to compare across age groups,[60] and so lack a framework for real engagement with the key questions about substantive equal treatment over a lifetime, such as:

- Is age a relevant consideration in the fair distribution of health provision?
- Is it OK to segment the provision of insurance by age, if it drives up costs for some and makes it unavailable for others?

[60] Though see also the Department of Work and Pensions survey of changes to British Social Attitudes to Retirement, at www.gov.uk/government/uploads/system/uploads/attachment_data/file/602539/dwp-analysis-of-british-social-attitudes-data-2008-2015.xlsx.

- Is age a relevant consideration in the provision of any other financial services?
- What does it mean for society and for us as individuals to keep on older workers?
- Who pays the cost of benefits to those well off but over pension age?
- Should we value experience and if so how when setting pay schemes?

What seems to happen is that the public largely treat the answer to these questions about intergenerational fairness as for someone else to worry about – until, that is, they affect them on an individual level. Regrettably, there has been a long history to this kind of muddled thinking in the general public discourse about age. If we look to the past, we can readily find examples of public indifference to addressing obvious age discrimination clearly, comprehensively and consistently.

For instance, in 2018 we were all reminded that it was the centenary of women's great triumph in winning the vote, yet it was also the anniversary of an egregious case of age discrimination, because the vote was only given to women aged 30 or more,[61] whereas universal suffrage was extended to all men at 21.[62] Several reasons were given at the time for justifying this combined age/gender discrimination – none of them survive the scrutiny of history. The principal reason for this discrimination was, it seems, because it was thought unacceptable to have an electorate of significantly more women than men,[63] just as the

---

[61] See s. 4 of the Representation of the Peoples Act 1918.

[62] This was when he was 'of full age', which was 21: see s. 1 ibid.

[63] See www.electoralregisters.org.uk/timescales.htm.

Great War, that caused such a loss of male life, was ending. In any case, Parliament thought it obvious that a woman at 30 had the same worldly sense as a man at 21. Of course, 10 years later the age difference was eliminated by the Representation of the People (Equal Franchise) Act 1928,[64] but even then age discrimination continued because only those of 21 had the vote.

We can see this indifference in other ways in our history. For instance, Parliament has for many years valued a life less than a vote. Since 1908[65] it had permitted the hangman's noose for those of 16 or more, only raising the age of maximum culpability to 18, 5 years after women got equal votes at 21.[66] As a result, teenagers have been hung in the United Kingdom well into my lifetime.[67]

I do not want to suggest that there is no discussion now going on about age equality. That would not be true; very fortunately, even if the public at large are not engaging with intergenerational fairness, some really important

---

[64] And by a similar Act for the Northern Ireland Parliament, see the Representation of the People Act (Northern Ireland) 1928.

[65] See s. 103 of the Children Act 1908.

[66] See s. 53 of the Children and Young Persons Act 1933.

[67] The death penalty was only abolished on 8 November 1965 by the Murder (Abolition of Death Penalty) Act 1965. It is believed that Francis Forsyth, then 18, became the last teenager to be executed in England and Wales, when he was hanged, together with 23-year-old Norman Harris, for the murder of Allan Jee at Wandsworth on 10 November 1960, while the last teenage execution in Scotland took place at Barlinnie Prison on 29 December 1960, when Anthony Miller, aged 19, was hanged for the murder of John Crimin.

commentators from civil society are. Excellent organisations such as the Resolution Foundation's Intergenerational Commission[68] and the Institute of Fiscal Studies[69] are trying to develop better public engagement. There have also been some excellent Parliamentary discussions on this issue.[70] The problem remains, though, that in our world of increasing populism, all the thought sensibly deployed in civil society will not be worth a fig, if its wisest insights cannot be communicated, discussed and understood by the public at large. That is evident from the public response to the kind of pressures that demographic change is now already causing Italy[71] or Japan[72] to face. That is why I think that we are all called on to play our part in this discussion and to take our views out to the public at large in any way that we can.

How are we to do it? The first thing is to sort out what is comparable and what not. As I shall show, we have a lot of unthinking to do!

---

[68] www.resolutionfoundation.org/advanced/a-new-generational-con
tract/.

[69] See, for instance, the Submission to Work and Pensions Committee Intergenerational Fairness Inquiry, from the Institute of Fiscal Studies, of 17 February 2016, at www.ifs.org.uk/publications/8246.

[70] See the Third Report House of Commons Work and Pensions Committee for the Session 2016–17, 'Intergenerational fairness', at https://publica
tions.parliament.uk/pa/cm201617/cmselect/cmworpen/59/59.pdf.

[71] See, for instance, https://econlife.com/2018/06/italys-aging-population/.

[72] See, for instance, www.ft.com/content/7ce47bd0-545f-11e8-b3ee-41e0209
208ec or www.economist.com/asia/2017/01/07/as-japan-ages-so-too-
does-its-workforce.

2.2 Looking for a Principle of Age Equality

I have already shown there have been some very entrenched stereotypes about age, particularly about the non-comparability of those above and below SPa. To move forward to a place where the legal principles of age equality are well known, well accepted and well used, these stereotypes will have to be challenged and their utility reassessed by logic and empiricism. When this is done systematically, then – as for gender or race and ethnicity or disability – new principles can and will emerge that do not lead to inappropriate decisions. The lesson from the steps to progress for the protected characteristics, such as gender, race, disability and sexual orientation, is that it takes a lot of hard work over a long period of time.

When Parliament was thinking about women's enfranchisement in 1918, there was no established legal framework within which to analyse those proposals that we can now see so clearly to have been age discriminatory, and that surely is why the stereotypes won out. It is true that there had been considerable discussion about how age might be used to define the legally permitted treatment of citizens, in different contexts. The problem was that the arguments had not been joined up into a consistent non-stereotyping general non-discrimination principle, equivalent to that for which women were arguing, and in due course won,[73] for gender. On previous occasions Parliament had thought in an elementary way

---

[73] See the Seventh principle identified in Article 427 of the Versailles Treaty, stating the importance to the High Contracting Parties

about age equality when it was aware that economic or social outrages had been borne most heavily by particular age groups. It is just that when it did, it reacted with specific legislation and did not seek to argue from a general principle of age equality.

Take child labour, for instance. It is particularly interesting, since it shows how hard and over such a long time has been the struggle to relinquish the idea that in the workplace children were in comparable situations to older persons.

In the early nineteenth century, girls and boys commonly worked in the Manchester cotton mills for 14 or more hours a day.[74] Those mill-owners saw nothing wrong in imposing working conditions on children that were comparable to those that their adult parents and relatives worked under. They lived in a highly competitive world and bought labour where it was cheapest and most malleable. If some children could work those hours, all could be expected to. Only eventually was it recognised that children should not be seen as being in a comparable situation to their elders.

Once this dreadful abuse came to be discussed in Parliament, the reaction was not based on deep principle that children, having the need to grow and develop and be educated, are not in the same position as elders. If that had been understood, a total ban on child labour would have

(including the United Kingdom) of 'The principle that men and women should receive equal remuneration for work of equal value'.

[74] N. Gould, *Information Concerning the State of Children Employed in Cotton Factories* (Manchester, 1818), printed for the use of members of both Houses of Parliament; see www.bl.uk/romantics-and-victorians/articles/manchester-in-the-19th-century.

followed. Rather, the reaction was to introduce specific regulatory measures on the employment of children and young
people in factories. For instance, the Factory Act 1833[75] held
that there were to be no child workers under 9 years of age,
children of 9–13 years could work no more than nine hours
a day, and children of 13–18 years were permitted to work only
up to 12 hours a day.[76] This Act did not, then, prohibit their
exploitation elsewhere, such as in service or agriculture. This
was, of course, an improvement, but it still considered that
children were sufficiently comparable to their elders to be
worked incredibly hard.

Other kinds of specific regulatory legislation followed, until in the early part of the last century it began to
be realised that what was needed were really *general* regulatory principles to protect children and young persons, to give
them a life that was neither rushed nor degraded by economics or social pressure nor subject to the imbalance of power
between them and their elders. Such principles, premised on
the non-comparability of children to their elders, defined the
need for special measures.

The first steps in this direction came just after the
Great War, just as women were campaigning for the vote,
when the League of Nations adopted a general Declaration of
the Rights of the Child, drafted by two British sisters,
Eglantyne Jebb and Dorothy Buxton.[77] In retrospect, we can

---

[75] 'An Act to regulate the Labour of Children and young Persons in the
Mills and Factories of the United Kingdom.'
[76] In retrospect, of course, this protection seems shockingly inadequate.
[77] See www.savethechildren.org.uk/about-us/our-history.

see this as a very significant milestone on the path to age equality, particularly because in due course it inspired the modern UN Treaty on the Rights of the Child.[78] Just how forward thinking this Declaration was can be seen against the fact that there was still a wide social belief that no special protection was really needed for children. Thus when Lord Kitchener raised his volunteer army, although Queen's Regulations did not permit recruits under 18, many 13- and 14-year-olds were signed up, and as many as a quarter of a million under-age males went to war.[79] Wars of course bring special and specific social pressures; nonetheless this extraordinary statistic represents not merely the determination of under-age boys to join their older brothers and friends, but the complicity between adult society and the state in ignoring the rules.

The fact is that we have not been challenging age stereotypes with the same intensity as we now bring to those for gender. Yet just as gender stereotypes have been deeply embedded, age stereotypes, too, run very deep in our

[78] However, the UK did not take this kind of universal approach to children's rights until it adopted the UN Treaty as a domestic law in the Children Act 2004. This has led to the kind of detailed consideration about the extent of the implementation of the general principle of the best interests of the child seen in 'The UK's compliance with the UN Convention on the Rights of the Child', the Parliamentary Joint Committee on Human Rights Eighth Report of Session 2014–15, see https:// publications.parliament.uk/pa/jt201415/jtselect/jtrights/144/144.pdf.

[79] See www.bbc.co.uk/news/magazine-29934965. It has been suggested that in many cases this was to avoid the monotonous and arduous work that lay ahead of them, though they must have had little idea of what they had signed up to.

collective psyche. This is not just a point about the SPa. Without perhaps reaching the level of the Confucian concept of filial piety, we have been brought up to believe that increased age will bring increased status, so that we should segment our comparisons across a lifetime.

Nowhere can we see this better summarised than in Shakespeare's classification for men at least[80] – in his 'All the world's a stage' soliloquy: infant, schoolboy, lover, soldier, Justice, followed by the less desirable older man, and second childhood.[81] The soliloquy is of course written as a description of the path through life of a male, so I must note that Julia Sneden[82]

---

[80] Shakespeare opens the passage (see footnote 81) with a reference to 'men and women' but a substantial part of the imagery is certainly directed to men alone.

[81] *As You Like It*, Act II, Scene vii. 'All the world's a stage, And all the men and women merely players; They have their exits and their entrances, And one man in his time plays many parts, His acts being seven ages. At first the infant, Mewling and puking in the nurse's arms; And then the whining schoolboy, with his satchel And shining morning face, creeping like snail Unwillingly to school. And then the lover, Sighing like furnace, with a woeful ballad Made to his mistress' eyebrow. Then a soldier, Full of strange oaths, and bearded like the pard, Jealous in honour, sudden and quick in quarrel, Seeking the bubble reputation Even in the cannon's mouth. And then the justice, In fair round belly with good capon lined, With eyes severe and beard of formal cut, Full of wise saws and modern instances; and so he plays his part. The sixth age shifts Into the lean and slippered pantaloon, With spectacles on nose and pouch on side; His youthful hose, well saved, a world too wide For his shrunk shank; and his big manly voice, Turning again toward childish treble, pipes And whistles in his sound. Last scene of all, That ends this strange eventful history, Is second childishness and mere oblivion, Sans teeth, sans eyes, sans taste, sans everything.'

[82] See the Senior Women's Web at www.seniorwomen.com/news/index .php/about-us.

has rewritten this passage for women. She has emphasised the extent to which a woman's life changes with age in different but also stereotypical ways, starting with a schoolgirl coping with puberty, and adding in a job-seeker, a worker coping with maternity, and an empty-nester.[83]

Yet neither her, nor Shakespeare's, list is much good as a working stereotype for life's stages, by which to define fully what social policy on age should be. Such stereotypes are, and were always, inadequate as means to generalise about lives. The full seven ages have been denied to most people, most of the time, since Shakespeare wrote. He died at 52^{84} without ever becoming a Justice, and in any event median life expectancy in Jacobean England was around 35 to 40.[85] Likewise by no means all women are working mothers, and some children seem even less likely to leave home![86]

These statements about the different stages of ageing are important as part of our inherited culture, but they are better seen as merely aspirations or expectations applicable to some, rather than typically descriptive

[83] www.seniorwomen.com/articles/julia/articlesJulia031905.html.

[84] In 1616.

[85] Max Roser, 'Life Expectancy' (2017). Published online at OurWorldInData.org. Retrieved from: https://ourworldindata.org/life-expectancy/. This was largely because of the high levels of infant mortality and the poor state of public health.

[86] The ONS reported that the percentage of young adults living with their parents in the UK had risen from just over a fifth (21 per cent) in 1996 to 26 per cent in 2017, rising from 2.7 million to 3.4 million in the past two decades, see www.ons.gov.uk/peoplepopulationandcommunity/births deathsandmarriages/families/datasets/youngadultslivingwiththeirparents.

of all. Even so, as aspirations, or expectations, we must recognise that they do still have great force in shaping our views about comparisons across a lifetime. They continue to underpin an approach to advancing age – shared by many – as being desirably transformative from the undeserving beginner, to the major contributor, to finally the deserving dependant of the state.

As a result, we really do not find it easy to consider that persons, in the stage of a lover or a justice, a girl entering puberty or an empty-nester, could be in a comparable situation. Yet as families extend, marriage or partnering takes place later in life, the range of years within which parental or other caring responsibility arrives, lives are prolonged, we shall have to do better than this. We now need to be able to identify the common issues that can be compared at any age. Some of these are obvious, such as the needs for a roof and income, for adequate health care and social support, and education, and the opportunity to enjoy our capacities to the full, at whatever age. At present there is a very unequal relationship between beneficiaries and funders when this is looked at by age profile.

And, in confronting these stereotypes, we must also recognise that not everyone will grow old, or even achieve average life expectancy, or have the opportunity to acquire the benefits typically linked to any specific age group. This matters hugely in any discussion about age discrimination, since it is only if everyone enjoyed the same sort of longevity, and with it the same sort of health and capacities, that it could be argued that age equality can, and will, be achieved in the long run. We need to bear in mind that there is, and will continue to be, a distribution around the mean for both longevity and years of full capacity, for every cohort.[87]

Let me show you a graph,[88] in Figure 3.8, submitted by the Intergenerational Foundation to the House of Commons Work and Pensions Committee when it was discussing 'Intergenerational fairness',[89] in order to illustrate how government spending has become so highly age specific.

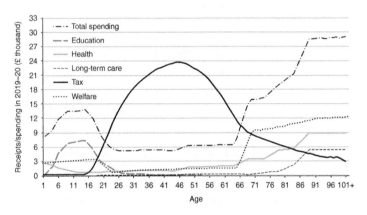

Figure 3.8 Representative profiles for tax, public services and welfare spending

[87] The vast majority of us will not enjoy a wholly healthy and disability-free life with our capacities undiminished. Although 'healthy life expectancy' and the related 'disability-free life expectancy' are rising, they are far off matching life expectancy: see 'Future of an Ageing Population', footnote 52 above, at p. 21 and ff.

[88] Based on information from the Fiscal Sustainability Report from the Office of Budget Responsibility for June 2015, see http://obr.uk/fsr/fiscal-sustainability-report-june-2015/.

[89] Ibid. See https://publications.parliament.uk/pa/cm201617/cmselect/cm worpen/59/59.pdf.

The Foundation argued from that graph that:

> the primary function of the welfare state is to distribute resources across lifetimes, rather than between generations. Within each generation, fiscal contributions (tax receipts shown in red) and withdrawals (total spending shown in purple) should tend to balance. The alternative is one generation effectively subsidising another over the course of their respective lifetimes.

There is much to be said for its approach. For our discussion, I think it is important to note from the graph how this distribution marks a national perspective on need. Interestingly, the Resolution Foundation's approach is beginning to have more traction. In a joint report of the House of Commons, Health and Social Care, and Housing, Communities and Local Government Committees published on 27 June 2018,[90] it was argued:

> 38 . . . provision of care for working-age adults amounts to over half of all spending on social care and is set to grow in future years. To be sustainable, reforms to social care funding, including decisions on where the funding should come from, need to take into account the costs of meeting the needs of working age adults.
>
> . . .

---

[90] See 'Long-term Funding of Adult Social Care', First Joint Report of the Health and Social Care and Housing, Communities and Local Government Committees of Session 2017–19, Ninth Report of the Health and Social Care Committee, Seventh Report of the Housing, Communities and Local Government Committee, HC 768, see https://publications.parliament.uk/pa/cm201719/cmselect/cmcomloc/768/768.pdf.

39. The evidence we heard revealed that, for a funding solution for social care to be perceived as fair across the generations, it would have to reconcile different attitudes across the age groups. These included the feeling among older people that they had 'worked hard during their lives, paid their taxes, paid into the system and it ought to be there for them when they need it in later life'. On the other hand, while recognising that not all older people are wealthy, in general older people's wealth relative to younger generations was seen as having increased in recent decades, with the current generation of young people being 'the first to be worse off than their parents', with many facing an extended period of paying in effect a 'graduate tax'. The further point was also made that, as older people will benefit from social care reforms, 'it would be reasonable to expect [them] to make some contribution'.

. . .

40. Intergenerational fairness needs to be addressed. Contributions towards the cost of care should be fairly distributed between generations. Some older people who stand to be the main beneficiaries of increased spending on social care may be relatively wealthy, with housing assets, savings and pensions, compared to younger generations. Young people often face higher housing costs, less stable employment and less generous pensions, and may be paying back student loans or have family commitments. Life expectancy has increased, which is a cause for celebration, but which again has implications for the balance of contributions between different age groups. Working age employed adults are a shrinking proportion of the total adult population. For these reasons, older people could be expected to continue, while taking into account the fact that they have contributed

throughout their working lives via taxation. However, over the longer term, the distribution of wealth between the different age groups may change, with corresponding implications for fairness, suggesting that a flexible solution is required. (footnotes omitted)

This is significant, but our views about welfare distribution must not determine all aspects of age equality, whether in employment or as consumers. The task of age equality law ought to be to try to even things up for everyone. That means providing equality of opportunity across lives that may be relatively long, or short, or anything in between, and which may be enjoyed in good, bad or indifferent health. It means shaking off these stereotypes and looking to the aspects that we have in common at any age, as well as being really clear about those which by reason divide us. So how well are we doing so far?

PART 3 AGE LEGISLATION TO DATE

This idea of an approach to age issues that was based on general principles has taken a long time to take hold, but at last it is making some real progress. The phrase of 'age discrimination' first emerges in our domestic case law in the summary of the judgment of the Court of Appeal of England and Wales in *Foster* v. *British Gas Plc*,[91] but that was analysed

---

[91] [1988] 2 CMLR 697, [1988] ICR 584; the phrase was not, however, used in the judgment. The issue was raised by female employees complaining about the different ages – 65 and 60 – at which men and women were forced to retire by British Gas. Understandably the case was brought as one of sex discrimination, though in truth it was a case of what is called

and resolved as a case of sex discrimination. The Industrial Relations Law Reports did not first use the phrase until November 1997, reporting a judgment as to whether a contractual prohibition on age discrimination in the Scottish Police Service continued once the contractual retirement age was reached, though the Employment Appeal Tribunal (EAT) held it did not.[92] The existence of such a contractual prohibition reflected in part a developing discussion in the 1990s about non-statutory measures to address age-related conditions in recruitment.

There had been some discussion here about the need to address overtly age discriminatory recruitment advertisements in a similar way to that taken in the United States. In June 1999, a non-statutory Code of Practice on Age Diversity in Employment was issued. At around this time, some workplaces began to adopt very basic age equality policies. By the early 2000s, these came under review. The government published a report, 'Winning the Generation Game',[93] with the intention of signalling its intention to encourage older people to remain actively involved in work. In 2001, the DWP published a report of a survey carried out for it setting out what it considered to be 'Good Practice in the

---

intersectional discrimination, where two factors intersect to cause a disadvantage. The case followed on the litigation by Mrs Marshall with Southampton Area Health Authority: see Case 152/84 [1986] QB 401, [1986] 2 WLR 780, [1986] 1 CMLR 688, [1986] ICR 335.

[92] *Secretary of State for Scotland* v. *Taylor* [1997] IRLR 608.

[93] Performance Innovation Unit, *Winning the Generation Game* (HMSO, April 2001).

Recruitment and Retention of Older Workers',[94] which it defined as those over 50.[95]

The first step towards a general enforceable law of age equality in Northern Ireland was taken by the Employment Equality (Age) Regulations (Northern Ireland),[96] made on 13 June 2006, coming substantively into force[97] on 1 December. These Regulations, which though amended are still in force, mirrored the similarly named Employment Equality (Age) Regulations applying to Great Britain, made on 3 April 2006,[98] and eventually coming into effect on the same date. Both Regulations were made under powers in the European Communities Act 1972 in order to transpose Directive 2000/78/EC.[99]

Although written in essentially general terms, as their names implied, both only applied to the field of employment law. They did not extend to the other areas within which discrimination is normally outlawed, such as goods, facilities and services, the provision of education, charities and other areas of civil society. This was because

---

[94] See http://webarchive.nationalarchives.gov.uk/20130323035828/https://www.education.gov.uk/publications/eOrderingDownload/rr303.pdf.

[95] Ibid. at p. 1.

[96] The Employment Equality (Age) Regulations (Northern Ireland) 2006 (SI 2006/261).

[97] See Regulation 1.

[98] See the Employment Equality (Age) Regulations 2006 (SI 2006/1031), now wholly repealed by the Equality Act 2010.

[99] Council Directive 2000/78/EC of 27 November 2000 establishing a general framework for equal treatment in employment and occupation.

the scope of application of Directive 2000/78 was similarly limited.

These Regulations largely followed the way that the Directive was written and this in turn depended on the Treaty powers to make it. It is worth looking a little more closely at those powers. The relevant source power was Article 13 EC,[100] introduced into the EC Treaty by an amendment agreed in the Amsterdam Treaty.[101] This Article was the first provision in European law (and so in our own domestic law) that specifically mentioned age as a ground that was protected against discrimination.[102] It was written in very general terms. It merely referred to 'age' and did not define in any way what 'age' meant. By agreeing to use such a general term, the

---

[100] Now Article 19 TFEU.

[101] As first agreed, Article 13 EC said: '1. Without prejudice to the other provisions of this Treaty and within the limits of the powers conferred by it upon the Community, the Council, acting unanimously on a proposal from the Commission and after consulting the European Parliament, may take appropriate action to combat discrimination based on sex, racial or ethnic origin, religion or belief, disability, age or sexual orientation.

2. By way of derogation from paragraph 1, when the Council adopts Community incentive measures, excluding any harmonisation of the laws and regulations of the Member States, to support action taken by the Member States in order to contribute to the achievement of the objectives referred to in paragraph 1, it shall act in accordance with the procedure referred to in Article 251.'

It was later amended and is now replaced by Article 19 of the Treaty on the Functioning of the European Union. See also Article 6 TFEU.

[102] The UK is a signatory to the International Covenant on Civil and Political Rights. Although Article 26 of that Covenant includes a wide range of explicit protected characteristics, it does not expressly mention 'age'.

Member States impliedly rejected two important notions that might have stymied the development of an effective law.

First, it did *not* say that age discrimination was principally (or even solely) an issue of discrimination in the workplace; and secondly, it did *not* say that age discrimination protections should be the preserve of the old or the older sections of the population, i.e. those above a certain age. In short it was clear from the outset that the Member States' intention in agreeing to this new Article and the powers it contained was that the prohibition on age discrimination should benefit all in an unlimited range of contexts.[103] This was truly radical. It bore no relation to anything gone before in the UK or Europe.

The Member States might have gone down a very different route and followed the basic[104] American model of protection from age discrimination. Thus, the United States of America, which had been among the first to address age discrimination at work, had enacted the Age Discrimination in Employment Act of 1967 (ADEA).[105] There now seems little doubt that the ADEA has been a cause of greater and longer participation in the workforce by older workers, but it was

---

[103] For a discussion of the way in which Directive 2000/78/EC came to articulate the aspiration in Article 13 EC, see H. Meenan (ed.), *Equality Law in an Enlarged European Union. Understanding the Article 13 Directives* (Cambridge University Press, 2007).

[104] It is true that this Act was followed in 1975 by the Age Discrimination Act and this went further and prohibited discrimination on the basis of age in programmes and activities receiving federal financial assistance. The Act, which applies to all ages, permits the use of certain age distinctions and factors other than age that meet the Act's requirements.

[105] 29 USC Section 621.

limited from the outset to protecting only certain applicants and employees aged 40 or more. Originally, the protection was capped at 65, although this has now been completely removed,[106] and many states have extensive local laws.[107]

The problem with the ADEA was that it provided nothing for those who suffered age discrimination below or above these ages, or in other contexts. Its focus was exclusively on those reaching what was stereotypically assumed to be the second half of their careers (the period between age 40 and 65) and the economic consequences of unemployment or under-employment at that time.[108] So the Member States are to be congratulated on avoiding this elephant trap in agreeing Article 13 EC. As a result, Great Britain (but not yet Northern Ireland) has been encouraged down a similar road in its own wider domestic legislation.

The Member States also rejected the more limited focus on the problems associated with just ageing – as opposed to age – described in the political declaration of the First UN World Assembly on Ageing held in Vienna, in 1982.[109] However, as we

---

[106] This upper limit was altered to 70 in 1978 and removed altogether in 1986.

[107] There are now many state and city laws outlawing age discrimination in employment which go further than this Federal law: see, for instance, in relation to New York the New York State Human Rights Law (Executive Law Section 290), and New York City Human Rights Law (Administrative Code of the City of New York), Section 8-101 et seq.

[108] See e.g. D. Neumark, *Reassessing the Age Discrimination in Employment Act* (University of California at Irvine, AARP Public Policy Institute, 2008); www.economics.uci.edu/~dneumark/2008_09_adea.pdf.

[109] The first World Assembly on Ageing was held in Vienna, between 26 July and 6 August 1982. It created a Vienna International Plan of Action on

shall see, this dichotomy between seeing age equality as a life-long right or as an issue solely (or principally) concerned with older peoples' rights has never been far away and has recently re-emerged as a key point in the development of age equality.[110]

Though radical, there was a very good reason for the Member States to take this whole-of-life approach. The attainment of a threshold age of 40 for protection under the ADEA was obviously arbitrary. If protection was necessary at 40, why was it not also necessary at 39 or 38 and so on? Indeed, it was also obviously discriminatory, in itself. It was clear that the ADEA fell afoul of one of the most important foundations of the rule of law: the principle of equality before and under the law. To replicate it would not be the best of starts to a new human rights dimension to European law making.

There is no doubt that the European Commission, the Council and the Parliament understood that this Article took a fresh approach to age equality. Thus, when Directive 2000/78 was agreed,[111] the Member States were permitted to opt for a 6-year period within which to transpose its obligations. The

---

Ageing as the first international instrument on ageing, and provided a basis for the formulation of policies and programmes on ageing. It was endorsed by the United Nations General Assembly in 1982 (resolution 37/51). See www.un.org/esa/socdev/ageing/documents/Resources/VIPEE-English.pdf.

[110] See https://social.un.org/ageing-working-group/.

[111] Council Directive 2000/78/EC of 27 November 2000 establishing a general framework for equal treatment in employment and occupation.

UK as well as other important states such as Germany took the full 6 years.[112]

In making the Directive, the European legislator moved cautiously on another front, beyond the period for transition. Although Article 13 EC said nothing at all about justification, the European legislator decided it should permit Member States, when transposing the legislation into national law, to provide that certain types of *direct* discrimination should be justifiable.

This was not inconsistent with the basic Aristotelian notion of equal treatment I have discussed in Chapter 1, but it was new. For no other protected characteristic had European law so explicitly permitted Member States such a broad scope for limiting the effect of European anti-discrimination law. Member States were offered this margin in their transposition by Article 6(1) of the Directive:[113]

> Member States may provide that differences of treatment
> on grounds of age shall not constitute discrimination, if,
> within the context of national law, they are objectively and
> reasonably justified by a legitimate aim, including

---

[112] Government Press Notice, 'Government will legislate to tackle age discrimination', 14 February 2001.

[113] Article 6(1). Article 6(2) added '2. . . . Member States may provide that the fixing for occupational social security schemes of ages for admission or entitlement to retirement or invalidity benefits, including the fixing under those schemes of different ages for employees or groups or categories of employees, and the use, in the context of such schemes, of age criteria in actuarial calculations, does not constitute discrimination on the grounds of age, provided this does not result in discrimination on the grounds of sex.'

legitimate employment policy, labour market and vocational training objectives, and if the means of achieving that aim are appropriate and necessary.

Such differences of treatment may include, among others: (a) the setting of special conditions on access to employment and vocational training, employment and occupation, including dismissal and remuneration conditions, for young people, older workers and persons with caring responsibilities in order to promote their vocational integration or ensure their protection; (b) the fixing of minimum conditions of age, professional experience or seniority in service for access to employment or to certain advantages linked to employment; (c) the fixing of a maximum age for recruitment which is based on the training requirements of the post in question or the need for a reasonable period of employment before retirement.

The text of the list exemplifying permissible exceptions may seem rather odd. It was in fact very hard fought over, as I recall from my involvement in these discussions at the time.[114] Baroness Greengross, then Director General of Age Concern UK, for instance, argued for a much more restrictive list.

The fact that the European legislator accepted the text of this Article – with potentially such a wide effect – reflected a need to go cautiously in relation to the situation on the ground in Europe. The novelty of the concept of age equality and lack of knowledge about what the impact of its

---

[114] I worked with both the European Commission and the UK government at the time in relation to the discussions on the text of this directive.

introduction would or could be were significant issues. Moreover, age discrimination had been built into much of labour relations in Europe: many collective agreements provided for age-related pay increments[115] and for age conditions for benefits in employment.

In Chapter 1, I noted the close connection between comparison and justification. Although the Directive spoke of the possibility of justifying age discrimination, I think that it really reflected a realisation that the hard work in deciding what was a comparable situation and what not had not been done. I doubt the Council would not then have been able to garner sufficient political agreement to define comparability for the purposes of the Directive further.

We can see this readily by considering what happened in the UK. When the time came to make Regulations to transpose the obligations in the Directive, the deeply entrenched view that those over and below SPa were not in a comparable position had to be confronted. Should it continue or should it be removed? Removing it in legislation seemed very radical to government and a step that it thought employers generally would not welcome. Article 6 of the Directive seemed to provide a possible way out of this dilemma, and the UK immediately sought to take advantage of it when making the first domestic age discrimination Regulations. Thus the Regulations (both in Northern Ireland and in Great Britain) had a convoluted limitation to

---

[115] Though it was increasingly realised that these were also often discriminatory on gender grounds: see e.g. Case C-17/05 *Cadman* v. *Health & Safety Executive* ECLI:EU:C:2006:633.

their application to those at or over the age of 65.[116] This limitation was directly related to the then SPa for men and the proposal to harmonise women and men's ages to 65. Secondly, these Regulations introduced a general right for employers to justify what would otherwise be direct age discrimination.

These decisions by the government immediately set a challenge for those opposed to the continuation of these stereotypes about SPa. Was the first limitation lawful under Article 6 of Directive 2000/78? What did the second mean?

A different order question was what could be got from the specified examples of justified exceptions in Article 6. Thus (a) seemed to be directed at forms of special measures and to be relatively unobjectionable on its face; (c) was concerned with the payback on training; while (b) was more opaque. The question was whether these three examples defined the class of justifications.

Together these questions led to these exceptions to the reach of the principle of age being challenged in a judicial review. Working with Age Concern,[117] we developed a strategy to bring the issue to the forefront of the public discourse by seeking to get this limitation reviewed

---

[116] See the Employment Equality (Age) Regulations 2006 (SI 2006/103), now wholly repealed.

[117] Particularly Andy Harrop, then Head of Policy at Age Concern, and Richard Baker, then National Development Manager, with both of whom I had worked on earlier challenges to the lack of protection from age discrimination.

in the European Court of Justice (CJEU). I was instructed[118] to seek a reference to the CJEU in a case colloquially known as *Heyday* after the new name of a marketing arm of the charity Age Concern that brought the case.[119]

The outcome has been very important in the history of UK (and indeed European) age equality law, though the ruling of the CJEU did not dispose of the issues in the case fully. We were unsuccessful in persuading the court to limit the possible justifications on a class basis defined by reference to the examples in the text of the Directive. Nonetheless the Court did set limits on the range of justifications that a Member State could advance for limiting the right to be free from age discrimination by holding that Member States must have 'legitimate social policy' aims for any limitation to the right to be protected from age discrimination in employment.[120] Thus the potential range of exceptions in Article 6 of the Directive came to be at least partially curtailed. The basis for challenging the specific limitation in the domestic Regulations to those under SPa was set up.

---

[118] With Declan O'Dempsey in my chambers, Cloisters (www.cloisters.com).

[119] Case C-388/07 *Incorporated Trustees of the National Council on Ageing (Age Concern England)* v. *Secretary of State for Business, Enterprise and Regulatory Reform* EU:C:2009:128; [2009] ECR I-1569, [2009] 3 CMLR 4, [2009] All ER (EC) 619, [2009] CEC 754, [2009] ICR 1080, [2009] IRLR 373.

[120] Ibid. Operative Part [2].

As a result, a more nuanced challenge was made when the case returned to the Administrative Court in London. The government responded by alleging that it did indeed have a social policy aim essentially to give business an opportunity to control the profile of its workforce. Of course, having such an aim was one thing; justification required that the steps taken to secure that aim had to be legitimate. This was a more moot question, and it had to be considered both on an historic basis; i.e. as in 2006 and when the Regulations were made, and also on a prospective basis.

This enabled Blake J to hold that the Regulations were *intra vires* when made, but because the expected benefits from aligning the reach of discrimination law up to but not beyond SPa had not emerged, the limitation was no longer legitimate.[121] This was a major win. The government went through an early and perfunctory consultation on changing the Regulations. The consultation closed on 21 October 2010, by which time most respondents were ready to agree to extend the protection from discrimination beyond the age of 65. Soon after, steps were taken to amend the Regulations to remove the 65 limit both in Northern Ireland and in Great Britain.[122]

---

[121] *Age UK, R (on the application of)* v. *Secretary of State for Business, Innovation & Skills & Ors* [2010] ICR 260, [2009] Pens LR 333, [2009] IRLR 1017, [2009] EWHC 2336 (Admin), [2010] 1 CMLR 21.

[122] See the Employment Equality (Repeal of Retirement Age Provisions) Regulations 2011, SI 2011/1069. The Explanatory Memorandum to these Regulations discusses the outturn on the consultation.

We can analyse this particular litigation from the point of view of comparisons. When enacted, the makers of the Regulations – essentially the Executive, though the Regulations were approved by Parliament – considered that there would be an unacceptable impact on business if those aged 65 and over were treated as in a comparable position to those under that age.

Public opinion about SPa changed rapidly in the 4+ years between 2006 (when the first Regulations were made) and 2011 (when this restriction on their reach was repealed). Part of the reason for this change must be ascribed to Age Concern's tactics in the *Heyday* litigation, which kept the issue in the public eye and raised the question: why should a person aged 65+ be treated differently from someone under that age? The uncertainty this caused businesses as to how to treat its employees at or over 65 caused many to rethink whether they really need to make this differentiation. Businesses began increasingly to employ those aged 65+ and found them useful, knowledgeable and willing workers. Part of the reason must also be ascribed to the beginning of a realisation by the public that there was a long time post-65 when many should be fit and well enough to work and may need to.

We can see that though the context for this debate was the legitimacy of the justification of lesser protections for those of 65+, in fact all these points went to the key issue of comparison. Should a person of 65+ be treated as somehow not comparable to a person below that age? What – at least in the context of employment – could really be the basis for this differentiation?

After the changes, following Blake J's judgment there was no reason to consider a worker as being in a different incomparable position just because she or he was at or over SPa. In the context of the statistics on demographic change this was obviously right. When the amending Regulations were made, the historic legal link between SPa and workers' rights was broken.[123] Now, it can truly be said in relation to the field of employment that there is no age at which, in ordinary circumstances, there is an *a priori* legal assumption that adults of different ages are not in comparable circumstances.

This does not mean 'work till you drop', but rather that, if you go on working beyond SPa, there is no reason in principle why you cannot compare your treatment with that of someone much younger. It also raises the critical question: if you can do that at work, then surely you should be able to do so in society more generally? As we shall see, Parliament (but not the Northern Ireland Assembly) has bought that argument, though only to a limited degree.

Let's look closer at how our age laws currently work. The Northern Ireland Regulations are still in place, but the law for Great Britain is now found in the Equality Act 2010. The concepts of direct and indirect age discrimination in both Northern Ireland and Great Britain are now expressed in terms common to other protected characteristics. In none of this legislation has the protected characteristic of age been

---

[123] It can be argued that these changes were also pushed by the need to recruit both older workers as well as those under 65 or pulled by the *Heyday* litigation. The answer is truly of only historic interest now; it is the effect of this change which is critical.

defined solely by reference to persons over or under a particular age.[124] Age is defined in very broad terms: references to age include particular age groups which can be defined by reference to a particular age, or to a range of ages.[125] The Northern Ireland Regulations explicitly include 'apparent' age,[126] and this is probably implicitly included in section 5 of the Equality Act 2010, which simply refers to 'age' without saying that it has to be the specific age of a litigant or rights-bearer. In short, subject to one point,[127] our UK legislation takes very much a holistic approach in defining the characteristic of age. It is generally about self-determination through life in the fullest sense. It is no longer anything to do with SPa.

Direct discrimination involves treating a person less favourably on grounds of age.[128] Principally that will apply when it can be shown that a person of one age is treated less favourably than one or more other is, or would be, treated in a comparable situation. However, even after *Heyday*, uniquely among the protected characteristics, as noted, in both Northern Ireland and Great Britain, a finding of direct age discrimination can be avoided if the less favourable treatment is justified.[129]

---

[124] Though the Equality Act 2010 limits the application of the right in relation to the provision of goods, facilities and services to those of 18 or more years of age.

[125] See s. 5 of the Equality Act 2010.

[126] See Regulation 3(3)(b) of the Northern Ireland Regulations.

[127] See the discussion as to the limit of the application of the Act to those aged 18 and above, below.

[128] See s. 13 of the Equality Act 2010.

[129] However, less favourable treatment of part-time or fixed-term workers may be justified pursuant to the Council Directive 97/81/EC of 15 December 1997 concerning the Framework Agreement on part-time

In situations in which persons are treated the same but they are not in a comparable situation, indirect age discrimination arises for consideration. This is defined as occurring when:[130]

a. a person (A) applies to another (B) a provision, criterion or practice (PCP);
b. A applies, or would apply, the PCP to persons with whom B does not share the characteristic;
c. the PCP puts, or would put, persons with whom B shares the characteristic at a particular disadvantage when compared with persons with whom B does not share it;
d. the PCP puts, or would put, B at that disadvantage; and
e. A cannot show the PCP to be a proportionate means of achieving a legitimate aim.

This scheme on its face treats justification as different from comparability. I think we need to explore how this has been interpreted to see if this is so clear in practice. There has been important litigation following *Heyday* to explore what justifications are permissible in the United Kingdom for direct and indirect age discrimination. Was the test for justifying

work concluded by UNICE, CEEP and the ETUC – Annex: Framework agreement on part-time work and Council Directive 1999/70/EC of 28 June 1999 concerning the framework agreement on fixed-term work concluded by ETUC, UNICE and CEEP. Certain classes of disability discrimination may also be justified. There are also certain specific defences to both direct and indirect discrimination, such as the imposition of genuine occupational qualifications which must be justified.

[130] See s. 19 of the Equality Act 2010.

direct age discrimination the same as that for justifying indirect discrimination? I was instructed in the two appeals[131] so far to the Supreme Court that have explored these issues: *Seldon* v. *Clarkson Wright & Jakes* (*Seldon*) and *Homer* v. *Chief Constable of West Yorkshire* (*Homer*).[132] *Seldon* concerned direct age discrimination and *Homer* indirect.

In the result the Supreme Court held – reiterating the judgment of the CJEU in the *Heyday* case – that a different test was to be used in direct discrimination cases. This makes life complicated for the non-lawyer and interesting for the lawyer. I can see how this has happened, but such a subtle distinction is hardly conducive to a general legal theory of age equality.

A leading commentator[133] has correctly summarised the position thus:

> Direct [age] discrimination – such as mandatory
> retirement – may only be justified if the relevant treatment
> or provision seeks to achieve a legitimate aim of a public
> interest nature related to employment policy, the labour
> market and vocational training, the legitimacy of which

---

[131] With Dee Masters in *Seldon* and Declan O'Dempsey in *Homer*, both of my chambers, Cloisters. I must pay tribute to both for much help in developing many of my ideas on this subject.

[132] The Supreme Court gave judgment on these two cases on the same day: *Seldon* v. *Clarkson Wright & Jakes* [2012] UKSC 16, [2012] 3 All ER 1301, [2012] 2 CMLR 50, [2012] ICR 716, [2012] IRLR 590, [2012] Eq LR 579, [2012] Pens LR 239; and *Homer* v. *Chief Constable of West Yorkshire* [2012] UKSC 15, [2012] 3 All ER 1287, [2012] ICR 704, [2012] IRLR 601, [2012] Eq LR 594. I was instructed in both of them by the Equality and Human Rights Commission on behalf of the two employees.

[133] See Harvey on Industrial Relations and Employment Law, LexisNexis, ISBN13: 9780406048110, at Division L, [364.01].

> member states must establish rather than individual
> employers. Analysis of the 'evolving' European case law
> demonstrates that a distinction must be drawn between
> those types of social policy objectives, and purely
> individual reasons that are specific to the situation of
> a particular employer such as cost reduction or improving
> competitiveness, which could not justify direct
> discrimination.

So the ultimate responsibility for permitting any justification of direct age discrimination within the scope of the Directive (i.e. in employment and occupation) lies squarely with the state.

As noted, both these definitions – of direct and indirect age discrimination – are designed to reflect European law obligations giving effect to the Aristotelian notion of equal treatment. Our laws, like those across Europe, require a situational analysis before it can be ascertained whether they have any proscriptive effect. Both definitions demand a forensic inquiry of the degree to which situations are *comparable*; treating different situations as comparable may be appropriate or inappropriate. What is taken to be an appropriate comparison, and what not, is therefore critical for the application of these laws. How is this decided?

3.1 Identifying Material Age Differences

For any given law proscribing age discrimination, it is the lawyers' task to argue, and the judges' to dispose of, the issue as to which comparisons are apt, and which are not. In both Northern Ireland and Great Britain, some guidance is given in general terms as to the comparisons that can and cannot be made, which I discussed in Chapter 1, for instance, in section 23(1) of the Equality Act 2010.

Similar provision is made in Regulation 3(2) of the Northern Ireland Regulations.

At first sight this provision may seem helpful, but in reality it merely displaces the problem: what does no 'material' difference mean in an employment age case? Some guidance, though not much, was given last year in Case C-143/16, *Abercrombie & Fitch Italia Srl* v. *Antonino Bordonaro*, when the CJEU repeated earlier guidance:[134]

> With regard to the requirement relating to comparable situations, it must be pointed out that, on the one hand, it is required not that the situations be identical, but only that they be comparable and, on the other hand, the assessment of that comparability must be carried out not in a global and abstract manner, but in a specific and concrete manner in the light of the benefit concerned.

In that case, the Court held that although an Italian legislative provision relating to on-call workers established two different regimes for access to, and conditions of, employment, and also their dismissal, according to the age category into which a worker fell, the workers' situations were comparable. This was a relatively simple case because it is obvious that the European legislation was intended to cover such a situation. However, not all cases will be so obvious. In the end it will be

---

[134] The court cited its judgment in Case C-267/12 *Hay*, EU:C:2013:823, at [33] for this proposition.

for the courts and tribunals to decide, but in seeking the answer to the question, they will not work in a vacuum. Their understanding and application of 'material' will be highly susceptible to the prevailing ideas about age equality and what is a good way to proceed. As I have shown, this is definitely not something about which there is universal (let alone historic) agreement.

3.2 A New Consensus?

The important point is that ideas about what age equality law is there to achieve are at a wholly different level of discussion and coherence than those, for instance, applying to gender or race equality. What should be prohibited in relation to discrimination on grounds of skin colour or gender is now a matter of broad and deep social acceptance: not so for age. I litigated those kinds of cases on many occasions during the 1970s, '80s and '90s, and I soon learnt that my task in doing so was often didactic, teaching the courts and tribunals about the importance of gender and race equality. I was clear from an early stage that the legislation was intended to be transformative. It had a social purpose the outlines of which are very clear if one took time to study the background to the legislation. Judges might or might not personally agree that women or those from ethnic minorities should have exactly the same life chances as white men. However, I could show by frequent reference to the White Papers that had been published before the Sex

Discrimination Act 1975[135] and the Race Relations Act 1976[136] that the legislation did definitely intend this.

Jurists are now being required to undertake a similar process in relation to age equality, but there are at least two new difficulties. First, there is no domestic White Paper explaining the purpose of Article 13 EC, or Directive 2000/78. Secondly, this process can really only take place in the context of the cases that are actually being brought to trial because judges and tribunal members are not taught age equality law and have little express guidance on it. There are some statutory guides published by the Equality Commission for Northern Ireland (ECNI) in relation to employment[137] and the Equality and Human Rights Commission[138] in relation to Great Britain, but they operate at a very high level of generality and neither engages with the social policy issues that the *Heyday* litigation showed were so important.

What is now driving the cases in which age equality is discussed? In short, it is mostly the typical situations of different sectors of society in which litigants reacting to the new demographic and economic pressures become concerned

---

[135] Equality for Women, Cmnd 5724, HMSO, 1974.

[136] Racial Discrimination, Cmnd 6234, HMSO, 1975, see http://filestore .nationalarchives.gov.uk/pdfs/small/cab-129-184-c-93.pdf.

[137] See www.equalityni.org/Employers-Service-Providers/Large-Business/ Registration-and-monitoring/Fair-Employment-Code-of-Practice.

[138] See www.equalityhumanrights.com/sites/default/files/employercode .pdf and www.equalityhumanrights.com/sites/default/files/supple ment_to_the_employment_cofp.pdf.

about retirement and pensions.[139] These pressures will look very different indeed at different ages and as people take different career paths.

Take a common example of the situation of an older woman (A) who has had her employment career interrupted by caring for children or elderly parents of her own. Faced with the realisation that she may live well into her 80s, she is likely to consider that she has an urgent need for work and benefits to secure her economic security at the end of her life. She is justified in thinking that her opportunities to get that security are limited and diminishing each year.

Consider now a young woman (B) who has just left college with a student loan, who wants to see a prospect of earning enough to be free from debt and be able to start on home ownership.

Suppose these two employees are equally competent and productive and that they work for a firm that is faced with having to make employees redundant and must choose between them.

In the context of limited financial resources, how does a commercial employer deal with this and how does A compare her situation to that of B? While she may be sympathetic to B's debt, she is also likely to think that B has time on her side, while she does not. A might also point out that it will be B who will benefit from her sacrifices in bringing up her children when in

---

[139] Some judges already know this, having commenced litigation to increase their pension rights: *Lord Chancellor and Secretary of State for Justice* v. *McCloud* [2018] 3 All ER 208, [2018] ICR 1039, [2018] IRLR 284. The judges were successful in their claim, and the state's appeal failed.

due course, long after A is dead, they work to fund B's social care. How does B compare her situation to that of A? She will consider perhaps that A has had her chances and made her life, whereas she has been saddled with a debt caused by decisions to allocate resources to A or A's parents or children.

Comparisons of the different perspectives from different age points can be multiplied in many ways. Yet it is the task of the principle of age equality to provide a rational solution to the frictions that such age-related choices give rise to. This example shows that to resolve such competing claims, we need to identify quite different premises from just those advanced by A and B in these arguments. A and B will each consider themselves justified in their own point of view, but if an employer must advantage one over the other, how is it to proceed and how is a court or tribunal to decide if such treatment is lawful? Case law is working on this, of course, but it is a big task, as Lady Hale acknowledged in *Homer*:[140]

> the [Equality Act recognises] that difficult balances have to be struck between the competing interests of different age groups. We all have a lot of learning to do.

There have now been many[141] reported direct age discrimination in employment cases. Mostly these have been decided on the approach to justification rather than comparability, for instance it has been held that age indirectly

[140] At [27].
[141] Westlaw records 46 law reports in the Industrial Case Reports where 'age discrimination' is the key word.

discriminatory transitional arrangements may be justified.[142] However, the problem of distinguishing comparability and justification that Attorney General Sharpston identified in Case C-227/04 P *Lindorfer* v. *the Council of the European Union*[143] came up for consideration by the Court of Appeal in *Lockwood* v. *Department of Work and Pensions*.[144] This case concerned a redundancy scheme that gave more than *pro rata* benefits for those dismissed at age 35 or over. Although this led to the 26-year-old claimant receiving only £10,849, when an employee aged over 35 with the same service would have received £17,690 more, it was held not to amount to unlawful age discrimination.

At first instance it was held that it was not a true comparison to use an over-35 fellow employee because of their different financial position and the greater difficulty they would have finding other employment. It was also argued that the different financial positions justified the different treatment. However, in the Court of Appeal Lewison LJ said:

> When she left her job Ms Lockwood received less money than a 36 year old would have received. Why? The answer is: because she was younger. The ET said that the statistics showed that someone like Ms Lockwood would be able to react more easily and rapidly to losing her job than a 36 year old. Why? The answer again is: because she was younger. They also said that someone like Ms Lockwood would be less likely to have heavy financial responsibilities than a 36 year old. Why? The answer yet again is: because

---

[142] See *Essop* v. *Home Office (UK Border Agency), Naeem* v. *Secretary of State for Justice* [2017] UKSC 27, [2017] 1 WLR 1343, [2017] 3 All ER 551.

[143] ECLI:EU:C:2007:490, ECLI:EU:C:2005:656, ECLI:EU:C:2006:748.

[144] [2013] EWCA Civ 1195, [2014] 1 All ER 250.

she was younger. Accordingly, all the suggested reasons for concluding that Ms Lockwood did not suffer age discrimination turn out to be factors consequent upon her age. They are, therefore, not legitimate differences for the purpose of deciding whether discrimination has taken place.

That was surely right, but surprisingly the Court of Appeal held that the different treatment was indeed justified. Their analysis is poor, though regrettably I do not understand this case to have been appealed.

In my view, the Court was right on comparison but quite wrong to let the employer evade liability on the basis of justification. Of course, financial commitments *can* increase as we grow older, but they do not have to. Moreover, significance of financial commitments depends on resources. A person such as B with a huge student debt would consider their financial commitments as a huge constraint on self-determination. Moreover, a person under 35 can have children, caring responsibilities and a mortgage, in the same way as a person over that age. A person over that age may find another job very easily, too. If these were material considerations at all, then they could have been much more closely targeted. In reality the court was offered a stereotype about life development which it accepted too uncritically.

The case therefore throws up some key questions:

- Is it really the task of the employer to engage in this kind of social engineering?
- Is it fit to do so?

- While the case law requires that an employer's justifications must match national social policy, what level of congruence is required?
- Indeed can employers really be expected to develop workplace policies to match the national social interests in any substantive way, given how undeveloped they are?

To answer these questions fully might require a paper discussing every aspect of the developing case law on justification for direct age discrimination under European law.

Yet there is some indication that, within certain limits, the CJEU is willing to permit states a broad discretion as to the kinds of social policy aims that may be invoked. Thus on the one hand it is clear that the CJEU continues to adopt the statement it made in the *Heyday* case:[145]

> mere generalisations concerning the capacity of a specific measure to contribute to employment policy, labour market or vocational training objectives are not enough to show that the aim of that measure is capable of justifying derogation from that principle and do not constitute evidence on the basis of which it could reasonably be considered that the means chosen are suitable for achieving that aim.

While on the other, the CJEU has permitted a considerable degree of flexibility in the way it controls reliance on such

---

[145] See Case C-388/07 *Age Concern England*, EU:C:2009:128, at [51]. This passage was cited with approval by Advocate General Bobek in his Opinion delivered on 23 March 2017 in Case C-143/16 *Abercrombie & Fitch Italia Srl* v. *Antonino Bordonar*, ECLI:EU:C:2017:235, at [94] and fn [55].

exceptions; thus in Case C-143/16 *Abercrombie & Fitch Italia Srl* v. *Antonino Bordonar* it said:[146]

> It must be borne in mind that the Member States enjoy
> a broad discretion in their choice, not only to pursue
> a particular aim in the field of social and employment
> policy, but also in the definition of measures capable of
> achieving it

These statements will have particular relevance to actions by the state in limiting the reach of domestic laws, as the UK did in the first iteration of the Age Regulations. If such legislation excludes certain claims it does not matter much, though, whether this is analysed as the state declaring such cases as non-comparable or justified. Often the law will simply state that they fall within exceptions. The practical normative effect may well be that the public may be deterred from developing an acute sense of age comparison. Though I well recognise that countervailing forces may immunise this effect if there is a dissonance between the public's expectation and the legislation concerned.

3.3 Is Age Discrimination in Goods, Facilities and Services Different?

Soon after the European legislator had made Directive 2000/78, working with the European 'Age Platform'[147] I started

---

[146] ECLI:EU:C:2017:566, at [31]. See also Case C-530/13 *Schmitzer*, EU:
C:2014:2359, at [38] and the case law cited there.

[147] www.age-platform.eu/.

campaigning for a new directive that would effectively extend the reach of European age equality law to other areas. Our motive was to try to secure a European level of protection against age discrimination that would be capable of addressing the obvious need we saw arising from demographic change. As well as arguing from the need for such protection, we pointed out that this would bring age into line with other European legislation in relation to race and gender.

Thus, we noted how the Race Directive 2000/43,[148] made under the same powers in Article 13 EC, had a wide field of application ('Scope') set out in Article 3(1):

> Within the limits of the powers conferred upon the Community, this Directive shall apply to all persons, as regards both the public and private sectors, including public bodies, in relation to:
>
> (a) conditions for access to employment, to self-employment and to occupation, including selection criteria and recruitment conditions, whatever the branch of activity and at all levels of the professional hierarchy, including promotion;
> (b) access to all types and to all levels of vocational guidance, vocational training, advanced vocational training and retraining, including practical work experience;
> (c) employment and working conditions, including dismissals and pay;

---

[148] Council Directive 2000/43/EC of 29 June 2000 implementing the principle of equal treatment between persons irrespective of racial or ethnic origin.

(d) membership of and involvement in an organisation of workers or employers, or any organisation whose members carry on a particular profession, including the benefits provided for by such organisations;

(e) social protection, including social security and healthcare;

(f) social advantages;

(g) education;

(h) access to and supply of goods and services which are available to the public, including housing.

We also pointed out that Directive 2006/54/EC[149] had a similar scope in relation to gender discrimination. We pointed, too, to the jurisprudence of the European Court of Justice that was increasingly describing the right to age equality as a general fundamental right. For instance, in Case C-144/04 *Werner Mangold* v. *Rüdiger Helm*,[150] the CJEU held:

> 74 ... Directive 2000/78 does not itself lay down the principle of equal treatment in the field of employment and occupation. Indeed, in accordance with Article 1 thereof, the sole purpose of the directive is 'to lay down a general framework for combating discrimination on the grounds of religion or belief, disability, age or sexual orientation', the source of the actual principle underlying the prohibition of those forms of discrimination being found, as is clear from

---

[149] Directive 2006/54/EC of the European Parliament and of the Council of 5 July 2006 on the implementation of the principle of equal opportunities and equal treatment of men and women in matters of employment and occupation (recast).

[150] ECLI:EU:C:2005:709.

the third and fourth recitals in the preamble to the directive, in various international instruments and in the constitutional traditions common to the Member States.

75 The principle of non-discrimination on grounds of age must thus be regarded as a general principle of Community law ...

Although this statement was somewhat controversial when *Mangold* was first decided, it is now established law following the ruling of the CJEU in Case C-555/07 *Seda Kücükdeveci v. Swedex GmbH & Co. KG*,[151] and Case C-441/14 *Dansk Industri (DI), acting on behalf of Ajos A/S v. Estate of Karsten Eigil Rasmussen*.[152] Finally the CJEU has noted that the general principle of non-discrimination on grounds of age was to be found in Article 21 of the Charter of Fundamental Rights of the European Union.

As part of this campaign, I was instructed to write a draft Directive for the Age Platform and to present to relevant committees of the European Parliament. Soon after, the European Commission published its own more comprehensive proposal for a Council Directive on implementing the principle of equal treatment between persons irrespective of religion or belief, disability, age or sexual orientation having a scope similar to the Race Directive

---

[151] ECLI:EU:C:2010:21, see [20]–[22]. The UK's Supreme Court noted this principle and its potential when addressing the Appellant's argument in *Walker* v. *Innospec Ltd & Ors* [2017] WLR(D) 477, [2017] UKSC 47, [2017] ICR 1077, [2017] IRLR 928; see Lord Kerr's judgment at [73]–[74]. However, the Court felt able to resolve the issue on the basis of other case law.

[152] [2016] 3 CMLR 27, [2016] Pens LR 299, [2016] ICR D9.

2000/43.[153] The idea was to level up all the characteristics mentioned in Article 13EC to the protections provided to race and gender.

Many states have supported this idea, but there have been issues, particularly concerning the extent to which disability protections should be granted. As a result, to date, although each state that has had the Presidency has given the proposal consideration, it is yet to become law.[154] The proposal is not, however, dead and I do believe that in time it will make progress. Thus the latest report on the Interinstitutional File[155] notes[156] that:

> almost all [delegations from Member States] . . . reaffirmed their support for the aim of the proposed Directive. Delegations also pointed at a number of outstanding issues, such as subsidiarity and the division of competences, legal clarity and consistency with other legal acts, the budgetary implications and costs, and the implementation. These discussions allowed the Presidency to take stock of the positions in the Council, and will feed into future work on the file.

Even though the proposal from the Age Platform has yet to reach fruition in the European Union, it did provide

---

[153] COM/2008/0426 final – CNS 2008/0140, see https://eur-lex.europa.eu/legal-content/EN/ALL/?uri=CELEX:52008PC0426.

[154] Somewhat desultory discussion continues, see www.statewatch.org/news/2017/feb/eu-council-equal-treatment-directive-gender-sexual-orientation-5428-17.pdf.

[155] Interinstitutional File: 2008/0140 (CNS), see the Progress http://data.consilium.europa.eu/doc/document/ST-9734-2018-INIT/en/pdf.

[156] Ibid. at [II.2].

some political pressure on the UK to start work on extending the protections beyond employment when the Equality Act 2010 was before Parliament as a Bill. In 2009–10 there was simply not enough Parliamentary time to complete this. As it was on the measures that were being consolidated and brought up to date, the debate on the legislation proceeded right up to the moment when Parliament was prorogued. Nonetheless, one significant step forward was taken; the Equality Act 2010 contained powers for it to be amended to extend its reach in relation to age. Two years later these powers were used in Great Britain,[157] though as the Act had limited reach to Northern Ireland, this part of the UK did not benefit.

The new provisions included protection from age discrimination in relation to goods, facilities and services, as well as membership of clubs, and the use of premises, but compared with other protected characteristics their reach was very considerably curtailed.[158] Exceptions were made in relation to:

- immigration;[159]
- regulated financial services;[160]

---

[157] By the Equality Act 2010 Commencement (No. 9) Order 2012 (SI 2012/ 1569).

[158] By the Equality Act 2010 (Age Exceptions) Order 2012 (SI 2012/2466).

[159] See para 15A of Part 4 of Sch 3 to the Equality Act 2010.

[160] See para 20A of Part 5 of Sch 3 to the Equality Act 2010. But this is subject to a proviso that, where the financial service provider conducts an assessment of risk for the purposes of providing the service, that assessment of risk must, so far as it involves a consideration of their customer's age, be done by reference to information which is relevant to the assessment of the risk and from a source on which it is reasonable to rely.

- concessions and preferential treatment (such as discounts) offered by traders and service providers;[161]
- the provision of pre-arranged holidays to groups of people limited by reference to age;[162]
- schemes operated by those selling or providing goods or services that are subject to age limits created by or under legislation, such as alcohol, tobacco or entry to a cinema in respect of particular films;[163] and
- those operating residential mobile home parks in respect of limiting occupation of mobile homes on the site to persons who have attained a particular age.[164]

Other exceptions include various forms of special treatment by associations by reference to age,[165] and things done in relation to the participation of persons in age-banded activities to which access is restricted by reference to age or age groups. These are defined to include sports, games and other activities and include both physical sports such as football and also more mental or intellectual activities such as bridge or chess.[166] A further limit to the application of these provisions is that in contrast to the provisions protecting from age discrimination at work, they only apply to those aged 18 or above.[167]

---

[161] See para 30A of Part 7 of Sch 3 to the Equality Act 2010.
[162] See para 30B of Part 7 of Sch 3 to the Equality Act 2010.
[163] See para 30C of Part 7 of Sch 3 to the Equality Act 2010.
[164] See para 30D of Part 7 of Sch 3 to the Equality Act 2010.
[165] See Sch 16 to the Equality Act 2010, as amended.
[166] See s. 195 of the Equality Act 2010, as amended.
[167] See s. 28 of the Equality Act 2010.

Some of these exceptions are obviously unobjection-able, but others are much more contentious. Each of them is worth further discussion but, in particular, I would ask why should financial services be so fully excluded? After all, gender discrimination in financial services is not permissible at all since the judgment of the CJEU in Case C-236/09 *Association Belge des Consommateurs Test-Achats*,[168] so why should financial services get an almost free ride when health care is not excluded at all? The short answer is that the finance industry objected too strongly and the voice of the consumer was too little heard. There was thus a failure of political will.

The Regulatory Impact Assessment[169] for these new age provisions provided very detailed evidence of the benefits to be won by their introduction in relation to health care. The assessment in relation to financial services was somewhat different. It is in fact a quite breathtaking read. On the one hand, the government acknowledged that older persons

---

[168] ECLI:EU:C:2011:100. In *Test-Achats* the CJEU ruled that Article 5(2) of Council Directive 2004/113/EC of 13 December 2004 implementing the principle of equal treatment between men and women in the access to and supply of goods and services was invalid with effect from 21 December 2012. This led to consequential amendments in Northern Ireland by the Sex Discrimination Order 1976 (Amendment) Regulations 2012 (SI 2012/462), and in Great Britain by the Equality Act 2010 (Amendment) Regulations 2012 (SI 2992/2012). The Gender Directive had provided by Article 5(2) that Member States might permit proportionate differences in individuals' premiums and benefits where the use of sex is a determining factor in the assessment of risk based on relevant and accurate actuarial and statistical data. That is no longer the case.

[169] The assessment is in two parts, both of which are available at www .legislation.gov.uk/uksi/2012/2466/resources.

frequently pay much higher prices – if they can get them at all – for certain financial services, as the Impact Assessment stated:

> In order to determine the extent of age discrimination occurring in the financial services industry [the GEO] commissioned independent research by Oxera (henceforth, 'the Oxera research'). The Oxera research, and research by Age UK in January 2010, which looked at the travel and motor insurance markets for older people, showed age was a significant factor in determining how prospective customers are treated in the sector, including whether a service is provided at all and at what price. Many older people have complained that they are discriminated against when trying to obtain various financial services; they say that they have a more limited choice of services and pay a higher price for them. They also say they have problems obtaining loans, mortgages and are particularly concerned about travel and motor insurance. Age Concern surveys suggest that people aged 75 and over are nearly ten times more likely to be refused a quote for motor or travel insurance than people aged 30 to 49. 13% of people over 80 said they were put off taking holidays because of worries about getting insurance or the cost of premiums.
> A separate SAGA Populus survey found that 25% of people over 65 had been refused travel insurance on the grounds of age. The CRA International research for the [Association of British Insurers] stated that 25% of customers aged 65 and over had been refused travel insurance because of their age, although 93 percent of these people were able to find another insurer who would provide cover. Age UK showed that for motor insurance

half of quotation attempts for people aged 80 and over were initially unsuccessful; however, a third were then offered an alternative provider. For travel insurance, one-third of quotation attempts for people over 80 were initially unsuccessful, though the majority were offered an alternative provider. The Oxera research also showed that the price of motor and travel insurance policies differs depending on the age of the customer, with older people paying more than any other age group to obtain similar cover. The research also showed providers of motor and travel insurance specialise. Targeting specific age groups and refusing to supply other age groups is therefore common practice. (footnotes omitted)

Yet in the very next paragraph the Impact Assessment then said:

Evidence indicates that there is no specific discrimination in financial services, but that certain groups do have difficulty accessing financial services. We therefore believe that an exception is still appropriate to allow the industry to continue all current practices and operate effectively, and that a voluntary scheme to improve access and transparency in respect of travel and motor insurance should be pursued.

Most would think that the previous evidence had been simply ignored in reaching that conclusion! In my view this is a critical area in which age equality law is wholly inadequate and is not even having any normative effect. Set against the demographic change that is just about to accelerate, this exception is wholly unacceptable. It is not merely that it might be possible to justify direct age discrimination in the provision of financial services but that the administration in Great Britain has simply denied even the chance to assert the comparability of older persons and younger persons in their rights to financial services.

Compare the approach to health care, where there had long been protests about discriminatory treatment of older persons. Here, detailed research supported the argument that there was considerable discrimination, but clear thinking about the importance of eradicating it has led to its full inclusion within the scope of the protections applying to Great Britain. Much credit must go to Sir Ian Carruthers OBE and Jan Ormondroyd for their report 'Achieving Age Equality in Health and Social Care'[170] and for making the case so well. They recognised clearly that the importance of a person's health is no different whatever age they may be.

The exclusion of those under 18 from the protection from age discrimination in relation to the provision of goods, facilities and services is also very puzzling. It is clear that it does not apply in relation to employment. For instance, a woman has succeeded in establishing unlawful discrimination when she was dismissed on reaching the age of 18, because she then became entitled to a higher national minimum wage.[171] So, why on earth should it be that, in relation to the provision of goods, facilities and services, such a restriction should apply? Why

---

[170] Achieving Age Equality in Health and Social Care: A Report to the Secretary of State for Health by Sir Ian Carruthers OBE and Jan Ormondroyd, October 2009, see www.cpa.org.uk/cpa/achieving_age_equality_in_health_and_social_care.pdf.

[171] Greer v. Coulter (t/a Alphreso Café) [2011] Eq LR 1108.

should a young person be without rights when refused – say – access to services from a driving instructor when 17 and lawfully in possession of a provisional driving licence, yet able to assert those rights a few months later?

No such 18-year limitations apply to the equality provisions of the Canadian Charter of Rights and Freedoms as enacted in the Canada Act 1982.[172] There are several examples of under-18s litigating service provision or equivalent issues. For instance, in *Schafer* v. *Canada (Attorney General)*,[173] the Court of Appeal for Ontario found that a provincial government benefit to support children adopted over the age of 6 months discriminated against younger babies on the grounds of age; and in *S (J)* v. *Nunavut (Minister of Health and Social Services)*,[174] the Nunavut Court of Justice granted an order declaring that a provincial Act was discriminatory because it provided a lower level of care to children in the state care system aged 16 and 17 than those aged under 16.

In 2013, Dee Masters[175] and I were instructed by the ECNI[176] and the NICCY to review the approach of some other jurisdictions to similar age equality legislation.[177] We noted

---

[172] www.legislation.gov.uk/ukpga/1982/11/schedule/B.

[173] [1997] 35 OR (3d) 1, http://canlii.ca/t/6hfo.

[174] 2006 NUCJ 20, http://canlii.ca/t/1pxm6.

[175] Also a member of my chambers, Cloisters.

[176] I must pay tribute to the support and encouragement that we have had from these organisations and from Roisin Mallon at the ECNI in particular.

[177] www.niccy.org/media/1302/expert-paper-age-gfs-protecting-all-ages-inc-cyp.pdf.

additionally how the Australian Age Discrimination Act 2004 had no such limitation, and likewise in Belgium.[178]

Our paper analysed the reasons given in the Parliamentary debates on the Bill that was to become the Equality Act 2010. One objection raised in Westminster as a reason for denying protection to people under 18 was a fear that it would undermine protection of children and young people. This is recorded in the report of the Joint Committee on Human Rights of the House of Lords and House of Commons entitled 'Children's Rights',[179] as is the Committee's scepticism that granting rights would diminish rights!

> 39. Many examples of different types of discrimination were raised with us. These included:
>
> - 16 and 17 year olds finding it difficult to access social services and mental health services, and falling in the gap between provision for children and adults;
> - children and young people not being taken seriously when reporting a criminal or calling emergency services;
> - children and young people being treated unfairly in public spaces, particularly in shops, using public transport or where 'mosquito' devices are in use to disperse crowds;
> - public places such as leisure centres, libraries and transport facilities being unfit for adults with babies and young children;

[178] Loi du 10 mai 2007 tendant à lutter contre certaines formes de discrimination (BS 30 v. 07), article 3 Communities and Districts.
[179] See the twenty-fifth Report of Session 2008–2009, HL Paper 157, HC 318, in the following terms at [39] and [44] to [45].

- discriminatory attitudes of medical professionals towards disabled children;
- fertility of disabled children restricted by use of non-essential medical intervention;
- high incidence of bullying of children with a learning difficulty; and
- difficulties for young Gypsy and Traveller children in accessing suitable accommodation, public transport, GP surgeries and safe places to play.

. . .

44. The Government is not in favour of extending age discrimination to the provision of goods, facilities and services to the under-18s arguing that this could have the 'unintended effect of diluting protections[s] that are in place' rather than enhancing them. We asked the Minister to explain how extending protection against age discrimination to children would dilute existing protections. She reiterated the Government's concern that by extending protection it might not be able to provide age-appropriate services aimed specifically at children or at children of specific ages.

45. We doubt that prohibiting age discrimination against children would have the unintended consequences mentioned by the Minister. In particular, we consider that it would be possible to draft an appropriate provision which would prohibit all discrimination on the grounds of age in relation to goods, facilities and services, except where it can be justified. This would allow age-appropriate services to be provided where there was good reason for doing so, such as to respond to the needs of a young child. We recommend that the Equality Bill be amended to

extend protection from age discrimination to people regardless of their age in relation to the provision of goods, facilities and services, except where discrimination on the grounds of age can be justified.

In our Opinion, Dee Masters and I concluded that there were many obvious reasons why the protection in Great Britain was itself unlawful and discriminatory when set against international norms. Moreover, it is obvious that no adverse undermining of the special measures providing very specific protections of minors when working has occurred as a result of the Equality Act 2010's application to them. If age discrimination at work should be prohibited for under-18s, neither of us could see any good reason why it should not be in relation to the provision of goods, facilities and services.

Nonetheless, there are no imminent signs of change in Great Britain, and the proposals from civil society in Northern Ireland have so far had insufficient cross-community traction among politicians to be brought into effect. In the end, though, I believe that those demographic statistics I have set out above will have their own force. Those over 65 may be becoming more numerous, but that must also mean that those under 18 will become an even more precious asset to society. As the examples given to the Parliamentary Committee I have cited above show, while there are differences in the lives lived by the young as compared to the old, there are also many points in common. Their lives will become so important as they become rarer as a proportion of the population that they will need to be courted and encouraged. Changing this law would be a good start, as

Dee Masters and I sought to demonstrate for the ECNI and NICCY.

The new legislation also contained a conundrum. The black letter test for determining whether there was either direct or indirect discrimination was exactly the same for these new provisions applying in Great Britain as it had already been for discrimination in relation to work. Understandably, commentators rapidly started asking whether, although there was no European obligation to include these new prohibitions, the European law test for justification for direct discrimination also applied here.[180] If so, then this poses big questions for commercial and other enterprises supplying goods, facilities and services in Great Britain. As noted above, the *Heyday* case had established that direct discrimination could only be justified by legitimate national social policy reasons. What were these in relation to the provision of goods, facilities and services when age was an issue?

One direct consequence of the extensive range of exceptions and the limited scope of this new legislation is that there has been – as far as I am aware – no litigation relying on the basic right. This ought to be very concerning, since I simply do not believe that there is no such discrimination. Moreover, I am sure it will take a series of test cases to tease out the effect of this new legislation. The lesson of the

---

[180] See D. Romney and D. Masters, 'Beginner's Guide to the Ban on Age Discrimination in Goods and Services', at https://482pe539799u3yn seg2hl1r3-wpengine.netdna-ssl.com/wp-content/uploads/2012/09/2012-september-dm-and-dr-age-disc-goods-and-services.pdf and *Law Society Gazette* (11 September 2012).

Heyday litigation is that a great deal of hard work is necessary to conduct even one such case.

Undertaking such litigation requires the resources to take a case the full distance, even to the Supreme Court, the tenacity of the litigant to continue down that long road, and one or more willing funders. So, one reason for the lack of litigation may be that the relationship between costs, quantum and merits means that this kind of litigation is rarely worth it on an individual basis. No legal aid is available; funding from one or more Commissions is dependent on the allowance in their budgets and the priorities in their current work plan. The compensation for injury to feelings for this kind of tort rarely exceeds a very few thousand pounds.

Yet, if it is impossible to enforce these rights, then they will soon become known to be toothless. The law will not merely be a dead letter; the lack of normative effect will be entirely counter-productive.

If this lecture achieves nothing else, I would like to hope that it provokes more thought about how the efficacy of this legislation can be tested in Great Britain, and how in Northern Ireland less restrictive and more useful protections against age discrimination in relation to goods, facilities and services can be created.

3.4 The International Campaign Against Ageism

Despite my gloom about the efficacy of our current laws against age discrimination, there is some good reason to hope that international standards are changing and will in the long run put pressure on the UK to do better. At present within the UK, jurists have barely engaged with these international discussions, but I would encourage them to do more. What is happening is a direct result of the problems that demographic change has brought to the fore, particularly in the context of austerity.

Just as we are losing the stereotype that SPa marks a moment when comparisons change and persons become entitled, questions about the real needs of the oldest are coming into focus. Nobody denies that at some point special measures are necessary at the end of life, any more than it is in issue that they are necessary at the beginning. They must, however, be of the right kind, empowering self-determination to the end. The wrong view of end of life is that the oldest in our society have had their time, and are no longer worthy of equal opportunity or respect. This kind of ageism which neither meets the special needs of the most old nor respects their continuing rights to self-determination is coming under a much more intense worldwide focus. This I believe can only help with the need I have discussed to have a greater understanding of age equality.

The UN has been concerned about the impact of ageing for some time. This concern had been developed in the Madrid International Plan of Action on Ageing, 2002[181] (the Madrid Plan), formulated at the conclusion to the Second

---

[181] See Report of the Second World Assembly on Ageing, Madrid, 8–12 April 2002 (United Nations publication, Sales No. E.02.IV.4), chap. I, resolution 1, annex I. See www.un.org/esa/socdev/documents/ageing/MIPAA/political-declaration-en.pdf.

World Assembly on Ageing. Some time later, on 21 December 2010, the United Nation's General Assembly approved the formation of an 'Open-ended Working Group on Ageism'[182] (OEWG).[183] The OEWG has received contributions from an internationally wide range of NGOs on many issues connected with the problems of ageism.[184] I am delighted that the UK has begun to engage fully with the OEWG. At the most recent ninth meeting of the OEWG this summer, the UK was represented by a significant team[185] from the Foreign Office,[186] which to my knowledge had taken great care to inform themselves in advance as to the issues concerning such a new convention and the obligations and possibilities it might create.

One major focus of the Madrid Plan was to secure comprehensive laws to outlaw age discrimination, as Article 5 of the Political Declaration in the Plan stated:

[182] See Resolution 65/182, at https://undocs.org/en/A/RES/65/182.
[183] See https://social.un.org/ageing-working-group/.
[184] I have contributed to these deliberations as part of a group brought together by Bridget Sleap of HelpAge International, including Andrew Byrnes (Australian Centre for Human Rights, University of New South Wales), Israel Doron (University of Haifa), Nena Georgantzi (AGE Platform Europe/National University of Ireland Galway), Annie Herro (Australian Centre for Human Rights, University of New South Wales), Dee Masters (Cloisters), Bill Mitchell (National Association of Community Legal Centres, Australia). See, for instance, https://social.un.org/ageing-working-group/documents/eighth/Inputs%20NGOs/Joint_Paper_Equality.pdf.
[185] As well as by the Permanent Representative to the UN, Dame Karen Pierce.
[186] Mr Samuel Thomas Grout-Smith, Ms Tamarin Stodart and Ms Laura Jean Holbach.

We reaffirm the commitment to spare no effort to promote democracy, strengthen the rule of law and promote gender equality, as well as to promote and protect human rights and fundamental freedoms, including the right to development. *We commit ourselves to eliminating all forms of discrimination, including age discrimination.* We also recognize that persons, as they age, should enjoy a life of fulfilment, health, security and active participation in the economic, social, cultural and political life of their societies. We are determined to enhance the recognition of the dignity of older persons and to eliminate all forms of neglect, abuse and violence. (emphasis added)

And in the Plan itself it was said at [13]:

The promotion and protection of all human rights and fundamental freedoms, including the right to development, is essential for the creation of an inclusive society for all ages in which older persons participate fully and without discrimination and on the basis of equality. Combating discrimination based on age and promoting the dignity of older persons is fundamental to ensuring the respect that older persons deserve. Promotion and protection of all human rights and fundamental freedoms is important in order to achieve a society for all ages. In this, the reciprocal relationship between and among generations must be nurtured, emphasized and encouraged through a comprehensive and effective dialogue.

So the work of the OEWG ought to be expected to give a big push to developing comprehensive age discrimination laws across the world including here in the UK. The OEWG has now met nine times. From an early stage NGOs from around the world have pressed for the OEWG to develop proposals for a UN Convention on the rights of older persons similar to the UN Convention on the Rights of Persons with Disabilities. Rather to the surprise of some European countries, the UN has agreed to the consideration of such an idea. Such a new convention would be *lex specialis* to be considered and interpreted as giving specific expression to the existing UN general civil and political and social rights conventions and the Universal Declaration on Human Rights.

The focus of the OEWG has undoubtedly been on the rights of 'older persons'.[187] Its initial formation has been followed in May 2014 by an appointment by the Human Rights Council of Ms Rosa Kornfeld-Matte as the first Independent Expert on the enjoyment of all human rights by older persons.[188]

This focus raises really important points about the protections against age discrimination that might be included in any such UN Convention: who are 'older persons'; and when should 'older persons' become entitled to specific protections and treatment that are not to be afforded to others on an equal basis?[189]

---

[187] See UN Resolution 72/144, adopted by the General Assembly on 19 December 2017, which reviewed the progress to date and set the overall agenda for the 9th meeting of the OEWG this year.

[188] See www.ohchr.org/en/issues/olderpersons/ie/pages/ieolderpersons .aspx.

[189] As to the kinds of special treatment that might be afforded, see the Report of the International Conference, on the Human Rights of Older Persons & Non-discrimination, held on 3 and 4 October 2017, in Santiago, Chile,

No one doubts that there is such a class and a point in life when this should happen, when it is no longer appropriate to treat persons comparably irrespective of their age. To take the point to the extreme that there should be a right to appropriate end of life care is not in doubt; however, the question remains how far back should such a right arise? We are all after all facing the end of our life at some point; it is just that it does not equally signify with us. The acceptance of this proposition therefore begs the question: when is someone to be treated as an older person whose entitlements are not comparable to those of others?

I have already argued that SPa is a poor marker for becoming 'old' and should be discarded as a stereotype because it simply no longer fits the dynamic of ageing in the UK. Yet many other countries around the world use 60 as such a marker.[190] I think we must move on. With others,[191] I have been able to engage with the OEWG and the UK's Foreign and Commonwealth Office to raise some of these issues. In particular, I am interested in the question whether a person should be considered 'older' and therefore entitled to special treatment on a non-comparable basis, on a social or chronological basis.

by the Center of Old Age and Aging Studies, Pontificia Universidad Católica de Chile, and the Office of the United Nations High Commissioner for Human Rights; see www.ohchr.org/Documents/Issues/OlderPersons/ConferenceSantiagoReport.pdf.

[190] See, for instance, the frequent reference to those of 60+ as older persons in the Report of the International Conference, cited at footnote 189 above.

[191] See footnote 184 above.

The first question may be put in this way: if a person looks 'old' in their particular social setting, is that enough? This is an attractive argument when set against the approach taken in the UK to the concept of disability. Here we treat disability as having both a medical and social component.[192] Could we take a similar approach to being 'older', casting such persons into a non-comparable class lawfully having entitlements not available to others? Personally, I worry greatly about this approach. It is much too close to the stereotypical division of the population into those below and of or above SPa, which I am sure cannot be maintained on economic grounds as demographic change proceeds.

I would rather that we enabled specific special measures for those at the end of life, but otherwise did not permit persons to claim non-comparability because a member of the class of 'older persons' until a threshold had been crossed. That threshold should be fixed so as to include a particular number of deciles of the population. This approach would enable any future UN Convention to make provision for countries with very different life expectancies. It would also allow for the dynamic effects of demographic change. For instance, if a person did not become an 'older person' until they entered the age group which contained the last 10 per cent of the population, the class would alter in size in proportion to the capacity of the rest of the population to support its members.

---

[192] See the definition of disability as a protected characteristic in s. 6 of, and Sch 1 to, the Equality Act 2010.

These and other issues are under discussion in the OEWG and will affect the approach to age equality in the UK as well as the rest of the world in due course.

PART 4 CONCLUSIONS

So, in conclusion there are essentially four points I want to make:

- To achieve true equality, the law will need to be able to make comparisons across all ages.
- This should be in a much larger range of activities than is permitted now.
- For the law to be effective, it must be understood and accessible, but right now the public are struggling with the nature of, and need for, such comparisons, and are not accessing these provisions.
- Too few jurists are engaged in the process of working out how to make the right to non-discrimination on grounds of age really effective.

It seems obvious to me that a sufficiently systematic, rational and comprehensive concept of age equality is needed to make the protection of this newly identified protected characteristic work for all. That means being quite aware of the need to make comparisons on the broadest front. The aim must be to develop a jurisprudence that is understandable by the public and so enforceable with sufficient legal certainty. As demographic changes lead to longer lives, the principle of age equality needs to be just as understandable as the law against unfair dismissal and just as effective as any of the other anti-discrimination provisions in securing normative outcomes from local and national government, and private providers of goods, facilities and services.

In developing these new laws, jurists and the legislature are presented with choices about the scope of application of age discrimination law, the permissible comparisons, the general definition of the kinds of justifications that may be permitted, and the specification of situations where the law should provide a defence even though discrimination is proved. This last category is really no more than a legislated short cut to justification. There should be as small a range of such justifications as possible and each of those now in place need to be subjected to a much heavier scrutiny and wherever possible repealed. If we can achieve this, then these laws can make a real difference.

Prescribing finally how this might be got right is much too big an aspiration for one lecture, yet I am convinced that it is an urgent task that we must engage with because it is simply too important an issue to let develop *ad hoc*. Poor and bad decisions about its development will bring untold grief for society; good ones could be transformative for all generations. So, I hope therefore that this lecture will stimulate yet more debate. I shall continue to be involved deeply in what is left of my life!

Chapter 4

Comparisons When Equality Rights Are in Conflict

1.1 Introduction

In the last Hamlyn Lecture, delivered in Middle Temple Hall, I discussed a new issue in equality law that has emerged as a significant problem only in this century. It concerns conflicting claims for protection of those human characteristics specifically recognised by equality law as being precious and worthy of respect. These are complex problems. In such cases, the demand made of equality law is great; it must go beyond merely judging whether there has been disadvantage or less favourable treatment based on a single protected characteristic, to address a different question. In these cases, once one person has established that they have apparently suffered a wrong protected by equality law, the issue becomes whether, in the particular context, affirming that person's rights involves unacceptably diminishing the equality rights of another.

In these situations, the rights of each must be compared and evaluated. So far there have been relatively few occasions on which this task has been undertaken and so

292

there is a lack of really good jurisprudence to guide us. In simple terms, we can see that to develop such jurisprudence some difficult questions now need to be asked:

- How has this been done, so far?
- How should we compare and evaluate such competing claims?
- What thought has gone into finding a secure basis for this kind of problem, which has generic application?

By turns, these questions have both vexed and intrigued me, and in this chapter I intend to discuss them rather more extensively than I had time to do in my last lecture in Middle Temple Hall.

I have been thinking about them for a long time. I had seen these problems coming even before the turn of the century, having had the opportunity to discuss them in a W.G. Hart Workshop at the Institute of Advanced Legal Studies, London, in 1999.[1] My paper on that occasion concluded by saying:

> It is almost unimaginable to consider how Tribunals will struggle to deal with the interrelationship of the right to . . . non-discrimination on grounds of sexuality with religious rights. . . . One example which I have recently had to consider in anticipation of the Human Rights Act 1998 is the extent to which a church organisation should be permitted to advertise for and recruit employees for jobs of

---

[1] R. Allen, 'The Contribution of International and Transnational Regulation in the Search for Substantive Equality in the Workplace: Clarity or Confusion?' in H. Collins, P.L. Davies and R. Rideout, Legal Regulation of the Employment Relation (Vol. 3) (Kluwer Law International, 2000).

marginal religious significance by imposing faith requirements which undoubtedly have an adverse impact on many racial groups. While I believe I gave the right advice in the instant case I can see that many Tribunals would be utterly confused.

1.2 Four Supreme Court Cases

Since then I have been privileged to be instructed by our Equality Commissions to argue four such cases, each of which has been 'difficult', and each of which has ended up in the Supreme Court, becoming something of a *cause célèbre.* Collectively these demonstrate just how wide is the range of circumstances in which such conflicts can arise. In this chapter, I shall outline the conflicts in these four cases and try to explore some of the issues that arose, with the hope that some work can get done towards answering the three rhetorical questions I have posed.

The first case in which I was instructed was *E (ota R)* v. *Governing Body of JFS & Anor,*[2] known more colloquially as the 'Jewish Free School case'. This was one of the first cases decided by the newly formed Supreme Court. Their judgment was given on 16 December 2009 by nine judges, and it involved a conflict between race and religion rights, neatly reflecting my concern expressed at the conclusion of my paper for the Hart workshop a decade earlier.

---

[2] [2010] 2 WLR 153, [2009] WLR (D) 366, [2010] 2 AC 728, 27 BHRC 656, [2010] ELR 26, [2010] IRLR 136, [2010] 1 All ER 319, [2009] UKSC 15, [2010] PTSR 147.

The Jewish Free School has long been a very popular publicly funded school for rightly describing itself[3] now as being:

> a co-educational inclusive, modern, orthodox Jewish school that strives to produce well-educated, faithful and proud Jews who will be responsible and contributing members of society. JFS is a truly wonderful school.

Prior to the conclusion of this case, it had given preference to those children whose status as Jews was recognised by the Office of the Chief Rabbi (OCR), that is to say to children of a Jewish mother or those who were Jews by conversion as recognised and accepted by Orthodox standards. In determining the answer to this test, the OCR looked to the child's ancestors on the matrilineal line, to the mother, grandmother, great grandmother and so on. Each of these had to have been Jewish in the view of the OCR.

We could say that in one sense the problem that arose in the Jewish Free School case was an entirely religious one, in that the school refused to admit a child whose mother was not recognised as Jewish by the OCR, even though she considered herself to be Jewish and attended a non-Orthodox synagogue. In the OCR's view, it did not matter that the child's father was considered Jewish and the family had considered themselves to be Jewish by religion, and the child's mother had undergone a form of conversion.

However, the key point in the case was that the OCR's concept of Jewish religious identity was intimately

---

[3] https://jfs.brent.sch.uk/about-us/.

connected to the presence or absence of an inherited characteristic, and so the qualification of a particular religious identity could also be seen as an ethnic or race characteristic.[4] Was the Jewish Free School permitted to select in this way? The school tried to argue that the rule it applied should be seen as one of indirect discrimination that was nonetheless justified by the Governors' rights to religious autonomy. However, in the end the child's father successfully argued that this rule was direct race discrimination which the law did not permit to be justified.

The central battleground in the litigation thus concerned the classification of the discriminatory act that had led to the refusal to admit the pupil to the school. The school believed that if it could be said to be indirect discrimination, it would be able to succeed on justifying its policy, whereas the parents believed that if the policy was seen to be directly discriminatory on grounds of ethnicity, this line of argument would not be available. Behind these technical points lay a different issue; it concerned which party's claim to protection of their equality rights should be considered paramount. It was this aspect that caught the interest of the press, the concern of the whole Jewish community, and led to the Supreme Court deciding that nine judges, instead of a more usual five, should decide the case. The Equality and Human Rights Commission instructed me to intervene as one of the fourteen counsel in court, and my

---

[4] Ethnicity is a particular aspect of the protected characteristic of race; see now s. 9 of the Equality Act 2010.

argument was straightforward that this was indeed direct discrimination.[5]

Nonetheless, this complex conflict could not fail to invoke sympathy for both sides' positions, whether Jewish or not. On the one hand, who would not be sympathetic to the school in wishing to conform to the Jewish religious authorities' determination of who was Jewish; and on the other hand who would not be sympathetic to the child's parents in wishing their child to have an education in accordance with their religious beliefs in such a well-known and successful school? In the end the court divided 5–4 in favour of the parents, and I am sure that very close outcome is testament also to the sympathy that the court felt to both sides.

Looking back, we can also see that the case showed how sympathy for one party or the other is a poor basis for resolving such conflicts. Of course, the advocates for both sides sought to win this sympathy argument. It was, though, the judges' job to apply the law as Parliament had laid it down, and to let Parliament or the parties resolve how they would then act in the light of that decision.

The next case in which I was involved that required a conflicts of rights to be resolved was *Bull & Bull* v. *Hall &*

---

[5] As part of my submissions for the Commission, I pointed out that the legislation prohibiting race discrimination had long been made with the understanding that Jewish identity raised issues of both religious identity and ethnicity: see e.g. H. Street, G. Howe and G. Bindman, 'Anti-discrimination Legislation: The Street Report. Political and Economic Planning' (1967), at [1.1] and [122.1] and passim.

Preddy.[6] This case was decided by the Supreme Court on 27 November 2013. The conflict was different, concerning a conflict between sexual orientation and religion rights.

Mr Hall and Mr Preddy, my clients, are a gay couple then in a civil partnership, who had been refused access to a double-bedded room which they had booked in Chymorvah Private Hotel in Marazion, Cornwall. This hotel was run by Mr and Mrs Bull, who are evangelical Christians, who sincerely believe, as the trial judge put it, that:

> the only divinely ordained sexual relationship is that between a man and a woman within the bonds of matrimony.

In 2008 they publicised their hotel's policy on its online booking form, saying:

> Here at Chymorvah we have few rules, but please note, that out of a deep regard for marriage we prefer to let double accommodation to heterosexual married couples only – thank you.

Unfortunately, Mr Hall and Mr Preddy were not aware of this policy when they booked a room and only discovered it at the door of the hotel when they turned up late at night, so we can only guess whether they would have bothered to book the hotel had they known. They were told that, although the hotel was prepared to let twin-bedded and single rooms to any person regardless of marital status or sexual orientation,

---

[6] [2014] 1 All ER 919, [2013] UKSC 73, [2014] HRLR 4, 36 BHRC 190, [2013] WLR(D) 454, [2014] Eq LR 76, [2013] 1 WLR 3741, [2013] WLR 3741.

they would not be allowed to take up the pre-booked double-bedded room. They were turned away and their weekend away was ruined and so in due course they sued. As the refusal occurred prior to the passing of the Equality Act 2010, they had to sue under Regulations[7] which were later re-enacted as primary legislation in the 2010 Act.

Again, a first issue was whether this was direct or indirect discrimination. The Bulls wished to justify their rule by reference to their religious beliefs; however, the Bulls also relied on their rights as set out in Article 9 of the European Convention on Human Rights to manifest their religion without unjustified limitation by the state. The Supreme Court held the Bulls had indeed directly discriminated against Mr Hall and Mr Preddy, so that there was no possibility of justification under the Equality Act 2010, but that did not answer the case made by reference to Article 9. This is how that issue was resolved by Lady Hale in her judgment:

> 43. [Counsel for the Bulls] ... put the human rights dimension at the forefront of his submissions. He emphasised that it was the state which had placed limitations, in the shape of the Regulations, on the right of Mr and Mrs Bull to manifest their religion by conducting their business in accordance with their religious beliefs; whereas it was Mr and Mrs Bull, private citizens, who had arguably interfered with the right of Mr Preddy and Mr Hall to enjoy respect for their private lives without discrimination on the ground of their sexual orientation. The state had not interfered with that right. In order to

---

[7] The Equality Act (Sexual Orientation) Regulations 2007, SI 2007/1263.

engage the state's responsibility, it would be necessary to erect a positive obligation to protect them from interferences by private citizens.

44. One answer to that is that the state has already assumed such a responsibility, by enacting the Regulations. Another, and simpler, answer is that the 'rights of others' for the purpose of article 9(2) (and indeed the other qualified rights in the Convention) are not limited to their Convention rights but include their rights under the ordinary law. The ordinary law gives Mr Preddy and Mr Hall the right not to be unlawfully discriminated against. It follows that, for the purpose of article 9(2), the limitation is 'in accordance with the law' and pursues one of the legitimate aims there listed.

45. The question, therefore, is whether it is 'necessary in a democratic society', in other words whether there is a 'reasonable relationship of proportionality between the means employed and the aim sought to be achieved' (see, for example, *Francesco Sessa* v. *Italy*, App No 28790/08, Judgment of 3 April 2012, para 38). [Counsel] makes an eloquent plea for 'reasonable accommodation' between the two competing interests. The mutual duty of reasonable accommodation unless this causes undue hardship originated in the United States and found its way into the Canadian Human Rights Act 1985. It can of course be found in our own disability discrimination law (see E Howard, 'Reasonable Accommodation of Religion and Other Discrimination Grounds in EU Law' (2013) 38 EL Rev 360).

. . .

51 . . . Mr and Mrs Bull cannot get round the fact that United Kingdom law prohibits them from doing as they

did. I have already held that, if justification is possible, the denial of a double bedded room cannot be justified under [the Regulations]. My reasons for doing so are equally relevant to the Convention question of whether the limitation on the right of Mr and Mrs Bull to manifest their religion was a proportionate means of achieving a legitimate aim. The legitimate aim was the protection of the rights and freedoms of Mr Preddy and Mr Hall. Whether that could have been done at less cost to the religious rights of Mr and Mrs Bull by offering them a twin-bedded room simply does not arise in this case. But I would find it very hard to accept that it could.

The case caused consternation among many for whom religious identity is really important. The Christian Institute[8] campaigned hard in support of Mr and Mrs Bull. Lady Hale plainly had some second thoughts about the outcome. A significant indication of those second thoughts came in 2014 when she gave the Annual Human Rights Lecture for the Law Society of Ireland on the topic of Freedom of Religion and Belief. She was attracted by the idea of 'reasonable accommodation'.[9] She said:

> It was argued in *Bull v Hall* that the hotel keepers had done all that could reasonably be expected of them – that there should be give and take on both sides. But we rejected that argument, holding that they were not justified in refusing

[8] www.christian.org.uk/.

[9] Some review of Canadian law on reasonable accommodation in conflicts cases had been made in *Bull and Bull* v. *Hall and Preddy*; see e.g. *Smith and Chymyshyn* v. *Knights of Columbus* 2005 BCHRT 544(E) and *Eadie and Thomas* v. *Riverbend Bed and Breakfast (No 2)* 2012 BCHRT 247.

to provide their services on a non-discriminatory basis.
I wonder whether that is something of a relief or whether
we would be better off with a more nuanced approach?

After reflecting more generally on Article 9 cases she concluded by saying:

> the moral of all this is that if the law is going to protect
> freedom of religion and belief it has to accept that all
> religions and beliefs and none are equal. It cannot
> realistically inquire into the validity or importance of those
> beliefs, or any particular manifestation of them, as long as
> they are genuinely held. It then has to work out how far it
> should go in making special provisions or exceptions for
> particular beliefs, how far it should require the providers of
> employments, goods and services to accommodate them,
> and how far it should allow for a 'conscience clause', either
> to the providers, as argued by the hotel keepers in *Bull
> v Hall*, or to employees, as suggested by the dissenting
> minority in *Ladele*.[10] I am not sure that our law has yet
> found a reasonable accommodation of all these different
> strands. The story has just begun.

As we shall see this final musing – 'The story has just begun' –
was indeed correct.

There can be no doubt that *Bull and Bull* v. *Hall and
Preddy* was a critical case in the long story of the steps taken to
remove some of the terrible discrimination that gay and
lesbian couples had faced for so long. Christians of all kinds
know well that their faith has played too great a part in that

---

[10] See here *Eweida and Others* v. *United Kingdom* (2013) 57 EHRR 213.

story, and I have no doubt that the Supreme Court were in part moved by this fact. However, the campaign by the Christian Institute and other evangelical Christian and indeed other religious organisations began to seek to cast them as now the oppressed group.

I think that this is significant. In Chapter 1, I have showed how quickly the framework, within which the rights of gay and lesbian couples had been considered as a wholly absurd and alien concept, has changed. The litigation and the different views in the wider world about the relative merits of each parties' position marked yet another step in the changing framework for viewing the rights to equal treatment of gay and lesbian couples. Thus, the speed of change had its own impact; religious organisations and others with antithetical views found it hard to change and began to complain about the new expectations being made of them as the law changed to recognise the rights of gays and lesbians.

In that first chapter I also noted how fast that framework changed from the point at which Sir Tasker Watkins dismissed my arguments during the late 1990s and early part of the noughties. There is little doubt in my mind that although the statutory provisions which were in play in this case were in favour of Mr Hall and Mr Preddy, the case fuelled a degree of sympathy for those evangelical Christians coming to terms with the fact that their beliefs about marriage were no longer held universally. Perhaps this was partly because their argument was cast in terms that they would be forced to sin if they were to permit this gay couple in a registered civil partnership to have access to a double-bedded room in their hotel. Perhaps it was because they were old and claimed that complying with this law would affect whether they were able to continue in business.

The third conflicts case, *FirstGroup Plc* v. *Paulley*,[11] in which I was instructed in the Supreme Court, I shall discuss in some greater detail below. At this point I shall simply sketch the conflict that arose to indicate that a point of difference between the Jewish Free School and *Bull and Bull* v. *Hall and Preddy* cases. It can be described very simply as concerning wheelchair access to a bus and a conflict between disability and maternity rights. Although this was just as much a case about a conflict of rights as the previous two, there was a wrinkle which made the advocacy in the case somewhat different. Mr Paulley, a wheelchair user, wanted to travel on a certain bus to Leeds; so did a woman with a baby in a buggy. The problem was that there was no room for both the wheelchair and the buggy. The issue in the case therefore became concerned with the steps that the bus company took and should have taken to resolve this conflict. Unlike the previous two cases, where the individuals whose protected characteristics were in conflict were both represented in court, in this case the woman who had refused to move, and who the bus company had permitted to block Mr Paulley's access to the wheelchair space, was not in court.

The final case is *Lee* v. *Ashers Baking Company Ltd and Mr & Mrs McArthur*,[12] often known as 'the Gay Cake Case',

---

[11] [2017] RTR 19, [2017] 1 WLR 423, [2017] IRLR 258, [2017] WLR(D) 22, [2017] UKSC 4, [2017] WLR 423, [2017] 2 All ER 1.

[12] [2018] 3 WLR 1294, [2018] UKSC 49.

which completed its stages through the UK's courts only shortly before my lectures in 2018. Mr Lee has now lodged a complaint with the ECtHR, so in one sense it remains unresolved. This case was rather more complex, involving a conflict between sexual orientation and political opinion on the one hand, and religion and a different political opinion on the other. Like *Paulley*, I shall discuss this in some detail in this chapter.

Before considering these two cases in detail, I think we should note what connects these cases together, because although the rights in issue were different, they did have several points in common.

First, they each concerned everyday life events:

- a school admission;
- a hotel booking;
- a bus journey; and
- the purchase of a celebration cake.

This shows how these kinds of conflicts of rights, which I feared back in the last century would soon arise, might occur in almost any context in which different people must interact. In short, we need to recognise that these conflicts are and will continue to be humdrum events. For this reason alone, it is important in my view that the law studies them and considers what it can do about them.

Second, the litigation in each case was prolonged and expensive, even though the amounts of money involved, if any, were tiny. This is another critical point. Everyone knows that the utility of the law has an inverse relationship to the cost of using it.

Third, there were special interests over and above that in ordinary discrimination litigation. These cases gave rise to more argument and emotion than any other kind of equality dispute with which I have been involved. Moreover, the losing side and its backers have, to a greater or lesser extent, felt that it is they who have suffered the grievous wrong, that the law is inadequate, and/or that it has let them down just when they needed it. The decision by Mr Lee to take his case to the European Court is just the most recent example of the concern expressed by the losing side. In the other cases, there has also been dismay and active political engagement to see if there could be a move to a different outcome.

For all these reasons, I think that such a sense of injustice to the loser is a serious matter, because it can all too easily be deployed by Equality Law's enemies, and that is a major reason for my wish to discuss these conflicts. Since I believe profoundly that effective Equality Law is an essential tool for social justice, I don't wish to see it rendered inaccessible or undermined by bad outcomes to difficult cases. In general terms it is easy to say what is needed to avoid this: first, a better way to explain to the public how such comparisons will be undertaken; and next, a legal process that will resolve such issues more quickly and easily, or where necessary will ensure that judges resolving the conflict do no harm to the general principle of equality. These points are easy to make and much more difficult to put into action. What we do not need is a game of Legal Top Trumps in which one kind of equality right always beats another, because equality law has no hierarchy. A Protestant is not worth more than a disabled person, or a Muslim, or a lesbian, and so on and vice versa. As

Lady Hale has pointed out, 'Democracy is founded on the principle that each individual has equal value.'[13] Advocate General Poiares Maduro has made the same point, saying that 'At its bare minimum, human dignity entails the recognition of the equal worth of every individual.'[14]

Before digging deeper into this problem, I must put one point to the side. It would be nice if such clashes could be easily resolved by an appeal to toleration, 'give and take' or 'do as you would be done by'. There is no doubt that the jurisprudence of the ECtHR emphasises that democracy is built on tolerance and broadmindedness,[15] and some further interesting work has indeed been done on developing such a legal principle by the European Council on Tolerance and Reconciliation;[16] but the truth is that the social traction of such an approach is very limited. Moreover, in conflicts cases such as this, opponents can and will *each* argue that it should be the other party doing the tolerating, while they should be permitted the doing. So, if society is to address these kinds of humdrum events effectively, its laws will need to do more than just appeal to the kindness of others, important though kindness is as a human virtue to be encouraged in all. Sometimes that may work; sometimes a gay couple may look elsewhere for a hotel; sometimes a wheelchair user may be happy with the next bus; sometimes a parent will like

---

[13] *Ghaidan* v. *Godin-Mendoza* [2004] 2 AC 557 at [132].

[14] See his Opinion in Case C-303/06 *Coleman* v. *Attridge Law and another* [2008] ICR 1128 at [8].

[15] See, for instance, *Alekhina* v. *Russia* (2019) 68 EHRR 14 at [197].

[16] See http://ectr.eu/ectrmembers.

another school; and sometimes another baker will do just as well. The problem is that sometimes they won't; what then?

1.3 The Fact of Diversity

Let's look closer as to why we should we be bothered about this. The answer can be encapsulated in one word – 'Diversity'. This is a fact of modern life in the UK. Even in these dog days of Brexit when, whatever happens, we all know that the UK will remain a very diverse nation. For instance, in the summer of 2018, when the English football team competed in the World Cup, nearly 50 per cent – 11 out of the 23 players – were not white. The England Manager Gareth Southgate saw this as a point of personal pride, saying:[17]

> We're a team with our diversity and our youth that represent modern England.

While Sunder Katwala, Director of British Future, a think-tank addressing identity, commented correctly that:[18]

> Few people [saw] anything new or unusual in that. After all, 85 black and mixed-race players have worn the 'Three Lions' on their shirt . . . since Viv Anderson first played for England in 1978.

Modern England certainly – but it is not much different in Wales, Scotland or Northern Ireland. If you look you will soon see – whatever your views about it – just how much

[17] See Tweet 26 June 2018.
[18] See https://inews.co.uk/sport/football/world-cup/england-world-cup-2018-squad-diversity/.

there is diversity in the makeup of each of the nations of the United Kingdom. Although in another country this might be dangerous, in fact the evidence is that support for diversity and inclusiveness as a means to secure fairness is already high and is growing daily.[19] This is of course good news, but we must also never forget that it is actually *necessary* for our society to work. Some simple social statistics will make this point for me:

- The 2011 Census showed that while 87 per cent of the UK's population is white, 13 per cent belong to 'Black, Asian, Mixed or Other' ethnic groups.[20]
- Although the UK is now among the least religious countries in the world,[21] it still has an extraordinarily wide range of different religious organisations and beliefs.
- Not less than 2.0 per cent of the adult UK population identify as lesbian, gay or bisexual, and somewhere around 4 per cent of those in the 16 to 24 age group do so.[22]
- Moreover, there are nearly 14 million disabled people in the UK, spread across all ages, though skewed to the older age

---

[19] See, for instance, N. Jones, C. Bromley, C. Creegan, R. Kinsella, F. Dobbie, and R. Ormston, 'Building Understanding of Fairness, Equality and Good Relations' (No. 53) (2010) EHRC research report, see www.equalityhumanrights.com/sites/default/files/research-report-53-building-understanding-of-fairness-equality-and-good-relations.pdf.

[20] See www.ethnicity-facts-figures.service.gov.uk/.

[21] See www.theguardian.com/world/2015/apr/12/uk-one-of-worlds-least-religious-countries-survey-finds.

[22] See www.ons.gov.uk/peoplepopulationandcommunity/culturalidentity/sexuality/bulletins/sexualidentityuk/2016.

groups: being 8 per cent of children, 19 per cent of working-age adults and 45 per cent of pension-age adults.[23]

- Into the mix must be added the fact that we are rapidly changing the way in which we must consider age and its related capacities,[24] as I discussed in my first lecture and in Chapter 3 – and now the government, prompted by the Women and Equalities Committee, is in discussions about enhanced protections relating to gender identity.

So, for the UK to be a modern peaceful country, Catholic and Protestant must be able to shake hands, live together and do business in Northern Ireland, Liverpool and Glasgow,[25] as much as anywhere else. Those in Bradford or Leicester, who identify as white British, must accept that they may be educated, served, employed and even entertained with those who identify as British Asian. The LGBT community must be able to work, shop and holiday, just like the straight community. And huge work must be done to ensure that the disabled are able to do the same. Likewise, religious persons must be able to live and work and enjoy themselves, as so must those transgendered or those who are non-binary, just as much as

---

[23] See https://assets.publishing.service.gov.uk/government/uploads/sys tem/uploads/attachment_data/file/692771/family-resources-survey-2016 -17.pdf.

[24] I discussed this point in the first Hamlyn Lecture: Lecture 1: The newest problem: Making a fair comparison across all ages, Tuesday 23 October 2018, Queen's University Belfast.

[25] There are many examples of this, but a recent one may be cited from Glasgow, where the singing of sectarian songs at a football match was held to be a criminal act: see the judgment of Sheriff S Reid on 29 March 2018 in *Procurator Fiscal, Glasgow* v. *K* 2018 SLT (Sh Ct) 179.

those who self-identify as male or female.[26] To say this is to say no more than to recognise that whatever our protected characteristics, we are entitled to the fullest possible right to self-determination – the ability to determine for ourselves, free of stereotypes and unjustified assumptions, how we are to live our lives. Yet recognising how well our society is coping generally with diversity, we must not ignore the fact that it still has its rubbing points – those occasions when the differences between us come into conflict and need to be resolved. And of course, to keep us going down the road where support for diversity and inclusiveness continues to grow, these rubbing points must be resolved and resolved well.

1.4 The Range of Protected Characteristics

Such conflicts occur not just because society has become so diverse. They also occur because of the now very broad range of personal protected characteristics which equality law protects. The cases I have noted above give some idea of the range of characteristics, but it is in fact much wider. Here is a list of them as set out in the Equality Act 2010:

---

[26] This is specifically recognised in s. 3 of the Equality Act 2006, which imposed a general duty on the Equality and Human Rights Commission to 'exercise its functions under this Part with a view to encouraging and supporting the development of a society in which – (a) people's ability to achieve their potential is not limited by prejudice or discrimination, (b) there is respect for and protection of each individual's human rights, (c) there is respect for the dignity and worth of each individual, (d) each individual has an equal opportunity to participate in society, and (e) there is mutual respect between groups based on understanding and valuing of diversity and on shared respect for equality and human rights.'

- Age.[27]
- Disability.[28]
- Gender reassignment.[29]
- Marriage and civil partnership.[30]
- Pregnancy and maternity.[31]
- Race (includes colour, nationality, and ethnic or national origins).[32]
- Religion or belief.[33]

---

[27] Section 5 of the Equality Act 2010 defines age thus: '(1) In relation to the protected characteristic of age – (a) a reference to a person who has a particular protected characteristic is a reference to a person of a particular age group; (b) a reference to persons who share a protected characteristic is a reference to persons of the same age group. (2) A reference to an age group is a reference to a group of persons defined by reference to age, whether by reference to a particular age or to a range of ages.'

[28] There is a complex definition of disability that is based neither on a wholly medical nor a wholly social model; see s. 6 of the Equality Act 2010.

[29] This is a reference to proposing to undergo, is undergoing or has undergone a process (or part of a process) for the purpose of reassigning the person's sex by changing physiological or other attributes of sex: see s. 7 of the Equality Act 2010.

[30] See s. 8 of the Equality Act 2010.

[31] This concept is addressed in ss. 17, 18, and 72–76 of the Equality Act 2010.

[32] See s. 9 of the Equality Act 2010.

[33] In s. 10 this is defined as '(1) Religion means any religion and a reference to religion includes a reference to a lack of religion. (2) Belief means any religious or philosophical belief and a reference to belief includes a reference to a lack of belief. (3) In relation to the protected characteristic of religion or belief – (a) a reference to a person who has a particular protected characteristic is a reference to a person of a particular religion or belief; (b) a reference to persons who share

- Sex.[34]
- Sexual orientation.[35]

If each of the compendious characteristics is unpicked, this is a list of some sixteen characteristics. Some, of course, are connected, but overall they allow for a pretty complex description of each of us. It is only in the noughties that the grounds have so rapidly expanded. This was required mostly – but not exclusively – by European law. The overall driver for this expansion was a developing recognition of the close connection between personal dignity and our right to self-determination, whatever combination of characteristics you or I may have. People instinctively recognise this – that their personal characteristics protected by equality law help define the contours of their capacities to live the life they want. That is a major reason why when equality rights come into conflict the dispute can get so heated.

---

    a protected characteristic is a reference to persons who are of the same religion or belief.'

[34] Section 11 of the Equality Act 2010 defines sex: 'In relation to the protected characteristic of sex – (a) a reference to a person who has a particular protected characteristic is a reference to a man or to a woman; (b) a reference to persons who share a protected characteristic is a reference to persons of the same sex.'

[35] Section 12 of the Equality Act 2010 defines sexual orientation '(1) Sexual orientation means a person's sexual orientation towards – (a) persons of the same sex, (b) persons of the opposite sex, or (c) persons of either sex. (2) In relation to the protected characteristic of sexual orientation – (a) a reference to a person who has a particular protected characteristic is a reference to a person who is of a particular sexual orientation; (b) a reference to persons who share a protected characteristic is a reference to persons who are of the same sexual orientation.'

Now this list of sixteen or so 'protected characteristics' is good. It is certainly much better than when I started as a barrister in 1974. Yet, in the context of the current discussions about equality law, it is not thought to be entirely satisfactory. For instance, although it refers to gender reassignment, the provisions of the Equality Act 2010 do not differentiate between concepts of birth or biological sex and lived gender. This is a significant issue within the trans community and can give rise to exactly the kinds of clashes with which I am concerned. I must add that the list has also been criticised as not really having caught up with the developing concepts of parental or caring responsibilities, and it does not include socio-economic status, even though the Equality Act 2010 itself recognised that discrimination can occur on that basis.[36]

These deficits may be met at least in part when other laws are in play, such as the Human Rights Act 1998 and Article 14 of the European Convention on Human Rights. The Charter of Fundamental Rights of the European Union has similar effects, though post-Brexit, the European Union (Withdrawal) Act 2018, may well diminish its significance.[37] We should also note how this close connection between the characteristics that equality law protects and the diversity of our population is now part of modern parlance – so much so that they are commonly linked in a single phrase, that trips off the tongue without distinction. 'Equality and Diversity' is often just reduced to the letters 'E&D' in public discourse.

---

[36] See Part 1 of the Equality Act 2010.
[37] See s. 5 of the European Union (Withdrawal) Act 2018.

We certainly frequently do that in the Committee I chair at
the Bar Council.[38]

PART 2 HOW CONFLICTS CAN ARISE

Once we are aware of the diversity of the UK and the range of
personal characteristics that are protected directly by domestic equality law or which the European Convention or Charter
might add to the list, it is not very difficult to see that one
person with a particular combination of personal characteristics might come into conflict with another with
a different set.

It is obvious that with not less than sixteen different
personal characteristics or even more – if the omissions I have
noted are counted in – there are likely to be other conflicts.

Some can be quite surprising. Here is an example.

2.1 Friday Night at the Indian

In 2000 I was invited to be a special legal adviser to the
Disability Rights Commission (DRC) by the Chair, the late
Sir Bert Massie. During my first interview with him, he
recounted an occasion in which the DRC had been confronted with a conflict of rights between, of all things,
a disabled man and a Muslim. The circumstances were these.

---

[38] Though there is a current tendency to move from E&D to D&I, meaning
diversity and inclusion. I think that this can be a cause for some concern.
That we should build an inclusive society is necessary to meet the rights
of all is not in doubt. What has concerned me, though, is that the D&I
formulation can lead to less emphasis on equal treatment.

He informed me that the Commission did not ordinarily take on cases about guide-dogs for the blind as they were too easy. The DRC merely gave advice and sent the disgruntled non-admitted customer to the County Court, where they would now always win. Then with a twinkle in his eye he said there were exceptions to this policy.

A recent case had emerged in which a blind man had not been admitted to an Indian restaurant for a beer and curry at the end of the week. The owner objected to admitting the man's dog. A letter before action had been sent, but a solicitor's letter had come in reply complaining that the proposed action infringed the restaurant owner's rights in relation to his religion and belief. The owner was a Muslim and objected on religious grounds on the basis that taking dogs into the house or home was not permitted. To enforce the blind man's rights against him would be discriminatory and did not respect his personal protected characteristic as a Muslim.

At first – not having any deep knowledge of Islam – I was highly sceptical, thinking that this was nothing but a try-on by the restaurant's solicitors. Later, I understood better. I am no Islamic scholar, but if I have it aright,[39] the basis of this view lies in certain Hadiths – or sayings – attributed to the Prophet Mohammed,[40] revered by Muslims. For instance, I understand Abu Talha recalls[41] the Prophet as saying:

---

[39] And must apologise if I sourced this view incorrectly.

[40] See, for instance, www.quora.com/What-does-the-Quran-say-about-dogs.

[41] Sahih Al Bukhari, 4:54:539.

> Angels do not enter a house which has either a dog or
> a picture in it.

I understand, however, that it can be accepted within Islam that dogs may be kept – not as pets within the house – but for practical reasons such as for hunting or guarding the home. A Hadith recorded by Sufyan bin Abi Zuhair Ash-Shani is to the effect that the Prophet said:[42]

> If somebody keeps a dog that is neither used for farm
> work nor for guarding the livestock, he will lose one Qirat
> (of the reward) of his good deeds every day.

Sir Bert told me that he had resolved this particular problem by obtaining a ruling – a Fatwa – from Islamic scholars that guide dogs fell into the latter category and were not to be considered as pets. This clever alternative approach to litigation resolved the problem between the blind customer and the restaurant owner. It was typical of Sir Bert to be so creative; having been struck with polio in his youth, he had learnt great skills in negotiating conflicts between his exercise of his rights to self-determination and a world largely unaware and unadapted to the needs of wheelchair users.

Sadly, this has not been the end of this type of conflict. Similar problems are regularly reported by blind and partially sighted persons with guide dogs wanting to use taxis where the driver is a Muslim holding similar religious views about dogs. It has become a commonplace for the driver to use diversionary tactics, arguing that the close proximity between driver and dog within the taxi is harmful to the driver's health,

[42] Sahih Al Bukhari, 4:54:542.

or that they are afraid of, or have an allergic reaction to, the dog.[43] Here the law has now intervened specifically by criminalising such refusals where there is no medical certificate expressly dealing with the issue and a suitable notice displayed in the taxi.[44] This brings me to the Cake case.

2.2 The Gay Cake Case

The Gay Cake Case brought Gareth Lee into conflict with Ashers Bakery in Belfast and its owners Mr and Mrs McArthur. What a conflict it was, given that it was just concerned with the icing that Mr Lee wanted on a cake he ordered from the bakery. On 10 October 2018 the Supreme Court finally gave judgment and once again the media went into overdrive to discuss the rights and wrongs of the case. Though it became a *cause célèbre*, the transaction at the heart of the dispute was no less mundane than the dispute over access to a curry house. Yet, unlike Sir Bert Massie's speedy intervention, in this matter the conflict was fought out in three different courts over 4½ years all the way to the Supreme Court. It may not end there, as Mr Lee has now taken the matter to the ECtHR.[45]

---

[43] See, for instance, www.bbc.co.uk/news/uk-england-birmingham-42732832.

[44] See s. 37 of the Disability Discrimination Act 1995, now replaced by ss. 168–169 of the Equality Act 2010.

[45] See the BBC news story of 15 August 2019: 'Ashers "gay cake" row referred to European Court'; see www.bbc.co.uk/news/uk-northern-ireland-49350891.

The facts of the case have not always been accurately reported. They are, however, important if the reason why the case was brought, what was at stake and why it took so long, are to be properly understood.

The oppression of gay and lesbian women in Northern Ireland has continued longer and in a more serious way than any other part of the United Kingdom.[46] It has had some devastating psychological effects.[47]

Mr Lee, who was gay, supported proposals for a change in the law on marriage in Northern Ireland. He wished to take a cake to an event at Bangor Castle celebrating the progress of the campaign for change. He went to a bakery he had previously visited to order the cake. This bakery – Ashers – offered a service to ice cakes with customers' designs. Its advertising material contained no apparent restrictions on the service offered; indeed, it showed Hallowe'en cakes with witches, and cakes designed to support particular football teams. Ashers' advertising gave Mr Lee no reason to think there would be the slightest problem when he handed over his design for the cake he wanted, showing Bert and Ernie from Sesame Street and the message 'Support Gay Marriage'.[48] He

---

[46] The Sexual Offences Act 1967 decriminalised consensual sexual relations between men within Great Britain but it took 14 further years until the judgment of the European Court of Human Rights on 23 September 1981 in *Dudgeon* v. *United Kingdom* (1982) 4 EHRR 1 for Northern Ireland to be forced to take similar steps. While Part 4 of the Civil Partnership Act 2004 extended to Northern Ireland, its Assembly has never passed legislation to permit same-sex marriage.

[47] Per O'Hara J in *Close & Ors, Re Judicial Review* [2017] NIQB 79 at [5].

[48] The Northern Ireland Court of Appeal expressly noted in its judgment that 'No case was made at first instance that this order was outside the

commissioned the cake and was charged and paid £34. However, unbeknownst to Mr Lee, the bakery was owned by two evangelical Christians, Mr and Mrs McArthur, who believe that the only form of marriage is that between one man and one woman. They opposed the political campaign in Northern Ireland for same-sex marriage. On reflection they decided that their company could not accept Mr Lee's order without compromising their beliefs. They did not like the fact that Mr Lee appeared to support gay marriage. They did return his money, but they took no steps to redirect him to another bakery or to help him out in anyway.

Mr Lee considered he had suffered discrimination and the ECNI agreed. They made a complaint to the bakery, but Mr and Mrs MacArthur's solicitors argued that the complaint did not respect the rights the couple had as a result of their particular religious and political beliefs about marriage.

Although four judges in Northern Ireland considered Mr Lee had suffered discrimination, the unanimous judgment of the five members of the Supreme Court was against him. The MacArthurs succeeded in their complaint that they – not Mr Lee – were the true victims. They argued that the judgments of the courts below the Supreme Court discriminated against them, and that Mr Lee's case against them infringed their rights to protection of their religious and political beliefs. Building on the arguments made for Mr and Mrs Bull, as the case progressed, they worked to establish their identity as the

normal range of the offer and there was no basis for allowing an amendment to introduce that issue at this stage'; see [2016] NICA 39 at [44].

victims in the case. Their cause was also taken up by the Christian Institute.[49] Even before the first hearing they attracted in excess of 2,500 supporters to the Waterfront Hall in Belfast[50] for an evening of organised support.

I suspect that in the future law schools may discuss the quality of the judgment by focussing down onto a comparison of the different judicial approaches in the courts below and in the Supreme Court, which heard the case when sitting for the first time in Belfast in Northern Ireland. Professor Hugh Collins, Oxford's Vinerian Professor of English Law, has already started this process, noting a query by a law student about the quality of the reasoning in the judgment.[51]

I will express my own views on the quality of the judgment below. Yet looked at from the point of view of supporting equality and diversity, I think the case has thrown up a no less important issue of a different kind which is typical of these conflict cases and that I want to discuss first.

Shortly after the Supreme Court's judgment, I was watching a colleague, Daphne Romney QC, being interviewed on the BBC Sunday Morning Live programme about the case. I was struck by the very first question that the interviewer on

---

[49] www.christian.org.uk/case/ashers-baking-company/.

[50] www.belfasttelegraph.co.uk/news/northern-ireland/gay-cake-row-christian-institute-rally-for-ashers-baking-company-held-at-the-waterfront-hall-31093145.html.

[51] See his blog 'A missing layer of the cake with the controversial icing', in which the reasoning in the case has been extensively criticised; see https://uklabourlawblog.com/2019/03/04/a-missing-layer-of-the-cake-with-the-controversial-icing-hugh-collins/.

this magazine programme asked her with a very puzzled look on her face:

Why has this taken 4 years?

Had I been interviewed, I could easily have answered the BBC's question on a literal basis, explaining all the applications that were made, the pressure on the courts to find time to deal with the matter, and the delay caused by the intervention of the Attorney General. I could have taken her through the steps we had sought to take to bring the litigation to an end swiftly and at the least cost. However, it was quite obvious that this was not at all what the interviewer was thinking about. The literal answer to her question would not only be boring TV, the detail would have been completely irrelevant to her viewers. Her question was really posed, on behalf of the ordinary mass of folk watching her magazine chat show, to make a practical point. More prosaically, she was making a question or statement on her viewers' behalf[52] about the law's utility in this type of case. We can rephrase it thus:

> Isn't it ridiculous that it has to take 4½ years to decide whether a very simple request for a commercial company to bake and ice a cake must be accepted?

And here is an important issue.

---

[52] The question had probably been drafted for the questioner by a BBC researcher. The BBC staffer would have been instructed to find a hook to hold the audience when the issue was raised. He or she must have been trying to identify a good point which had not been aired before but which would be a real issue to the audience.

I absolutely agree that it is not acceptable that every time that there is a serious conflict of different equality rights, the case should have to go to the Supreme Court, or worse from there to the ECtHR or the Court of Justice of the European Union. While lawyers love appeals, surely litigants want speedy justice and certainty, and we should consider that their desires are far the more important. I too think this time-frame is quite ridiculous – indeed completely unacceptable – in our modern diverse society. A conflict about a transaction between complete strangers about buying a cake should have been over and forgotten within a matter of days. There is a certain madness about it being the subject of deep debate and disagreement, taking such a long time to resolve. Indeed, to some the length of time to final judgment on this issue seems to make our equality law appear almost irrelevant. That I believe is very dangerous. In the diverse country in which we live, it ought to be completely clear whether the owners of the bakery could say 'No' or were required (perhaps through gritted teeth) to bake and ice the cake that Mr Lee ordered and paid for.

So, a key point is that if debates of this kind – about the resolution of conflicts of equality rights – are going to take such a long time to resolve, then equality law is a pretty useless tool for most people to rely on when they go out shopping or seek to buy services of any kind and unexpectedly are pitched into a disagreement. Does this matter? I think it very much does. Indeed, for several reasons I am completely sure it does.

In the first place, if we are to protect the right to self-determination free from discrimination on such a collection of protected characteristics and for such a diverse community, we need much better tools than this to resolve the inevitable conflicts. This is a broad point, of course. We need to take it to the next level, and to do so I think we need to make some distinctions about the kinds of problems that equality law must address. We can, I think, readily see one class of problem as being concerned with treatment denying equal opportunity that has potentially dire long-term consequences so that the losses that have to be addressed are very large. Typically, this arises when discrimination occurs in relationships that either have been, or are expected to be, relatively long term. Employment and housing discrimination are good examples. Here, when there is a complaint that has to be addressed, it may matter less that the law takes its time. The principal remedy sought is usually compensation for a past wrong. That can be relatively large and so where the merits are good, claims that are expensive to run and which will often involve complex forensic inquiry can be justified. Although other remedies may be sought, taking these cases is justified by the need for substantial compensation for substantial losses.

The Cake Case was not of that type at all – at least for Mr Lee.[53] As it happened, fortunately, Mr Lee was able to find another baker, who was indifferent to the issue of printing the

---

[53] It is more difficult, perhaps, to say what it was like for the MacArthurs. They did not themselves have to make the cake; they had staff who would do that and who were not as concerned about the concept of marriage. It was a one-off purchase and if they did not wish their business to do another such cake, they could easily have changed their advertising material. On the other hand, they considered that for them even to permit their business to make such a cake would be sinful.

message 'Support Gay Marriage', in time to attend the function at Bangor Castle for which he wanted the cake. That's why it was agreed throughout the litigation that he had only suffered temporary injury to feelings, for which an almost nominal sum of £500 was due satisfaction.[54]

I have no doubt that to some extent this fact has affected many commentators discussing the case. There is a view that says, 'What do his rights matter – given he was not greatly inconvenienced?' This view is understandable, but it misses the point. Mr Lee was not interested in getting huge damages; he just did not wish to be treated in this way. Like all of us, he just wanted to be able to shop and buy services free of concern about who he was seeking to buy from. If we can empathise with this point of view, we shall get a clearer understanding as to why this case and others concerning small, short-term transactions matter.

It is a fact that because such small sums are typically the only monetary value to be put on many complaints about discrimination in the provision of goods, facilities and services, they are very infrequently litigated. After all, what private person would litigate a case where the most that could be expected in compensation for a one-off act of discrimination was only £500, but the law was not clear, and the other side had the resources and might wish to take it to the Supreme Court? The relationship between costs and potential

---

[54] Counsel for the bakers was in due course to describe this sum as a state-imposed penalty; it was in fact agreed without argument between counsel as the right sum to assuage Mr Lee's injury to feelings, on the assumption that they had been unlawfully hurt by the Defendants to his claim.

benefit would be so disproportionate that few individuals would litigate even if the merits were close to 100 per cent. This is particularly true of what I will call commercial transactions – those contracts we make day in day out, buying the goods and services that we need or want to get us through life. This is where we need to remind ourselves of important principles underpinning the rule of law.

First, it really does matter that when a law is made it is respected. The rule of law operates as a single structure. An unenforced or unenforceable law is a weak law that diminishes the strength of the whole. More specifically, if laws to stop discrimination in the provision of goods, facilities and services are in this category, they weaken the value of all equality law. Those closely involved know this well. The humdrum facts of the cases I have mentioned at the outset all involved little financial value to justify taking them. Where the parties were backed by the Commissions, this was only because they sought to obtain normative outcomes that they hoped would either change the way society works or reinforce desired social rules that had come under challenge. Both the ECNI and I considered these points to be extraordinarily important – they certainly were in the Cake case. This is typical of these conflict cases; they engage deeply with the way in which society works and ought to work. These are cases where the framework I have discussed in previous chapters matters hugely. I need to explain this better in relation to the Gay Cake Case since, although I made extensive submissions in relation to what I considered to be the relevant framework, they were in practice ignored by the court. In my view this was a bad mistake and one which a future court cannot afford to make.

In Great Britain we know only in general terms that Northern Ireland is a very divided community, but in Belfast the divisions across those communities are the stuff of daily life. Personal identities are constantly reinforced in stark oppositional terms as Republican or Unionist, Catholic or Protestant, Believer or Atheist. It is a little like the discussions that we have here in the Temple as to whether someone is a Brexiteer or Remainer, only much, much more so. This kind of oppositional personal identification determines where you will go to school, where you will live in Belfast and what kinds of signs you will pass painted on the ends of terrace walls before you get there. It affects who your friends might be, the names they will have, the flags you might or might not fly above your house, and the marches you might attend or avoid. Explore below the surface of the personal life of almost every single person in Northern Ireland and you will find personal tragedy not far away: a family member or friend killed or wounded in the Troubles, a relation who has left the area because of fear of violence, or a career that has been stultified by prejudice. Any one or more of those kinds of issues have affected everybody. They are the social facts of Northern Ireland that the 1998 Good Friday Agreement[55] was designed to address and, in many ways, has done much to resolve.

---

[55] The Belfast Agreement, also known as the Good Friday Agreement, was reached in multi-party negotiations and signed on 10 April 1998; see www .gov.uk/government/publications/the-belfast-agreement.

Yet this is not job done; in Northern Ireland judges still even now get personal protection to and from court, and they can all remember the events that led to some of them being killed in the Troubles.[56] In short, the work of resolution – of building a new Northern Ireland – is a daily mission for all people who are not actively opposed to the Good Friday Agreement. Now this is where the importance of free trade comes in. The former Lord Chief Justice of England and Wales, Lord Thomas of Cwmgiedd, has recently pointed out how important trade is and how certainty in the application of commercial law is essential to enable it to flourish.[57] When the free flow of commerce is encouraged, there is no doubt it can bring communities together.[58] The Equality Commission and the Northern Ireland judges were all well aware of this.

[56] During the Troubles the IRA murdered five judges overall: Rory Conaghan in 1974, William Doyle in 1983 and Lord Justice Sir Maurice Gibson in 1987; resident magistrates, William Staunton and Robert McBirney, were also victims of the IRA, murdered in 1972 and 1974 respectively. The IRA also murdered Lord Justice Gibson's wife Cecily, as well as Mary Travers, the daughter of Judge William Travers. Judge Doyle and Ms Travers were both shot dead as they left Catholic churches. See http://news.bbc.co.uk/1/hi/northern_ireland/8351344.stm.

[57] See 'Developing commercial law through the courts: rebalancing the relationship between the courts and arbitration', The Bailii Lecture 2016, 9 March 2016; see www.judiciary.uk/wp-content/uploads/2016/03/lcj-speech-bailli-lecture-20160309.pdf.

[58] Sir Roy Goode has explained the importance of trade in this way: 'One of the most powerful influences on human activity is the driving force of trade. Governments may be overthrown, wars may break out, large areas of a country may be devastated by natural disaster, but somehow traders find ways of establishing business relationships', in E. McKendrick,

They understood that securing a fully open commercial sphere in which all could participate without concern about protected characteristics had great social force in eliminating the divisions they saw every day around them. They understood that ensuring the population could engage in commerce on such a free and open basis enabled everyone to live fuller lives. They recognised that such free commerce has a healing effect, binding up such social divisions, so that through engaging in commerce, people of all kinds of different background would be encouraged to learn to live together in other ways, in education and housing, and political life.

So, in taking the Cake case, the Commission wished to underscore that commerce in Northern Ireland should be like this. They saw a positive outcome in the case for Mr Lee as strengthening cross-community relations in Northern Ireland. That may sound strange to those who have sided with the MacArthurs; but I hope they can understand how the Commission wanted to ensure that in ordinary simple commercial dealings, purchasers did not need to be concerned with the personal identities of the providers, and providers should not take into account the personal identities of the purchaser. Vague notions such as personal conscience that cannot be examined by the court should not be permitted to disrupt transactions.

It is a matter of great regret to me that in the end I was not able to secure this outcome for the Commission. Though I made this point in my submissions, it seems to have been

Goode on Commercial Law (Penguin, 2010) at 3. See footnote 2 to Lord Thomas' speech, cited at footnote 57.

lost on the Supreme Court. Certainly, to the extent that they took it into account at all, it was not determinative: they did not discuss my submissions on this to any material extent in the judgment, even though I put all the travaux that led to this legislation before them. So how did the Court proceed?

Mr Lee's case was brought on the basis that there had been both sexual orientation and religion and belief discrimination. The Supreme Court rejected the complaint of direct sexual orientation discrimination on the basis that the treatment of Mr Lee concerned discrimination against the message on the cake and not him. In my view, this distinction is hard to understand on the ground. It certainly does not help build up a free commerce; rather, it is bound to open up further arguments in later cases – if they are brought – when the delivery of goods and services is denied.

This route through the litigation was not available to the Supreme Court in relation to Mr Lee's complaint of religion and belief discrimination, because Presiding District Judge Brownlie had concluded as an unappealable fact that the refusal to serve him was also caused by the fact that the MacArthurs' considered he supported the political idea of same-sex marriage. In this respect the discrimination concerned the man and not just the message.

In the end the Supreme Court decided that the conflict between Mr Lee and Mr and Mrs McArthur was to be resolved by reference to the right to freedom of expression in Article 10 of the European Convention on Human Rights – not Mr Lee's rights but those of the MacArthurs.

They held that Mr Lee could not enforce his rights because Mrs McArthur feared someone could think she was associated with the message on the cake,[59] notwithstanding Judge Brownlie having concluded, at first instance, that no one could objectively have reached that conclusion.[60] It was enough that Mrs McArthur was personally worried. In short, her conscience was on this occasion a trump card; her fear that she should be thought to be sinning by letting the cake be made and iced in this way was comparatively more significant in law than Mr Lee's rights as enshrined in the legislation on which he relied.

It does not take a genius to see that this approach opens a complete can of worms. Not only did this litigation take 4½ years, but it has made it almost certain that there will be more disputes in the future. We will have to see whether anyone has the energy and resources to litigate them. We can already see how this has had an effect on commerce though.

One such dispute occurred on the day of judgment, as the *Independent* news site reported. Apparently, the Christian Institute, which had backed the Ashers Bakery and the MacArthurs, had booked a photographer through an internet booking site called Perfocal.[61] No doubt they were attracted by its strapline 'Book a photographer for anything'. The 'anything' the Institute had in mind was someone to come to the

---

[59] See [2008] UKSC 49 at [53] to [55].   [60] See [2015] NICty 2 at [95].

[61] www.perfocal.com/?utm_source=google&utm_medium=cpc&utm_cam paign=brand&campaignid=2046626053&adgroupid=72694991272&adid =375788834595&gclid=CjwKCAjwxOvsBRAjEiwAuY7L8kCMbWHgiw_ RK2FvdwaH6j-ic-QSNEd7hzAUB3QTvuioGQ2jw1Cr1RoCkGoQAvD_ BwE.

Supreme Court on the day of judgment to take photographs of the MacArthurs' triumph after the judgment was given.

The booking online simply said this was for a 'business event' and listed only a few details about the brief, with no mention of the specific court case or the individuals to be photographed. The photographer came and took the photos, but later Perfocal realised who its client was. Perfocal had a big weddings business for all. Its founder – a man called Tony Xu – no doubt became worried that he and his business could be associated with the Christian Institute which is so opposed to gay marriage. The images were then withheld, and a refund was issued.[62] You can understand how, after the Supreme Court's resolution of the conflict of equality rights, Mr Xu felt he could and should take this line. He called it 'tit for tat'.[63] He said:

> This isn't just about standing up against discrimination,
> I hope our stance serves as an example of exactly where this
> kind of judgement could lead us. Where does it end?
> One of our photographers was recently booked for
> a 'business event'. As the screengrab of the booking . . .
> shows, we knew little more than the time, date, location
> and key points of the photography booking. It is not
> uncommon to be booked to photograph media events, and
> we were unaware of the details of the case being heard. The
> customer information we had was a name and number.

[62] Perfocal's tweet explaining its actions can be seen at https://twitter.com /perfocal/status/1050322799255011328.

[63] Perfocal's statement can be seen here: www.irishtimes.com/news/crime-and-law/photo-service-withholds-images-of-gay-cake-bakery-owners-in-protest-1.3660546.

We later found out that the customer was charity and lobby group Christian Institute, paying all fees for the family that owned the bakery embroiled in a four-year long legal case, after taking a booking and then refusing to make a cake with the slogan 'Support Gay Marriage'.

It's been accepted in the highest court in the UK that private companies can accept bookings and then, if they feel that it goes against their morals, refuse that booking if it offends their sensibilities and it not be counted as discriminatory.

As such, I have made the decision to refuse to hand over the photographs and fully refund the Christian Institute.

The photographer booked on the day has been paid in full for their time. The Christian Institute paid for a 3-hour shoot package including editing, all original JPEGs and 24-hour Delivery add-ons as opposed to the company's usual 48-hour service. This statement is within that 24-hour period, and the customer has been contacted with our decision.

We appreciate that this looks like tit for tat, and it is. We are proud to have been booked for many religious ceremonies, including Christian, Jewish and Muslim celebrations. We've also been booked often for same-sex weddings, including high-profile individuals. In short, we welcome customers from all backgrounds.

When our photographer on the ground learned what it was while doing the job, they felt immediately uncomfortable with the situation, as many members of the public are, but remained professional. As soon as I found out though, I realised this was an opportunity to highlight exactly why this kind of result is damaging.

> This isn't just about standing up against discrimination,
> I hope our stance serves as an example of exactly where this
> kind of judgement could lead us. Where does it end?

I am tempted to smile about this, but the truth is that this is not good for equality law. The Christian Institute ought to be able to buy photographic services, just as much as Mr Lee ought to be able to buy cakes – without worrying about the providers playing their conscience as a trump card. Mr Xu's statement shows exactly the fault in the Supreme Court's approach. In London it may seem that this may not yet matter too much. However, pause for a moment and think about the divisions shown up by the Brexit debate and the consequences of concluding that commerce can be denied on this basis.

PART 5 DIFFERENT APPROACHES TO RESOLVING CONFLICTS

Can we find other ways to ensure that the law is respected in a practical way? Is there another way to resolve such conflicts in the commercial sphere where cases are very difficult to litigate but the importance of equality law is so great? I think that there has to be, and I am not alone.

5.1 Legislated Conciliation

It is a striking fact that the very first UK enactment to address discrimination was deeply concerned with exactly these kinds of small-scale incidents of discrimination which occur not in employment but in the small daily transactions we all need to make. The approach that was taken was enhanced compulsory conciliation. In 2018, the nation recalled how it was 70 years since the Empire Windrush arrived at Tilbury Docks, on 22 June 1948, and the first workers came from the Caribbean islands to relieve a post-war labour shortage. Although the country needed their labour, it was deeply hostile to accommodating these black immigrants into society at large. This was not a conflict of rights, of course, but a basic hostility that had little justification beyond the fear of the other – the previously unknown.

This hostility was seen in myriad ways – colour bars in housing, pubs and clubs, refusal of service and so on. It was a huge social problem and a national disgrace, and legislation in the form of the Race Relations Act 1965 was passed to address it. That Act focussed on the danger to society at large from denying these workers and their families the opportunity to live their non-working lives fully and freely. Its primary focus was on seeking to eliminate discrimination in the provision of services and the like in places of public resort. Its enforcement mechanism was a little clunky and soon enhanced by a further Act in 1968, but it was always intended to be intensely practical, seeking quick local solutions. To achieve this the Act sent disputes to local conciliation committees set up by a Race Relations Board. Only later, and if absolutely necessary, after consideration by the Attorney General, was the Race Relations Board to take legal enforcement action.

Although this first system for addressing social conflict around equality rights can be criticised on other grounds, the focus on early reconciliation was, I believe, right. I don't know if such a conciliation committee if set up in Northern Ireland would have resolved the dispute between Mr Lee and the MacArthurs, but it might. Any such committee would not necessarily have had the imagination and skills of Sir Bert Massie, of course. But it must also be remembered that so much political dispute in Northern Ireland has already been resolved by discussion and negotiation. Conciliation lies at the heart of current political settlement in the Good Friday Agreement.

The merit of the 1965 Act was that it forced the parties to come to conciliation. Now – outside employment, where ACAS has a role – this will only happen when both parties to a dispute agree to try it and there are resources to pay for it. This does not ordinarily happen, but it should. In the Republic of Ireland enforced early mediation has been very successful in resolving very many equality disputes,[64] including those with conflicts, and I see no reason why it should not be used successfully in cases such as these too. There are also ways in which the courts can encourage different forms of conciliated resolution, as Mr Paulley's case shows.

5.2 Judicial Solutions

While religious differences do provide a fruitful context for many such conflicts, it would be a mistake to think religion is always the driver of division. There are other divisions in our

---

[64] See www.workplacerelations.ie.

society that may seem less obvious but where a speedy resolution is equally essential.

Those with full mobility are often quite unaware how little the environment meets the needs of those with mobility impairment. But, if you are a wheelchair user or someone who cannot use escalators or climb stairs or needs to sit down when you travel, you will be aware every day of the problems your mobility limitations cause you. There are now some solutions to those problems, but these can easily give rise to conflicts. Together with Catherine Casserley, a junior barrister in my Chambers, I argued the case for Doug Paulley, a wheelchair user, in the Supreme Court in 2016, which did just that. It is interesting for this lecture because of the form of its outcome.

Doug Paulley wished to catch the 9.40 bus from Wetherby to Leeds. He turned up in good time to board. As required by law, the bus had a designated wheelchair space, but you should know also that the designation carried no formal powers of enforcement by, for instance, the criminal law. That space was occupied – not by another wheelchair user but by an unnamed woman, travelling with her baby in a buggy.

It is not that easy to travel in the early stages of maternity, as should be obvious; new mothers (and for that matter fathers) need spaces to put buggies when they travel. Most buggies do of course fold down, but many parents are loathe to wake a sleeping baby, for very good reason. So, we must accept that this woman had equality rights too, like Mr Paulley. Nonetheless, she was not only occupying the wheelchair space, that space was the only place on the bus where Mr

Paulley could travel, whereas it was at least theoretically possible for her to move, and still stay on the bus.

The bus driver asked her to move but she refused without reason. She did not try to make any adjustments for Mr Paulley and as the bus driver did not press her, and there was nowhere else for Mr Paulley to place his wheelchair safely, he could not get on. As a result, he missed a train connection in Leeds and a family occasion was ultimately spoilt.

Subsequently, backed by the Equality and Human Rights Commission, Mr Paulley sued the bus company. It was not with the hope of getting on the bus, of course – the bus had long since gone – but in order to get change to inadequate policies and so help wheelchair users have much better access to buses. The gist of the argument was that the company's bus driver should be trained to address such conflicts more thoroughly and put greater pressure on persons occupying the designated space. One part of the bus company's defence was to argue that it needed to allow for other travellers who – despite the fact that this was a designated wheelchair space – might wish to occupy it and even be able to assert that they had equality rights to do so.

Mr Paulley's case was based on a specific kind of discrimination that applies in the case of disability, where a service provider is under an anticipatory obligation to make reasonable adjustments to the services provided to make it easier for disabled persons to access them.[65] This fact allowed the debate about the case to focus in a more

---

[65] See s. 20 of, and Part 12 to, the Equality Act 2010.

generic way on the procedures that the bus company should take to secure access.

On this occasion a seven-judge Supreme Court went some way to holding that bus companies should have a policy in place that would resolve this kind of conflict speedily and readily. They held that it was not enough for the bus company to instruct its drivers simply to request non-wheelchair users to vacate the space and to do nothing further if the request was rejected. The appropriate approach for the driver to take could depend on the reason for the refusal to move. Where the driver concluded that the refusal was unreasonable, the bus-operating company should have a policy that required some further coercive step by the driver, including in some circumstances stopping the bus until there was compliance.

So, although this case also took 4 years to resolve in the highest court, the result has been useful.[66] It really did try to get to grips with the kinds of conflict of rights wheelchair users face. It focussed on finding a general means to resolve such conflicts in a practical and immediate way. Though the Supreme Court were not exactly mandating a conciliation effort by the driver, they were clear he or she should engage with the problem there and then when the wheelchair user needed an intervention. This judgment therefore has some parallels with the prescription adopted by the Race Relations Act 1965. It saw the need for a speedy solution when conflicts between equality rights concerned with the provision of goods, facilities and services arise.

---

[66] Not just in legal terms. It is now a commonplace to see both designated wheelchair and buggy spaces on buses.

And I don't think that this judgment will have adverse consequences in the sense of giving rise to further long-term litigation all the way to the Supreme Court. A wheelchair user would be unlikely to take a case if a driver – following the Supreme Court's judgment – had really tried with some sense of active purpose to resolve such a conflict in the future. Nor do I think that a Commission would want to back such a case. So, I am pleased with this outcome, as – I believe – are many of the travelling wheelchair community. The task they now face is to keep the bus companies up to the mark set by the judgment. Many such wheelchair users are resourceful and well able to take this task on.

That is not to say I am entirely satisfied that the problem of such conflicts for wheelchair users has been resolved, because what is really needed is legislative change to ensure more clearly that wheelchair users have real priority rights to access the bus space.

This brings me to the role of legislation in resolving conflicts of equality rights, because Parliament and the Executive have tried to do their bit to anticipate some such conflicts of equality rights and to decide how they should be resolved. This is entirely consistent with Human Rights law – indeed it has been commended by the ECtHR in a case called *Animal Defenders* v. *the UK*.[67]

---

[67] [2013] EMLR 28, (2013) 57 EHRR 21, 34 BHRC 137, (2013) 163(7564) NLJ 20.

5.3 Legislated Resolutions

Sometimes legislation says in terms what is to happen in specific contexts. Parliament then decides that a particular protected characteristic will exceptionally be allowed to operate as a top trump without a discussion of the competing claims that might arise. Sometimes the legislation does somewhat less than that, but measures the competing equality rights and determines the margin between them. Sometimes it does something in between. The situation faced by wheelchair users on buses almost fell into the first category but not quite. Regulations had been made even before wheelchair users got equality rights to give them a degree of protection when travelling.[68] The problem for Mr Paulley was that these Regulations did not quite go the distance that he needed to secure that the bus driver got the woman to move. In this respect there is a distinction between Mr Paulley's case and one part of Mr Lee's. As I have said, he complained of sexual orientation discrimination in the provision of goods and services as well as the similar provisions in relation to religion and belief.

The Equality Act (Sexual Orientation) Regulations (Northern Ireland) 2006 (SOR) on which Mr Lee relied had been made after a long period of consultation with the public in which the question whether Christian businesses could be exempted from its proposed prohibitions was widely discussed. A key question emerging from the consultation was the extent to

---

[68] See the Public Service Vehicles (Conduct of Drivers, Inspectors, Conductors and Passengers) Regulations 1990, SI 1990/1020, as amended by the Public Service Vehicles (Conduct of Drivers, Inspectors, Conductors and Passengers) (Amendment) Regulations 2002, SI 2002/1974.

which 'Christian businesses' could be permitted to discriminate without incurring liability under the proposed regulations.[69] The position of the Northern Ireland Office on this issue was explained in the Explanatory Memorandum to SOR thus:

7. Policy background

7.1 The Equality Act 2006 at section 82 gave the Department a power to make Regulations, based on the Race Relations (Northern Ireland) Order 1997, to outlaw discrimination on the basis of sexual orientation in the provision of goods, facilities, services, education, public functions and the disposal of property.

7.2 The regulations will protect people from direct discrimination i.e. where a person treats another person less favourably because of his sexual orientation. They also prohibit indirect discrimination, where the discrimination is often an unintended consequence of the action and harassment on the ground of sexual orientation. They also prohibit victimisation, to ensure no-one feels that they cannot bring, or support a claim, under these Regulations.

7.3 The main areas where the Regulations will impact include, . . . ; in the area of religion, where the Government has acknowledged a difficulty with doctrinal teaching and practice and provided an exemption within the Regulations for such bodies. The Regulations will also impact on hotel and bed and breakfast owners, who will not be able to deny a same sex couple accommodation on the basis of their sexual orientation. The Government has

---

[69] See the Explanatory Memorandum for SOR at [7.5]–[7.6].

also extended the Regulations to cover private members clubs.

7.4 The Department undertook an eight week consultation, which ended on 25 September, with statutory consultees and the public generally. The response was encouraging with 375 responses. However, of these a significant majority addressed only the questions concerning exemptions for religion and religious organisations.

7.5 There was, therefore, no significant opposition from the consultees to the basic premise behind the Regulations, which is to ensure equality of treatment for all sections of society. Of the concerns that were expressed regarding exemptions for religion the Government believes that those concerns have been addressed by the wording of the exemption at regulation 16.

7.6 Those that were not covered by the wording of the exemptions in the Regulations were generally asking for something that could not be defined legally, such as a 'Christian business' or asking for exemptions that were too wide and would have made the Regulations unenforceable.

. . .

That is why, in the end, the legislator decided that to provide an exception for Christian businesses based on their conscience alone would permit closet discrimination. This would be permissible for purely religious organisations but where the organisation was engaged in commerce that was not acceptable.

The equivalent regulations in Great Britain took the same line and did not permit a Christian business exception. This proved fatal to the defence by Mr and Mrs Bull to the claims by Mr Hall and Mr Preddy, where the Supreme Court had no trouble in holding that their complaint of sexual orientation was of a kind anticipated by the legislator and so should be upheld.

If Mr Lee had been able to show that the refusal of his order was based on his sexual orientation, and not merely the message on the cake, then this ought to have been a problem for the MacArthurs. However, he was not so able and so his case stood or fell in relation to the issue of religion and belief discrimination.

This kind of discrimination was outlawed in Northern Ireland by the Fair Employment and Treatment (Northern Ireland) Order 1998 (FETO).[70] There had been lengthy consultation on this too, but it did not focus so clearly on whether Christian businesses should be permitted to avoid liability on grounds of conscience. This legislative reticence opened up a space for the MacArthurs' argument and the Supreme Court's judgment. Though of course I pointed out that using this space would be inconsistent with Parliament's approach to the conflict between sexual orientation and religion, this did not feature in the Court's final judgment.

I should add that the Fair Employment and Treatment Order was made in Northern Ireland on the recommendation of the Standing Advisory Committee on Human Rights,[71] which was fully aware of the need to bridge the gap between religious

[70] The Fair Employment and Treatment (Northern Ireland) Order 1998, SI 1998/3162 (NI 21).
[71] See 'Religious and Political Discrimination and Equality of Opportunity in Northern Ireland' (the Second SACHR report), published in 1990 Cmnd 1107, presented to Parliament by the Secretary of State for Northern Ireland as a Command Paper in June 1990.

communities and to avoid the ghettoisation of service provision. So, the absence of any such clause might have been taken to imply that it was not thought appropriate at all.

I am sure it was for these reasons that the four Northern Ireland judges would not countenance the argument that Mrs MacArthur's personal subjective fear that she could be identified with the message on the cake was a defence to Mr Lee's claim. They saw no place for the conscience exception that the Supreme Court ultimately granted to the MacArthurs.

In my view legislation is now needed to answer this question comprehensively and to secure that commerce is something that all can participate in equally. The approach taken in SOR to conscience issues should be replicated in FETO.

That brings me to the current discussions about the rights of transgendered persons or those who consider themselves non-binary. There is much concern by some women, particularly those running or connected with women's refuges, that they will not be able to refuse access to male to female transgendered persons. Those with a female birth status fear that this could be dangerous and oppressive for the women in the refuge.[72] The counter-argument is that a transgendered person should be treated as having the new gender for all purposes and treated accordingly. At present there is a halfway house in the legislation well described by the Equality and Human Rights Commission on its website.[73]

---

[72] See, for instance, *Kimberly Nixon* v. *Vancouver Rape Relief Society* 2005 BCCA 601.

[73] See www.equalityhumanrights.com/en/advice-and-guidance/gender-reassignment-discrimination.

I am sure that legislation is really the best way to solve this problem. A legislated solution may not be acceptable to all, but it would bring legal certainty and should avoid long, expensive litigation.

PART 6 CONCLUSIONS

Litigation about conflicts of equality rights may resolve the facts of a particular dispute, but will rarely resolve all the kinds of conflicts that can arise between different protected characteristics. Litigation is expensive and usually leads to great delay, both of which make it undesirable to rely on cases being brought to solve these problems.

It would be much better to have a formalised system of conciliation for such disputes, but most importantly, whenever possible Parliament or the Executive should make clear what the outcome should be in any legislation that addresses foreseeable disputes.

If litigation has to happen, the judges must be aware that when they decide such cases they have a key role in contributing to the growth in confidence in the diversity of our UK. They must of course decide cases by reference to their judicial oaths and I do not doubt they try to do so. Yet I would suggest that leaving it as a matter of conscience whether a person should obey the law is a poor way to proceed. Resolving conflicts of rights in this way is the first step to a hierarchy of rights, and that is neither good for equality law nor society.

I emphasise that we cannot allow a new hierarchy of protected characteristics to emerge. Judges must therefore be absolutely acute to this possibility. Religion and belief are important aspects of the personality of each and every one of us, but they are not sacrosanct characteristics which must be protected to such a degree that they can be deployed to trump all other claims based on protected characteristics.

We should never forget that it was this overweening claim for religion and belief that underpinned Apartheid and limited the extent to which women and gays and lesbians could live as full and fulfilled a life as any other.